SUPERNATURAL
SERIAL
KILLERS

SUPERNATURAL SERIAL KILLERS

CHILLING CASES OF PARANORMAL BLOODLUST AND DERANGED FANTASY

SAMANTHA LYON &
DR DAPHNE TAN

ARCTURUS

Corbis Images: 203 (Reuters); 270 (Bettmann)

Getty Images: 8 (Time & Life Pictures); 158 (Popperfoto); 169 (Popperfoto); 182 (Paul Harris); 217 (Taro Yamasaki); 284 (JIJI PRESS); 290 (JIJI PRESS); 306 (Terry Smith); 315 (Terry Smith)

Mary Evans Picture Library: 40; 53; 83 (Sueddeutsche Zeitung Photo)

Topfoto: 66 (Charles Walker); 114 (Topham Picturepoint); 123; 134 (Topham Picturepoint); 147 (Topham Picturepoint); 260 (AP)

ARCTURUS

This edition published in 2017 by Arcturus Publishing Limited
26/27 Bickels Yard, 151–153 Bermondsey Street,
London SE1 3HA

ISBN: 978-1-78599-124-0
DA004743UK

Printed in China

Contents

Introduction

Our Fear of and Fascination with Serial Killers

Criminals and their dark deeds have held a grim fascination for people from all levels of society for centuries. This can be seen in the enormous popularity of the true crime genre and crime fiction and in the way the press has always reported crimes in painstaking detail to satisfy the macabre curiosity of many readers. Going further back in time, people gathered in their masses to attend public hangings, eagerly watching, waiting and cheering when the convict dangled and twitched as he took his last breath. The nature or severity of the crime was not always particularly important. It might have been murder; it might have been stealing cattle or witchcraft: whatever the crime, the gruesome punishment was considered prime entertainment for everyone.

In the UK, executions eventually stopped being public spectacles and were carried out in private. Then, in 1964, they were abolished altogether when the focus of criminal punishment shifted towards deterrence and rehabilitation, rather than pure retribution. In the US, certain states still have the death penalty, but the executions are not feted as

An engraving of a werewolf devouring a young woman.

a public spectacle. Along with legal systems and societal norms, our social perception of violence has also changed.

Professor David Schmid, who has studied society's interest in true crime and serial killers, stated, 'We have largely lost our ability to be appalled. It takes a very, very extreme crime for us now to recover that.' In this modern era, though most of us are removed from experiencing it first hand, violence is often depicted gratuitously and in extreme forms both in fiction and non-fiction and all the various mediums they employ. It takes a great deal now to shock and to disgust us – but this has in no way quelled public interest in crime. It simply means that the crimes that captivate and terrify us most are the truly terrible ones. It takes an unthinkable murder, a merciless serial killer, someone we barely consider to be human to really capture our interest.

Serial killers have existed for centuries, although the term itself was not coined until the 1970s and is commonly attributed to an FBI Special Agent named Robert Ressler. What is it about mass murderers that inspires such public fascination? Thanks to the media, especially film and television, we are accustomed to vicarious displays or reports of violence and depravity. It is not until we hear of someone who has so heinously traversed social norms and boundaries, such as in the case of serial killers, by coldly murdering a succession of innocent people often in the most despicable ways, that we feel shaken to our core. Most people would, justifiably, find it difficult, if not impossible, to understand how or why someone could possibly commit such terrible acts. But the need to understand still niggles at us, preys on our minds, and our endless questions about who did it, when, where, how and *why* demand answers.

If you are the type of person who regularly watches crime-themed television programmes or documentaries about serial killers, or who has an impressive library of true crime or crime fiction, rest assured you are not alone. There is a huge demand for crime-themed content and there are many keen followers of the crime genre. If there were not, there would be significantly fewer documentaries about true criminal cases, and popular television series such as *Hannibal*, *Bates Motel* and *Dexter* would not exist. These shows give us an insight into the mind of a killer. They make these otherwise mysterious and villainous characters not only understandable, but also relatable and, dare we say it, in some instances, likeable.

Interestingly enough, real-life serial killers can be very likeable, too. They have stalked our streets for centuries claiming their victims, often fitting in with the rest of their community and appearing every inch the normal, even pleasant, neighbour or the caring father or friend. If we consider Ted Bundy (1946–89), who had the capacity to charm many of the people in his life, then the chilling ability some killers have to flip a switch from decent to terrifying becomes all too clear. Bundy was, at one point, described as 'kind, solicitous and empathetic', and this was a man who raped and killed countless women before sexually assaulting their dead bodies. The married and supposedly respectable John Wayne Gacy (1946–89) ran his own construction business and was so skilled at emotionally compartmentalizing and keeping up the appearance of an honest family man that he got away with murder and rape for six years. It could well be this disconcerting dichotomy that fuels both our interest and fear. These men and women are, to all appearances, just like us, and there are elements of any serial killer that are human and relatable. The attempt to reconcile this with their horrific crimes can be a confusing and unsettling process. It also throws up some significant criminological and psychological questions, such as whether these people became twisted over the years, were victims of their environments or whether they were, quite simply, born evil.

When describing serial killers, especially those who killed in particularly grisly ways, we very often use words such as 'evil' or 'monster'. A monstrous nickname is, in fact, often applied to them by the press, which the public comes to know them by, such as 'The Brooklyn Vampire', 'The Werewolf of Wysteria' or 'The Boogeyman'. All these names were given to Albert Fish, who committed crimes of child molestation, rape, murder and cannibalism in the early twentieth century (see Chapter 6). Nicknames or pseudonyms are usually awarded when the murders have been discovered, but the identity of the killer is not yet known, and it is useful for the media, in their coverage of the story, to have a sensational epithet with which to refer to the as-yet-undiscovered perpetrator.

This process and need to label these men and women as something inhuman is understandable to a certain extent. They have performed acts that are truly monstrous. Their crimes are unforgivable and unimaginable to most reasonable people. To write serial killers off as monsters or think of them as innately evil is easy and, perhaps, in a sense, comforting: it is reassuring to be able to attribute some kind of *otherness* to these killers that separates us from them. They were born that way. They are not like us. We could never be capable of something like that – except, of course, that is not entirely true. It is, in fact, an over-simplification and unhelpfully reductive. Though these killers have crossed beyond the threshold of all civilized and human decency, it does us no good to pretend that they are not, also, members of the human race. They were born innocent, like the rest of us, but something happened in their lives that subsequently pushed them off course. A sobering insight that inevitably arises from studying the often traumatic formative years of serial killers is that, given the necessary corrupting cultural and environmental influences and developmental, medical or psychological issues, any one of us might be capable of murder.

How does one become a serial killer? According to Stephen Giannangelo in his 1996 book, *The Psychopathology of Serial Murder: A Theory of Violence*, it is a long and complicated process. Giannangelo proposes a *Diathesis/ Stress Model of Serial Killing* that suggests that serial killers have an innate tendency to behave and think in ways that lead to serial killing, given the right environmental stressors. They have problems with self-esteem, self-control and healthy sexual functioning, all of which result in the development of dysfunctional social skills. The person retreats into a private, murderous fantasy world, in which his or her fantasies are indulged to their extreme. When he or she begins to seek out real life victims on whom to enact these fantasies, the actual act of murder fails to meet expectations, so more victims are sought: the cycle is repeated and usually becomes ritualistic in nature. This process, evident in many of the stories of the serial killers examined here, provides an intriguing insight into the complex issues at work in their psychological make-up. Furthermore, understanding the men and women that we have historically labelled as monsters serves a forensic and psychological function. Examining their stories and gaining a more profound insight into the factors that shaped them and their murderous urges can play an important role in early detection or even the prevention of similar crimes from occurring in the future.

Supernatural Serial Killers aims to look at the various elements that have come together to create the killers to which society has attributed supernatural associations. These were given to serial killers who committed particularly gruesome or terrible murders, especially those of a sexual or cannibalistic nature and those involving child victims. The 16 chapters of this book deal with 16 serial killers who were either associated with or influenced by supernatural forces. We examine the stories of people such as Richard Trenton Chase, 'The Vampire of Sacramento', who suffered from schizophrenic delusions and terrorized citizens of Sacramento, California with his killing spree in the 70s, and Friedrich 'Fritz' Haarmann, 'The Werewolf of Hanover', who preyed sexually on young boys and teens in post-First World War Germany.

Killers are not created in a vacuum, nor is evil simply born into existence. It is created via myriad pathways. In this book, we look both at the acts of the killers and at these pathways, by exploring their minds and the psychology behind their chilling behaviour.

Why Killers Kill

Abusive childhoods and traumatic experiences

Not all serial killers had an abusive childhood or experienced trauma. More importantly, not everyone who suffers an abusive childhood and traumatic experiences ends up exhibiting criminal tendencies or behaviours. A common denominator for the majority of the killers in this book, however, is an unhappy, neglectful or violent start to their lives.

The early years are, of course, integral to a child's development. Research shows that the first five years of life are critical and form the foundation of a child's emotional and social development. During this time, children learn incredibly quickly and develop a sense of trust and security, meaning they need a nurturing and caring atmosphere to thrive. Without it, children may find it difficult to maintain healthy relationships with others. Children who have suffered a dysfunctional childhood can become loners and socially isolated and do not develop their skills of normal socialization and empathy. Neglected children are also more likely to develop habits of risk-taking and alcohol and drug abuse, as well as emotional and interpersonal problems and mental health issues, such as depression.

They can also exhibit worrying and dangerous behaviours, such as theft, arson, sexual promiscuity and general aggression and hostility. This may go a long way to backing up the assertion that serial killers are made and not born. In addition, many of the serial killers examined here share a history of sexual dysfunction and trauma in their childhoods and adolescent years, which later manifested in the markedly sexual nature of their murders.

Head injury

Many of the killers discussed in this book share another common factor: a blow to the head, usually in the form of an accident suffered in childhood. Studies have proved that this can have a lasting impact on a developing brain and shows a correlation with subsequent violent or aggressive behaviour.

Homicidal triad

In psychiatrist J.M. Macdonald's 1963 paper 'The Threat to Kill' (published in the *American Journal of Psychiatry*), it was suggested that certain childhood behavioural traits could possibly indicate or predict future violent tendencies or serial offences. This is the 'Macdonald triad', also known as the homicidal or sociopathy triad. It consists of three behaviours, and evidence of all three, or a combination of any two, are said to be predictive of future offences. The three behaviours are:

1. persistent bedwetting over the age of five
2. fire setting
3. cruelty to animals

Mental Illness

Much like childhood abuse and trauma discussed above, not all serial killers are possessed of a diagnosable psychiatric condition and not everyone who experiences mental illness ends up developing criminal tendencies. Although there is a widespread public perception that people with mental illness are more likely to display violent behaviour, many studies into the correlation between mental illness and violence have shown that this is simply not true and, in fact, unjustly stigmatizing. Something that a number of the men and women in these chapters do have in common, however, is that they were caught in the grip of psychiatric illnesses resulting in such symptoms as delusions or hallucinations inciting their murderous urges, or had psychological problems stemming from early traumas, drug use or other factors. Given the severity of their crimes, many of these killers were, nonetheless, not found to have a defence of legal insanity and were ultimately sentenced to death.

Categorization

In this book, we will be categorizing our killers using the 1998 Holmes and DeBurger typology. These categories are not definitive, however, and a serial killer may on occasion display evidence of more than one category at different times.

1. A Visionary-type killer hears voices in his or her head or sees visions that prompt murder. Most serial killers are not insane, although those who belong to this category will almost certainly be psychotic and have auditory or visual hallucinations.
2. The Mission-type killer, unlike the Visionary type, does not generally have any mental illnesses, although he may be found to be legally insane. He has made the conscious, premeditated choice to kill and is on a 'mission' to kill a certain type of person who is deemed bad or unsavoury. The Mission killer usually believes he is killing for a very good reason.
3. The Hedonistic type of killer is someone who murders because of the pleasure it gives him, or because of the rewards that he gains through the killing. There are three subtypes of Hedonistic killer: the Lust killer (someone who experiences erotic satisfaction from murder), the Thrill killer (someone who feels a rush of excitement when he kills and who enjoys the feeling of evading capture or baffling authorities) and the

Comfort or Profit killer (sometimes known as 'Gain killers', these people murder usually because they will gain something from the act, such as money).
4. The fourth and final type is known as the Power/Control killer. This is the kind of killer who murders because they like the feeling of being in control and of having someone completely at their mercy.

Our Fascination with the Supernatural

Over the past ten years or so, vampires and werewolves have come to dominate our screens and our bookshelves. *Twilight*, *The Vampire Diaries*, *True Blood* and *Teen Wolf* are obvious examples of popular television series in which vampires and werewolves are depicted as tragic and beautiful romantic figures. Today, more often than not, these supernatural protagonists are imbued with redeeming qualities to humanize them to their audience and, armed with super strength and impossible agility and charmingly burdened with the curse of their mythology, they come across more as sympathetic and lovable superheroes than the villains they were historically. Before *Twilight*, we had *Buffy the Vampire Slayer*, where vampires Spike and Angel and werewolf Oz won the hearts of viewers around the world. Before *Buffy*, there was *Interview with a Vampire*, which, though darker in tone, many argue gave vampire lore a romantic and sensual makeover. Our fascination with the supernatural is not, however, a new phenomenon.

The further back in time we go, the less charismatic and charming the vampires and werewolves are. Historical portrayals tend to more appropriately reflect the gorier and more dangerous villains of lore that terrify children, such as in Bram Stoker's classic *Dracula*. If we go back even further, long before film and television were invented and novels were in common circulation, we enter a time where vampires, werewolves and other supernatural beings were not considered simply fictional. People believed they existed and placed responsibility for gory crimes at their door. This prompted a significant period in legal history where it was entirely possible to be convicted as a werewolf. Unable to fathom how a fellow human being could have committed certain terrible crimes, society and legal systems of the time decided that something else, something inhuman and otherworldly, was responsible.

Werewolves

The word 'werewolf' comes from the old English 'were', meaning 'man', and 'wulf', meaning 'wolf'. Others have asserted that the word derives from '*wargwulf*', which is an old English name for an 'outlaw' wolf – a wolf that would kill simply for pleasure, rather than food. Some historians claim that the legend itself may have originated with the Viking Berserkers, whose name is thought to derive from 'bear-shirts' and who were also known as 'wolf-skins' or 'wolf-coats', referring to the bear or wolf skins that they wore in order to terrify their enemies. Berserkers were often said to change into animal form, or to take on the ferocious qualities of a wolf or bear, during battle.

Whatever its etymological origin, the werewolf myth has been around for centuries. Over that time, it has seen several transformations. At one time, it was said that men were able to transform into wolves with the aid of a ring, an item of clothing, herbs or salves. One source suggests that one became a werewolf after eating the meat of a human mixed with the meat of a wolf. Some legends say that one became a werewolf if conceived under a new moon, or after having consumed water that was touched by a wolf. According to folklore, Zeus turned King Lycaon into a wolf after Lycaon killed his own son, Nyctimus, and served Zeus his roasted flesh in order to test whether or not Zeus was truly omniscient. The belief that one can become a werewolf via a bite is actually a very recent construct and was born from the film *The Werewolf of London* (1935).

Our fascination with werewolves is a longstanding and strong one. Why was it a wolf that prompted the myth? This could be due to the fact that wolves were the most dangerous land predator in Europe for thousands of years. They were not extinct in England until the 15th century. In other parts of the world, though tales of werewolves persist, there are other examples of human to animal transformations, based more on the dominant predator of the area, such as stories of werehyenas in African culture.

Though we may never know for certain how the tale of the werewolf originated, the mythical creature has been a scapegoat for evil for centuries. Superstitious societies in history have turned to the paranormal to explain away the evil that they witnessed and endured. This is how the werewolf and witch trials began in the late Middle Ages. The great 'monsters' of criminal history were, in particular, werewolves. Countless murders were attributed to them in the past, usually crimes that involved mutilation, cannibalism or the sexual abuse of children. These crimes were so unthinkable, and took place in a society so much more superstitious than the one in which we now live, that even the courts accepted that they must have been perpetrated by something not of this world. In the first three chapters of this book we examine three such cases from the 16th century. At that time, men and women in their droves were found guilty of the crime of being a werewolf and were executed, and their dead bodies put on display as a deterrent to other criminal shape-shifters in the region.

A werewolf was believed to have been a man or woman who had made a pact with the devil in order to mutate into a wolf and, as a result, they were also considered to have committed the crime of witchcraft. These werewolf and witch trials began in Switzerland in the 15th century and spread throughout Europe, as crimes of cannibalism, rape and murder continued to spread. They peaked in the 17th century and finally subsided in the 18th century. When the alleged werewolves were tortured into confessing, there would commonly be talk of a 'man in black' who had given them their ability. This was widely believed to be the devil. Many sources have claimed that werewolves were considered the most pressing social menace of the time. Throughout Europe, 30,000 cases of lycanthropy were reported between the years of 1573 and 1600.

Numerous people have confessed to being a werewolf over the centuries. Some may have been forced to confess through torture but some may well have been suffering from a medical or psychiatric condition. Clinical lycanthropy is now recognized as a rare psychiatric condition that gives sufferers the impression that they have the ability to transform into, or indeed already are, an animal. People have been known to growl, run around on all fours and howl. As well as cases involving people believing they were wolves, there are also cases of those who believed they were a tiger, cat, hyena or other non-human animal. In the past, due to their insistence that they had, at some point, turned into a wolf, they would quite likely have been burned alive as werewolves.

Vampires

Although vampires did not play as much of a role in our culture until approximately the 18th century, they are now so deeply ingrained in our collective psyche and popular fiction that without them the horror genre would look fairly bleak and thin. The original vampires of legend were gaunt and terrifying to behold, all of which contrasts dramatically with the roguish, seductive vampires we know and love today.

At one time, thinking about a vampire in a romantic sense would have been absurd. Over the years, in fact, the most chilling of murders have been attributed to vampires. Associations between serial killers and vampires have changed over time. It used to be the case that people genuinely believed an attack had been committed by the supernatural entity. However, as time passed and society became aware that these creatures were the stuff of myth and fantasy, the word 'vampire' became a label or a pseudonym for those who had committed terrible crimes. We still attribute to our killers the epithet of 'vampire', but what we really mean is that the human being behind the crime has a frightening amount in common with the bloodsucking creature of legend. They might be ruthless, calculating and cold-blooded in the execution of their crimes. The connection might be even more direct: frequently, the crimes attributed to 'vampires' involved murderers who drank their victim's blood or incorporated an element of cannibalism in their murders. It is easy to see how such a killer would earn such an appropriately inhuman title.

Though we have evolved as a society and generally accept vampires to be a myth and nothing more, it is not difficult to imagine how our ancestors once believed they actually existed. Science was not nearly as advanced then and knowledge of diseases and decomposition was in its infancy. Many diseases had the appearance of being caused by a monster out for blood. Anaemia, a condition well known and commonly treated today, would have looked suspiciously like the after effects of a vampire attack in centuries past with symptoms that include fatigue, paleness, fainting and shortness of breath. A loss of appetite is also common and some believed this meant that the sufferer was transitioning into being a vampire.

Another condition, coined 'Vampire's Disease' by some, is porphyria, in which chemical substances called porphyrins build up in the body, resulting in neurological or skin problems. Cutaneous porphyrias, where porphyrins accumulate in the skin, result in photosensitivity with severe pain and burning when the skin is exposed to sun, and can also cause a characteristic blistering on the skin, which can result in painful open sores. This disease reminded many people of the sunlight-related aspect of the vampire myth.

One ailment that may be partially responsible for the origin of the vampire myth itself is catalepsy, a symptom of conditions affecting the nervous system, such as Parkinson's disease, epilepsy and cocaine withdrawal.

Catalepsy results in muscular rigidity and a loss of voluntary movement, as well as decreased sensitivity to heat and pain. The sufferer is, effectively, trapped inside themselves, able to see and hear things occurring around them, but unable to interact or move. Gradually, someone suffering from catalepsy will experience a slowing of bodily functions, such as a decreased rate of breathing. Though this condition is temporary and will eventually abate, people suffering from catalepsy were occasionally thought to be dead and were subsequently buried, only to 'come to' at a later time and claw themselves out of their graves. To everyone else, it would appear as if the dead had returned to life.

No matter how the vampire myth evolves and adapts, vampires are stereotypically portrayed as creatures that circumvent our rules and social boundaries, frequently without much care or thought. With the promise of immortality, they exist truly on their own terms, free of inhibition. Yet they are creatures divorced from humanity, symbolizing the death of what we consider to be good and honourable – they have an innate urge to kill, and survive and thrive on blood and violence. For these reasons the label of 'vampire' in serial killer literature is reserved for those men and women whose crimes truly leave us chilled to the bone.

Chapter Structure

Throughout this book, 16 supernatural serial killers are discussed, one in each chapter, including those labelled vampires, werewolves, monsters, Satan worshippers and those involved in the occult. The chapters are arranged chronologically and each begins with a detailed **Introduction** on each killer. This examines their child-hood, teenage years and life before their murderous crime sprees began so we can begin to understand how their formative years and developmental psychology may have impacted on their later criminal tendencies and violent behaviour.

Each chapter then goes on to discuss their **Crimes**, describing the murders, the events leading up to them and the actions of the killer afterwards. Often the details of these murders will be graphic and potentially disturbing, but it is necessary to comprehensively recount the actions of each killer in order to provide a full and accurate picture of their crimes.

The **Trial and Sentence** of the criminal in question is then discussed. The chapters cover the capture, the ques-tioning, the trial, the sentence and the execution or incarceration of each serial killer. Some of the killers included in this book committed their crimes centuries ago and information on their legal proceedings will not be as exhaustive as those who killed more recently. In such cases, however, historical sources are referenced that recount the legal processes of the time, which provide a fascinating context to the social and legal backdrop of these early crimes.

Finally, the chapters conclude with a **Discussion** about the killers and their crimes, where their psychological and criminological background are considered, together with possible mental health issues and legal complications that may have affected their case and the impact of their criminal activity. In this section, we also place each killer within the Holmes and DeBurger typology.

CHAPTER ONE

Michel Verdun, Pierre Bourgot and Philibert Montot – The Werewolves of Poligny

'I was at first horrified at my four wolf's feet, and the fur with which I was covered all at once, but I found that I could now travel with the speed of the wind.'

Pierre Bourgot

Introduction

In the mid-1500s, the French countryside was a place rampant with crime, ranging from minor property offences to rape and murder. It was also rife with superstition. The prevalent belief at the time was that these crimes were committed not merely by human beings, but also by supernatural ones, which were considered by many to be one of society's most threatening menaces. Werewolves, in particular, were blamed for a great number of the country's social and criminal problems. Europe in general was gripped by a fear of other-worldly maleficence: an estimated 30,000 werewolf attacks were reported in the continent between the years of 1520 and 1630.

This belief in the existence of werewolves was not held merely by the superstitious or the gullible; it was, in fact, backed up by law. It is astonishing to believe that it was once possible to be arrested and convicted of the crime of lycanthropy – in other words, being a werewolf. Such an idea is bizarre, even unbelievable, to a rational and modern society possessed of the certainty that werewolves, vampires and monsters are merely fantastical figures of fiction. In the 1500s, however, werewolves were readily accepted as a dangerous threat and legal systems throughout Europe endeavoured as best they could to curb the increasing – and increasingly brutal – murders believed to have been carried out by these vicious, shape-shifting beasts.

The first supernatural serial killers we will examine are the Werewolves of Poligny: three Frenchmen who admitted, under severe torture, to be bloodthirsty werewolves who had taken a great number of lives over a number of years. The impact of their crimes persists into modern times and has even influenced traditional fairy tales: *Little Red Riding Hood*, for example, is thought to have been inspired, in part, by the Poligny story.

This case revolves around Pierre Bourgot (commonly known as Gros Pierre), Philibert Montot and Michel Verdun, who, in 1521, were all accused of making pacts with the devil and of the crimes of lycanthropy, murder and cannibalism. These three infamous men, who became collectively known as the Werewolves of Poligny, are now considered among the most notorious and savage werewolves of the Middle Ages.

Crimes

The crimes of Bourgot, Montot and Verdun and their subsequent trial occurred in the 1500s and, as such, any records or details that remain are few and far between. The facts we do know are largely taken from a confession from the three men, obtained under excessive torture, as was permissible in France at the time as part of the pre-trial process. What is detailed in the following pages is the most commonly held account of what happened centuries ago.

According to Pierre Bourgot's own confession given during his trial, the story began in January 1502, when Bourgot attended a New Year's fair in the town of Poligny (roughly 19 years before he and his fellow werewolves were finally apprehended). A sudden wild and violent storm came upon Poligny; the fair was ruined and the flock of sheep that Bourgot had been herding panicked and ran, scattering in different directions. Along with many of his fellow townsmen, Bourgot braved the storm to go in search of his livestock. The search was long, frustrating and, ultimately, fruitless. At the end of it Bourgot found himself in an unfamiliar location, near an almost deserted road.

It was on this road that he saw three men on horseback, dressed all in black. They approached and one of them asked what he was looking for. Bourgot explained his predicament, and the ringleader of the trio said that he could help find the sheep. He offered Bourgot a deal: if Bourgot would return to this same place in five days to meet him, not only would he guarantee that the sheep would be found, but they would also be protected: if a wolf or other animal were to attack them, they would suffer no injury: not a single one would die. As further enticement, the mysterious stranger offered Bourgot some money. Bourgot accepted the deal. As the man had promised, the flock eventually found their way back to him. So, five days later, Bourgot returned to the deserted spot to meet the stranger, as agreed.

During this second encounter, it became clear to Bourgot that this stranger was no mere Good Samaritan. He told Bourgot that he was a servant of the devil. In exchange for all he had done, he asked Bourgot to accept him as lord and master. He demanded that Bourgot renounce everything he had once held sacred – God, Heaven and the Holy Virgin, to renounce Christianity and to refrain from visiting any church, unless he knew he would not come into contact with holy water or experience Mass. The stranger said that, in return, he could offer Bourgot an ideal life, with money and good fortune. Once again, Bourgot accepted the deal. The stranger gave his hand to Bourgot to kiss, which Bourgot described as 'black and ice-cold as that of a corpse'. Bourgot then 'fell on [his] knees and gave in [his] allegiance to Satan'.

For one year, Bourgot devoted his life to Satan. He did everything that was demanded of him by his master, whose name he afterwards learned was Moyset, avoiding church, not letting holy water touch him and staying away from Mass altogether. He no longer had to worry about his flock as it was under the protection of the devil; not one of his livestock fell prey to wild wolves, illness or ailments. It was not long, however, before Bourgot became bored with his Satanic ways and lack of responsibilities, and reluctant to keep up his end of the bargain. In Bourgot's own words:

'This freedom from care ... made me begin to tire of the devil's service, and I recommenced my attendance at church.' It was at this time that he met Michel Verdun, who 'brought [him] back into obedience to the evil one', asking him to continue to observe the terms of his agreement with the promise of more money. Verdun then brought Bourgot into the forest of Chastel Charnon.

Bourgot provided a detailed description of that night: the clearing that the two men ventured into was lit by candlelight and filled with people, each of them dancing and holding green candles, which emitted a blue-black flame. Bourgot understood that Verdun had led him to a pagan sabbat[1]. Verdun reiterated Moyset's pronouncement that Bourgot would receive great luck and a substantial amount of money, and went further, stating that he would also have a freedom unlike anything he had ever experienced before, in the ability to be fast and be light on his feet. It was here that Bourgot was initiated into the world of lycanthropy: Verdun asked that he strip entirely naked, and then rubbed a 'magic ointment' on his body[2]. Soon afterwards, Bourgot said, he found himself mutating: his arms and legs became covered with thick fur, and his

---

1   There are eight sabbats, or festivals, in the pagan calendar year, set out by the Wheel of the Year, an annual cycle of festivals: Yule (midwinter), Imbolc, Ostara (vernal equinox), Beltane, Litha (midsummer), Lammas, Mabon (autumnal equinox) and Samhain. The celebrations usually occur as a communal gathering of pagan followers, characterized by feasting, dancing and offerings to the gods. In more archaic times, animal sacrifices and orgiastic rituals were also practised.

2   Ointments and wearable items, such as belts (as will be seen in the chapter on Peter Stumpp), were often associated with the ability to change shape or form, usually into that of a wolf. In most cases, these belts or salves were said to be given to the shape-shifter directly from a demon or the devil himself.

hands grew and changed before his very eyes, becoming wolf-like paws. Once the change was complete, he had fully transformed into a wolf, though he retained his human awareness. Initially frightened, he soon found comfort in the myriad new and liberating sensations he experienced: 'I was at first horrified at my four wolf's feet, and the fur with which I was covered all at once, but I found that I could now travel with the speed of the wind.' He and Verdun ran together as 'wolves' through the countryside, looking to satisfy a newfound lust for blood.

During this time, Verdun and Bourgot allegedly committed terrible crimes. On one occasion, they preyed upon, caught and killed a seven-year-old boy, whom they tore to pieces together. They also killed a woman who was gathering peas in her garden. When a man named De Chusnee tried to rescue her from her attackers he, too, was murdered. On another occasion, the two kidnapped a defenceless four-year-old girl, whom they savaged, murdered and consumed, leaving only one of her arms uneaten. In another incident, a young boy of six or seven years was able to make a lucky escape, dodging Bourgot's attack. The werewolf had been ready to sink his teeth into the boy's flesh, but the boy had begun screaming for help. Bourgot ran away, resuming his human form by rubbing his skin with various herbs as he had been taught, in case he was spotted.

The true number of Bourgot and Verdun's victims is not known, but additional murderous tales include the death of a young girl of about eight or nine, whom Bourgot killed in a vegetable patch by biting through her throat, drinking the blood that poured from her neck. On a separate occasion, the two men killed a victim before tearing a hole in his abdomen with their jaws, making it easier for them to drink his blood. When they were unable to find fellow humans to kill and eat, they preyed on livestock; on one occasion, Bourgot came across a goat in a field belonging to a man named Pierre Bongre, and satisfied his bloodlust by cutting its throat with a knife.

Bourgot and Verdun's murderous rampage finally came to an end when, in 1521, a traveller came passing through Poligny. The man was attacked by what he initially believed to be a wild wolf. He managed to injure the animal, wounding one of its front legs and scaring it away. The traveller was uncomfortable, however, leaving an injured wolf wandering the surrounding area, where it could easily attack again. He was particularly worried about it encountering a young child, who would be completely unable to fight it off, even wounded as it was. He therefore followed the trail of blood that the wolf had left in its wake, wanting to hunt it down and kill it. Before long, the blood brought the traveller to the edge of a village, then to the doorstep of a house. He let himself in, worrying for the safety of the people inside. Upon entering, he saw a man with a wound on his arm similar to that which he had inflicted on the wolf's front leg, being tended to by a woman, whom he later discovered to be the injured man's wife.

The traveller believed this to be a sympathetic wound – an injury that followed a werewolf from his wolf form into his human form – and so fled the village, immediately going to the authorities and informing them that the man in the house, later revealed to be Michel Verdun, was a shape-shifter.

Trial and Sentence

As will be seen again and again in the chapters of this book, regardless of historical period and place, in the wake of a bloody and high-profile outbreak of violence, the public becomes anxious to see the culprit brought to justice and held accountable for the atrocities that have occurred. The case of the Werewolves of Poligny was no different: the local people were distraught over the loss of their fellow townsfolk and their livestock, fearful for their own lives and in desperate need of an arrest to set their minds at ease.

Once an accusation of lycanthropy (and, by association, since a deal with the devil was integral to the process, witchcraft) was made, it was difficult, if not impossible, to dissuade the court of the accused's guilt. In retrospect, the logic used to come to the conclusion of werewolfism seems bizarre, but public belief, superstitions and the law in the 1500s were very different from what they are today. In nearly all cases where one was accused of witchcraft and/or lycanthropy, severe torture was freely utilized in order to procure a confession. The confession was usually necessary for the case to go to trial and for a conviction, due to what was often a lack of strong supporting evidence. This admission would need to include a deal with the devil that granted an inhuman ability to trans-mute, as well as an unquenchable desire for blood and destruction. The torture applied was severe and unremit-ting, often taking place on several occasions and, more often than not, the accused was tortured to obtain the names of fellow werewolves.

The pre-trial proceedings experienced by Verdun were

fairly standard for the time. Following his arrest, he was tortured at length and, ultimately, gave a confession. He admitted that he was a werewolf and had committed terrible crimes. After still more torture, he gave up the names of two fellow werewolves, Bourgot and a man by the name of Philibert Montot. The crimes he admitted to committing in the company of these two men included diabolism (devil worship), cannibalism and murder.

Following Verdun's torture and confession, both Montot and Bourgot were apprehended and subsequently tortured for a number of days. The men also, in time and under severe torture, admitted to the fact that they were shape-shifters, and confessed to the crimes that Verdun had described. In his confession, Bourgot reportedly spoke of killing and eating a four-year-old girl, declaring that her flesh had been 'succulent'. The other two men spoke of their time with real wolves, saying that they had mated with them on occasion and that they had experienced 'as much pleasure in the act as if we had copulated with our wives'. It is worth noting, however, the discrepancies in their confessions. All three men, when questioned, gave varying accounts of their crimes. There was little consistency in their descriptions of the sequence of events, further adding to the overall unreliability and, some would argue, the futility of the confessions.

The trial began in December 1521. All three men went to court at Poligny, and the case was presided over by Jean Boin, the Prior of the Dominican convent of Poligny, and the Inquisitor General for the diocese of Besançon (the capital and principal city of the Franche-Comté region in eastern France). During the trial, Bourgot recounted his story, describing how he had become involved with the devil and lycanthropy, and the murders that had occurred following his transmutation. Throughout the trial, it was never entirely clear which murders he had committed in human form and which in wolf form. Bourgot also described how Verdun, who was portrayed as the ringleader, would help them change back into human form with the use of more ointments and herbs: 'when we had been one or two hours in this condition of metamorphosis, Michel smeared us again, and quick as thought we resumed our human forms'.

The few rational words that the men received in support of their case came from Johann Weyer, a Dutch demonologist and physician[1]. Weyer claimed that the confessions given by the three men were forced through torture and therefore should not be allowed to stand. Despite this, all three were convicted of the crimes of lycanthropy and murder. They were then sentenced to death and burned alive at the stake. To make the story gloomier still, Verdun's wife was also implicated: despite there having been no concrete evidence or case to suggest that she was a shape-shifter like her husband and his accomplices, the court did not want to take any chances so she, too, was sentenced to death.

There is no record of the mysterious stranger and 'master', Moyset, being apprehended or brought to justice. We will never know whether this man actually existed, or whether he was fabricated or imagined by Bourgot. Following their execution, pictures of each of the murderers

---

1 Weyer was one of the first few people to publish material arguing against the prosecution of witches. He aimed to show how it was impossible to be a witch, and that the people who confessed to the crime were, in fact, suffering from mental illness.

were hung in the local Jacobin Church at Poligny, as a constant reminder of the evil men who had committed such unforgivable acts and a warning to other werewolves who might consider transgressing in a similar way.

Discussion

In terms of allegations of werewolfism, this case was merely the tip of a very large iceberg. For decades after this trial, thousands of lycanthropy-related criminal proceedings occurred and, often, when a werewolf was suspected, governments involved would issue edicts permitting villagers and townsfolk to hunt down and shoot werewolves at will.

One common trait that links most werewolf cases is the involvement of cannibalism: because France was devoutly Christian at the time, cannibalism would have been regarded as one of the most unforgivable acts. Starvation, however, was not unfamiliar to the people of the Middle Ages. In the area of Franche-Comté in particular, food was often scarce and children did go missing, conceivably to end up as a meal. If the crimes covered in this chapter did, in fact, occur, they would have most likely been the result of the fight against starvation, rather than of a magical balm that turned the perpetrators into wolves.

The crimes allegedly committed by these particular serial killers were horrific and, in cases such as these, it may have been easier, even comforting, for the public to assign blame for the bloodthirsty murders to a supernatural entity, rather than a fellow human being. It was vastly preferable to choose to believe in the existence – and the evil – of a supernatural being than to believe in the inherent evil of a friend or neighbour who had harboured a deeply hidden proclivity for killing and violence: to believe, in short, that such evil could arise from human nature rather than supernatural forces.

Compared with his two fellow werewolves, Philibert Montot rarely gets a mention in the records of this case. His crimes are mysterious and potentially non-existent. Regardless of this, these three men have gone down in history together as examples of 'real life' werewolves that savaged and wreaked havoc upon their local communities.

While categorizing these killers into types using the Holmes and DeBurger model, different perspectives must be considered: if we assume that the men committed their murders simply because they enjoyed the kill and they had an insatiable desire for human blood and flesh, they would belong to the Hedonistic type of serial killer. Hedonistic serial killers typically kill either because it is innately pleasurable for them or because it somehow enhances their personal or social status.

If, on the other hand, we assume that the three men truly believed they were shape-shifting monsters, then it could be argued that they belonged to the Visionary type, where mentally ill killers, who murder as directed by hallucinated voices or visions, can comfortably be placed. As Visionary serial killers, their case would raise the question of whether or not they could truly be held accountable for their crimes. Today, Verdun, Bourgot and Montot might have been diagnosed as suffering from a psychiatric or neurological condition prompting them to believe they were shape-shifters: a delusional belief arising from a delusional disorder or psychosis. Psychiatric disorders giving rise to psychotic symptoms include schizophrenia, bipolar disorder or severe cases of depression. Psychosis may also have neurological causes as far-ranging as dementia, brain tumours, diseases such as Parkinson's or Huntington's disease, infections which affect the brain or some forms of epilepsy; it may even be drug- or alcohol-induced. It is impossible to say with any certainty now, however, which of these conditions each may have been suffering from.

A psychological understanding and medical explanation of werewolfism itself was not to develop until the 17th century, when Robert Burton put forward a rational assessment of lycanthropy in his *Anatomy of Melancholy*, first published in 1621, in which the condition was described as a kind of madness[1]. In modern-day psychiatry and psychology, clinical lycanthropy has come to be recognized as a rare psychiatric syndrome, manifested in psychotic episodes involving a delusional belief that one has transformed into an animal. The delusion is not specific to wolves – though it is named after the mythical condition of lycanthropy, in which physical human-to-wolf shape-shifting occurs.

Today, an in-depth medical and psychological examination would, in all probability, have revealed some psychopathology and the three men may well have been declared legally insane. Unfortunately for the Werewolves

---

1   Interestingly, however, the link between lycanthropy and mental illness may have been made as early as in the Old Testament, where King Nebuchadnezzar is described in the Book of Daniel as losing his sanity and living in the wild like an animal for seven years before, as he himself says, 'my sanity returned to me' – a period now considered by some to have been an attack of clinical lycanthropy.

of Poligny, they lived in a time before these advances in our understanding of criminal psychology and the accompanying nuances in the law regarding mental illness.

Of course, a third possibility exists: that all three men were completely innocent of the crimes for which they were put to death and confessed simply to avoid further torture. The justice system at the time was far from perfect, and it is likely that a desire to ensure that a speedy and effective sentence was served led to many miscarriages of justice.

Whatever the case, and regardless of what mental or neurological illness, if any, the men suffered from, we know now that the legal assertion that they were werewolves was inaccurate and quite impossible.

CHAPTER TWO

Gilles Garnier – The Werewolf of Dole

'Being in the form of a wolf . . . [he] slew her with both hands, seemingly paws, and with his teeth carried some flesh home to his wife.'
                                                    Gilles Garnier

Introduction

Amid the deluge of attacks attributed to werewolves during the mid-16th century, France was to provide criminal history with one of the most gruesome cases of lycanthropy on record, in which such violent crimes were committed that they are considered by some to overshadow even those of Jack the Ripper. Although the killer in question is known by a number of aliases, including 'The Werewolf of Dole' and 'The Hermit of St Bonnot', he was known in his lifetime simply as Gilles Garnier, a recluse from the small French village of Dole, near Lyon, who confessed to making a pact with the devil and brutally murdering and cannibalizing a number of innocent children in the year leading up to his execution.

Lucas Cranach's engraving of a werewolf carrying off a child watched by the infant's helpless mother.

As Garnier's crimes took place so many centuries ago, most of the details about his life and his offences are lost to time. What we do know about Garnier comes mainly thanks to a pamphlet published in Sens, France, in 1574.

This pamphlet paints a vivid picture of Garnier's crimes, conviction and punishment with the specific intention of highlighting to the public the ever-present danger of werewolves, as well as demonstrating to potential culprits what would happen to them if they were ever to be caught. Though it provides us with most of what we know about Garnier, it is worth remembering that this pamphlet was published at least in part to sensationalize and that the facts surrounding the case may have been played up to achieve this effect.

Garnier's appearance has been described in great detail: he walked in 'a stooping attitude' and was 'ill-looking', with a 'pale face, livid complexion and deep-set eyes under a pair of coarse and bushy brows, which met across the forehead', as well as a long grey beard. It is worth noting that this fits well with the belief at the time that werewolves could be identified by certain physical characteristics, including a heavy monobrow and hairy palms, which, it was believed, they would shave to disguise their true nature. This was likely an attempt to give villagers and general members of the public a sense of safety: if they knew what characteristics to look for, they would be able to more easily identify the monsters among them.

Garnier enjoyed a solitary existence in the years prior to his marriage, rarely speaking to anyone. There is little evidence to suggest that he exhibited any criminal behaviour before his alleged spate of murders. In his 1865 book, *The Book of Were-Wolves*, Sabine Baring-Gould describes Garnier's house as being situated 'in a retired spot near Amangos, half shrouded in trees . . . a small hovel of the rudest construction; its roof was of turf, and the walls were blotched with lichen. The garden of this cottage was run to waste, and the fence around it broken through. As the hovel was far from any road, and was only reached by a path over moorland and forest, it was seldom visited.' Why a man with, by all accounts, such a reclusive personality decided to take a wife and start a family is unknown. Until he married, Garnier had only to provide for himself and was not a natural family man or caregiver; soon after his marriage, his problems began.

Crimes

In 1572, Garnier decided to settle down and marry a young woman by the name of Apoline. Little is known about their private life, but it is thought that, especially once the couple had children, Garnier found it nearly impossible to provide sufficiently for both himself and his growing family. Often he ventured out in search of food but returned home empty-handed.

Soon Garnier became desperate. His predatory instincts grew and he began to direct them not only at animals, but also at human beings. Young children in and around the village of Dole began to go missing and their lifeless, eviscerated bodies were discovered soon afterwards. Garnier killed both boys and girls between the ages of nine and 12. His preferred method of killing was manual strangulation, followed by ripping the bodies apart and devouring parts of them. The bodies of his victims were discovered horribly mutilated and, on occasion, dismembered, when he wanted to bring a limb or some flesh home for his wife to eat. There is no evidence to suggest that this meat was shared with their children.

Different sources disagree over the number of Garnier's

victims, with some reporting two victims and others as many as four or five; the last is the most commonly agreed number.

His first murder is said to have taken place on the first day of Michaelmas 1572 (approximately 29 September), roughly 1.5 kilometres from Dole. On Gorge farm, adjacent to the Le Serre Woods in the vineyard of Chastenoy, Garnier met a young girl of about ten years of age. He strangled the girl to death, reportedly in the guise of a wolf, before dragging her body into the woods and stripping her of her clothes. He proceeded to devour her, eating a good amount of her flesh, predominantly from her thighs and arms. He then kept some and brought it home to share with his wife.

Garnier's second murder is thought to have occurred only eight days after the first. Whether it was a newly acquired taste for human flesh or a feeling of power in the act of killing that prompted it, this second murder took place near the meadowland of La Pouppe. As before, the victim was a young girl, and the pamphlet describes that 'he slew her, tearing her body and wounding her in five places of her body with his hands and teeth'. He would most likely have eaten her, as he had his first victim, had it not been for three peasants from Chastenoy, who happened to be walking near the scene of the attack on their way home from work. They heard screams and wolf-like noises and immediately ran towards the commotion. They claimed that they saw a little girl desperately trying to defend herself from what looked like an attacking animal. Once the attacker noticed the men, it ran, on all fours, into the forest. Due to the growing darkness of the evening, no one involved could be entirely certain about what they had seen: some of the party thought the attacker had been an animal, while others thought that they had recognized the form of Garnier. The young girl who was rescued by the three men survived briefly after the vicious encounter, but was badly wounded and soon succumbed to her injuries and died, marking Garnier's second murder.

Garnier struck again, reportedly on 1 November 1572, between the communes of Gredisans and Menotey. This time, the victim was a ten-year-old boy, whom Garnier strangled to death. He was able on this occasion to satiate his appetite, ripping into the boy's body with his teeth and devouring his thighs, arms and abdominal flesh. He also ripped off one of the boy's legs and brought it home for his wife.

The penultimate attack took place one week later, near the village of Perrouze. The victim was a boy of 12 years whom Garnier abducted on the road and quickly killed before dragging him into a thicket under a pear tree. He may have gone on to eat the boy's flesh as he had done before, but again he was interrupted by a number of villagers passing by. The pamphlet, interestingly, expressed great affront that the incident had occurred on a Friday, as eating meat on a Friday was considered sacrilegious and in direct contravention of common Catholic custom at the time.

Although Garnier was not generally suspected at this time, the number of murders became too excessive for the Court of Parliament and the villagers of Dole to ignore. So the authorities of the Franche-Comté province promptly issued an edict allowing and urging the locals to track down, apprehend and even kill the werewolf that was causing such devastation:

'According to the advertisement made to the sovereign Court of Parliament at Dole, that, in the territories of Espagny, Salvange, Courchapon, and the neighbouring villages, has often been seen and met, for some time past, a were-wolf, who, it is said, has already seized and carried off several little children, so that they have not been seen since, and since he has attacked and done injury in the country to some horsemen, who kept him off only with great difficulty and danger to their persons: the said Court, desiring to prevent any greater danger, has permitted, and does permit, those who are abiding or dwelling in the said places and others, notwithstanding all edicts concerning the chase, to assemble with pikes, halberts, arquebuses, and sticks, to chase and to pursue the said were-wolf in every place where they may find or seize him; to tie and to kill, without incurring any pains or penalties.'

Despite the edict, one final murder was to take place in Chastenoy in January 1573. In this case, some residents of Chastenoy were returning to the village when they heard a child's desperate screams and the baying of a wolf. The villagers hurried towards the noise and arrived in time to see the attacker fleeing the scene. It is uncertain if the victim was a boy or girl, but he or she died shortly after being rescued. The incident was remarkably similar to the second murder; this time, however, a number of the witnesses claimed to have recognized the attacker before he escaped into the darkness, as he had attacked in human form. Not long after the incident, Garnier was caught and arrested.

Trial and Sentence

Shortly after Garnier's arrest he was assessed, in what may seem a surprisingly modern legal procedure, to determine his sanity and ability to stand trial. Although he apparently presented some symptoms of mental illness, the details of which are unavailable, a panel of experts decided that he was sane enough to be tried. This was due to the fact that, despite believing himself to be a werewolf – something he would later confess to after experiencing a significant amount of torture – he was coherent and seemingly rational, apparently knowing right from wrong and remembering in detail the events of his misdeeds.

Before the trial began, both Garnier and his wife were questioned and tortured in order to procure a confession from them. As discussed in the previous chapter, torture was often used in situations such as these, as well as where witchcraft was suspected. Without the advances in investigative and forensic science that we have today and with evidence based purely on vague eyewitness accounts, as in this case, it was difficult to prove that the culprit had committed the crimes of which they were accused without a confession.

At the time of Garnier's criminal spree, judicial torture in France was regulated by The Ordinance of Villers-Cotterêts, a piece of legislation created in 1539. According to this legislative edict, torture could be carried out on two occasions during a trial: before it began and after the verdict had been passed. Pre-trial torture was known as 'preparatory questioning' and could only be carried out once. It was usually conducted in order to secure a confession so that the case could proceed to court. 'Preliminary questioning', on the other hand, generally occurred after the criminal received his or her conviction and was performed in order to obtain the names of accomplices; at this stage, as the convict had been sentenced to death, there were no restrictions regarding how many times torture could be carried out.

In addition, torture in France had to first be threatened before actually being meted out, so that the accused was given the opportunity to confess without having to experience much discomfort. In Germany, this was known as torture '*mit gute*', meaning torture 'without pain'. Garnier did not confess to any crimes prior to being tortured. Considering the agony he would have experienced under torture, it is entirely possible that he might have admitted to crimes he had not actually committed simply to put an end to his suffering.

The exact manner of torture that Garnier experienced is unknown; however, given the most prevalent torture methods of the day, we can make a good guess as to the amount of suffering he was made to endure. At the time, the authorities did their best to induce extreme pain without causing death, usually by distressing the nervous and musculoskeletal systems. Of all the forms of torture available, the most common was the *strappado*, a means of punishment where the hands of the accused were tied behind their back and strapped to a ceiling-mounted pulley with a rope. The accused was then raised off the floor, suspending them in mid-air by the wrists, the most likely result of which was dislocation of the shoulder or arm joints, with continued and sustained pressure on the dislocated joints. Sometimes weights were added to the accused's body to amplify the effect. Contraptions such as thumbscrews and leg braces were also often used, which were specifically designed to crush limbs. Other common forms of torture included the rack, which stretched the body to the point of dislocating joints and tearing flesh, and fire applied to the soles of the feet.

In Garnier's case, the resulting confessions from both him and his wife proved to be the most persuasive testimony at trial. He confessed to murdering four children in both the form of a wolf and a human, as well as eating their remains.

The trial began in late 1572 and was conducted under the jurisdiction of the Parliament of Franche-Comté. Garnier's pre-trial testimony, which he upheld in court, was an extraordinary one. According to the account given in the pamphlet, he claimed that one night, early in his marriage and while hunting alone in the forest, he encountered a spectre (some sources interpret this to be a demon, others some kind of spirit). This spectre offered him a solution that would solve all his problems in the form of a special ointment. Once applied, this ointment would give him the power to morph into the shape of a wolf, facilitating his ability to hunt.

The general belief at the time was that in order to become a werewolf, one had to make contact with the devil, which meant that werewolfism constituted a kind of witchcraft. Garnier's confession, submitted pre-trial, was backed up by more than 50 witnesses, all of whom claimed to have personally seen him attack and kill children or consume human flesh. Some witnesses claimed to have seen him in his human form, while others had seen him as a *loup-garou* ('werewolf' in French).

Rather than attempting to deny his participation in the killings and subsequent cannibalism, Garnier tried to lay the real blame for the murders at the devil's door. He claimed to have been under the influence of demons and that their evil presence had prompted behaviour that he would not normally have displayed. The court accepted Garnier's claim of having been under the influence of demonic spirits, but rather than seeing this as a defence, the court decided that it was his own fault, as he had invited these supernatural forces into his life.

Garnier was ultimately convicted of murder, lycanthropy and witchcraft and was handed over by the court to the Master Executioner of High Justice. It was instructed by the courts that he should be 'drawn upon a hurdle from this very high place unto the customary place of execution, and that there by the aforesaid master executioner, he shall be burned quick and his body reduced to ashes'.

The sentence was carried out on 18 January 1573, when Garnier and his wife – who may well have been entirely innocent and unaware of her husband's alleged crimes – were both burned at the stake. Although he was not a man of means, what few possessions he had were confiscated by the state and used to pay for his trial and execution. Nothing is known about the fate of his children.

Discussion

The story of Gilles Garnier can be seen as horrific or tragic, or both, depending on whether Garnier actually committed the crimes of which he was accused. It is entirely possible that Garnier was nothing more than an innocent eccentric who suffered due to the superstitious atmosphere of his time and thus became a scapegoat for crimes he did not commit. It is equally possible, however, that Garnier was, in fact, a vicious killer with debilitating mental illnesses who caused great suffering to the innocent children who died at his hands.

If we take the view that his confession was true, we must assume that this man genuinely believed that he had the power to turn into a supernatural being at will. If so, as in the case of the Werewolves of Poligny before him, it poses the question of whether he was mentally ill and, therefore, whether he was unfairly convicted of and sentenced for his crimes. Under medical or psychiatric examination today, Garnier would quite likely have been diagnosed as suffering from a psychiatric or neurological condition manifesting in a delusional belief that he could shape-shift at will between wolf and human forms. This delusion is a hallmark of psychosis, which, as described in the discussion in the previous chapter, has a wide range of possible underlying medical causes.

That Garnier exclusively chose child victims is significant. There is no evidence to suggest that he attempted attacks on adults, who would be more able to defend themselves. Instead he targeted the most vulnerable members of society. Though his actions may have been born of a desperate need to provide for a starving family, Garnier crossed beyond all the boundaries of societal mores and moral decency. In the Holmes and DeBurger typology, Garnier may be classified as a Hedonistic killer, specifically of the Comfort killer subtype. These killers kill for 'creature-comfort' reasons, such as financial or other material gain. Another way of classifying him may be as a Visionary serial killer – if he did indeed suffer from a mental illness causing psychosis, with delusions that motivated his murderous impulses.

Finally, one might question why the court would have accepted a confession procured under the pain of torture when a strong possibility existed that it had been falsified. This is a complex area of archaic law with roots in a legal system long obsolete and often criticized, both during and after its abolishment. The criminal courts at the time were under great pressure from the general public to produce a culprit to blame for high-profile crimes and provide them with a sense of satisfaction in seeing justice carried out. Some people are of the opinion that Garnier was completely innocent and that he was simply an easy target for the courts and an attractive scapegoat, given the fact that he was a recluse who lived on the margins of society, was known to display strange behaviour and was seen as a dispensable member of the community in which he lived.

CHAPTER THREE

Peter Stumpp – The Werewolf of Bedburg

'Never was known a wretch from nature so far degenerate.'
from *A True Discourse Declaring the*
Damnable Life and Death of One Stubbe Peter

THE LIFE AND DEATH OF PETER STUMP

Peter Stumpp's story is shown in a series of 16th-century engravings.

Introduction

In the autumn of 1589, a small country town around 45 kilometres west of Cologne (in what is now Germany) became the setting for one of the most lurid and notorious werewolf trials in history. In the 16th century, before Germany or indeed the modern nation-state system came into existence, the town of Bedburg in the Electorate of Cologne was still a part of the Holy Roman Empire. On trial, and at the centre of the infamous crimes leading up to it, was a local man who came to be known as the 'Werewolf of Bedburg'.

Peter Stumpp (variations of his name include Peter Stube, Peter Stubbe, Peeter Stubbe or Peter Stumpf[1]) was a Rhenish farmer from a small village named Epprath, near Bedburg. Of all the murderers we will discuss in this book with a werewolf association, Stumpp's story is perhaps the best-known. Charlotte F. Otten, English professor at Calvin College and author of a number of books on lycanthropy, describes him as being among 'the most notorious criminal werewolves'. A regular feature in non-fiction work, his gruesome crimes have also captured the imagination of fiction writers: he was mentioned in William Peter Blatty's book *The Exorcist*;

---

1 These different versions of his name have been used in various works concerning him over the years. There are those who believe that stumpf (German for 'stump') may not have been his real name, but a nickname applied to him in reference to his missing left hand, which had been cut off, leaving only a stump. The wolf he purportedly transformed into was said to have a missing left forepaw, an injury which matched that of the man and was therefore used as evidence of his guilt. Another name used in connection to him, thought by some to be his birth name, is 'Griswold', with his given name being Abal, Abil or Obel. Throughout this book, however, we will maintain consistency with the name 'Peter Stumpp'.

he was the titular character in Sean Hutchinson's short story *On The Death of Peter Stubbe*, and he was also the focus of a fictionalized account of a werewolf trial, written by Scott Wolf. Stumpp's story has even been the inspiration for a song, *The Werewolf of Bedburg (Peter Stumpp)* by US death metal band Macabre, the lyrics of which describe his gruesome crimes and fate.

The story of Peter Stumpp is undoubtedly a compelling one, yet it remains shrouded in mystery and uncertainty: local church registers and public records of Stumpp's birth and life were completely destroyed in the 17th century during the Thirty Years War. Even basic details of his life, such as his date of birth and birth name, are lost to us today. Consequently, the most comprehensive surviving source of information on his story is a 16-page pamphlet published in 1590 in London, the English translation of a German original of which no copies now exist. The English pamphlet, entitled *A True Discourse Declaring the Damnable Life and Death of One Stubbe Peter*, was written approximately a year after his execution and discovered by occultist Montague Summers in 1920. Only two copies survive today, one in the British Museum and the other in the Lambeth Library.

A True Discourse Declaring the Damnable Life and Death of One Stubbe Peter contains vivid descriptions of Stumpp's life, alleged crimes and trial, and includes statements from witnesses to his crimes. Although it was written not long after the events actually took place and could reasonably be thought to be fairly accurate, the pamphlet was, essentially, an extract from a tabloid, written specifically to entice, entertain and horrify the public of the time. Like the pamphlet detailing Garnier's crimes, discussed in the previous chapter, Stumpp's pamphlet contained, in all likelihood, a story that was exaggerated and sensational-ized. Much of the literature compiled on Stumpp is educated guess-work and extrapolation from this source. The information included in this chapter represents the general consensus on Stumpp and his misdemeanors, and unreferenced quotations are taken directly from the pamphlet.

Dirk C. Gibson, author of *Legends, Monsters, or Serial Murderers?*, in which Stumpp is discussed, estimates Stumpp's date of birth to be some time in 1525. He was reportedly a farmer in the rural village community of Epprath in the 1580s, and is said to have been a widower and a father of two adolescent children: a girl named Beel, or Sybil, who was allegedly involved in his crimes, and a son, whose name is unknown.

It is believed that even before Stumpp possessed the power to transform into a werewolf, he had already been greatly inclined to evil acts and the practice of 'wicked arts from twelve years of age'. The folklore around Stumpp, as detailed in the beginning of the pamphlet, is that the devil himself saw the farmer's great capacity for torment and wickedness and appeared to him, promising to give him whatever his heart desired.

Stumpp asked for neither riches nor personal advance-ment, but instead requested that 'at his pleasure he might work his malice on men, women, and children, in the shape of some beast, whereby he might live without dread or danger of life, and be unknown to be the executor of any bloody enterprise which he meant to commit'. The devil, deciding that he was a 'fit instrument to perform mischief as a wicked fiend', gifted him with a single girdle, or belt, made from the pelt of a wolf. This belt gave Stumpp the ability to transform into a wolf: with it on, he became a physical reflection of the monster that he already was inside. Wearing his wolf pelt belt, Stumpp assumed 'the likeness of a greedy, devouring wolf, strong and mighty, with eyes great and large, which in the night sparkled like brands of fire; a mouth great and wide, with most sharp and cruel teeth; a huge body and mighty paws'. Upon removing the belt, he returned to his human state and assumed the guise of a civil, respectable man and a decent fellow villager.

Crimes

Grisly accounts of Stumpp's crimes and brutal murders are detailed in the pamphlet and referenced throughout the literature on his story. Stumpp was reportedly an 'insatiable bloodsucker', gorging on the flesh of sheep, goats, lambs, cattle, men, women and children. At his execution, upon being tortured, he confessed to having murdered and eaten 14 children as well as two pregnant women, whose unborn fetuses he tore from their wombs. Of the two fetuses it was described that he 'ate their hearts panting hot and raw, which he accounted dainty morsels and best agreeing to his appetite'.

It seems that Stumpp favoured small children as victims. He would begin by strangling them or bludgeoning them before tearing their throats open with his bare hands, disembowelling them and partially consuming them. One of the 14 was Stumpp's own child – the result of an incestuous relationship with his daughter, Beel. After enticing the boy out onto the fields and then into a forest outside of Bedburg, Stumpp is reported to have assumed the form of a wolf, attacked and killed him. He cracked open the boy's skull and ate his brain – a child who was both his own son and grandson, in an act described in the pamphlet as 'the most monstrous act that ever man heard of, for never was known a wretch from nature so far degenerate'.

Among the collection of terrible tales contained in the pamphlet is one chronicling the murder of two men and a woman, whom Stumpp came upon as they walked in the woods outside of Bedburg. As he was outnumbered, he concealed himself and, when they approached his hiding place, called out to one of the men, whom he knew by name. The man, thinking that it was a prank by a friend, left the group to find the source of the noise and was quickly and quietly murdered. After a time, the second man went to look for his companion, and was similarly disposed of. The woman, now alone and sensing that some evil had befallen the men, tried to escape but was overtaken and caught by Stumpp, who raped and then murdered her. What remained of the bodies of the two men was afterwards found mangled in the woods as if savaged and partially eaten by some wild animal, but the woman's remains were never found. Stumpp had completely devoured her body, which he 'esteemed both sweet and dainty in taste'. The savagery of this account, as well as the fact that he had had no cause to wish the three dead, would have made him all the more terrifying. His victims met their fate completely by chance, acquired, as Gibson describes, 'in an unsystematic and haphazard way', meaning that anyone and everyone in the vicinity was at risk.

In addition, Stumpp's crimes were not simply violent;

there was an underlying, darkly sexual side to his killings. He was reported to have sexually violated – or even tortured – his female victims before tearing them apart. Though many of the facts and details of Stumpp and his misadventures are uncertain, when he is mentioned in books and essays, his depraved, insatiable sexual nature is a constant theme. The unanimous belief is that Stumpp's perversity was not limited to his murders – his sexual life was almost as shocking. His sexuality was vividly described by Gibson as being a 'sojourn into sadistic and aberrant intimate behaviour', with many mistresses, both mortal and other-worldly. Among his many charges was that of incest: he confessed to having an incestuous relationship with his daughter, Beel, as well as a distant relative, Katharina Trompin. As a result of this confession, both women were later sentenced to be executed together with Stumpp. In addition, he confessed to having had intercourse with a succubus – a seductive female demon or supernatural entity – sent to him by the devil.

Trial and Sentence

According to the pamphlet, a group of men from Epprath led their dogs on a hunt for the predator, which was attacking and savaging their livestock and fellow villagers. After days of tracking, the men sighted a wolf and set their dogs to chase it down. When the dogs had the wolf cornered, the men approached. They were amazed, however, when it transformed before their very eyes into the shape of a man: Stumpp, knowing that there was no escape for him, had taken off his wolf pelt belt. Had they not recognized Stumpp as one of their fellow villagers, they would easily have believed him to be 'some Devil in a man's likeness'. Instead, still not quite believing he was the man he claimed to be – whom they all knew to be an upright member of their small community – they brought him back to his own house, in a bid to verify whether or not another, the real Peter Stumpp, was to be found at home – which of course there was not. Upon 'finding him to be the man indeede, and no delusion or phantasticall motion', they brought him before the magistrates of Bedburg. Stumpp was brought to trial charged with the aforementioned crimes of werewolfism and murder. However, it was only under pain of torture on the rack[1] that he confessed to all the heinous crimes with which he was charged. His torture-derived confession was enough to secure a guilty verdict, which was delivered on 28 October 1589. During the trial, Stumpp explained the absence of his magical belt by claiming that he had cast it aside on the day he was caught, while running from his pursuers. The magistrates sent men to look for the belt, but it was never found; the explanation given in the pamphlet was that after Stumpp had been exposed, the Devil himself had summoned the belt back to hell.

Three days after the verdict, on 31 October 1589, Stumpp's spectacular, public and gory execution took place. He was placed on a wheel and had his skin pierced

---

1   The rack was a torture device consisting of a rectangular frame and cylindrical rollers at either end. The victim's feet were chained to one roller at the ankles, and the hands to the other at the wrist. Via the turning of a ratchet sending the rollers in opposite directions, the tension on the chains was increased very slowly, inducing a slow-building, excruciating pain. If the interrogation took a long enough time, the sufferer's joints were dislocated and ultimately separated entirely.

by red hot pincers – or tongs – in ten different places, which ripped his flesh from the bone. To ensure that the supernatural being was, in fact, deceased, and would not return, his arms and legs were broken with the blunt side of an axe. Finally, his head was cut off. His body was burned on a pyre, together with his daughter, Beel, and his mistress, Katharina Trompin, who were deemed to have been accessories to his murders.

By the order of the magistrates, a monument to Stumpp was erected. The wheel upon which he had been tortured was placed on top of a long pole. Atop it was placed an image of a wolf and above this, on the sharpened tip of the pole, was attached Stumpp's severed head. From the wheel was hung 15 m (50 ft) long pieces of wood, representing each of his known victims. This 'monument to all ensuing ages' served as a warning to all potential future devil-worshippers or werewolves and was graphically illustrated in the 16th-century pamphlet.

News of Stumpp's extraordinary story and trial travelled quickly throughout Europe, and the case became a far-reaching precedent for a series of werewolf trials in France, Switzerland and Franche-Comté which followed.

Discussion

Stumpp's criminal career reportedly spanned two and a half decades: in addition to being tried and convicted as a werewolf, he was eventually found to be guilty of numerous other crimes, among them murder, cannibalism, rape, filicide, adultery and even sorcery. Most of these crimes resonate with us in the modern world and are relevant to our current legal systems. Werewolfism and sorcery, however, have since been relegated to the stuff of myth and fiction.

The historical context of Stumpp's crimes is vital to understanding these archaic charges against him – and it was not a happy one. His crimes, trial and eventual execution took place against a backdrop of political and religious strife between warring groups of Protestants and Catholics, resulting in warfare within the Electorate of Cologne with the armies of both sides invading Bedburg. Furthermore, Europe was, at the time, mired in superstition and a deep fear of supernatural forces. As Gibson writes, 'people were conditioned to believe in and fear werewolves, and they interpreted serial murder through that supernatural prism'.

This context is all the more relevant – and controversial – when considering that the lack of detail surrounding Stumpp has led many to debate his guilt for the crimes of which he was accused. It has been suggested that Stumpp, as a Protestant convert, may have been used by the Catholics as a political pawn following their victory over the Protestants in 1587. Confronted with the existence of a frightening and demon-like Protestant killer, those who remained in the Protestant faith might well be tempted to convert to the safety and protection of Catholicism. Even if one were not superstitious, the gratuitous public execution of a known Protestant might have served as a warning to others of the same denomination. In addition to these factors, it is worth noting that Stumpp's confession was procured either during or under the threat of severe torture and, as a result, may have been at least partially fabricated in an attempt to stave off more pain and injury.

Furthermore, the combination of the sadistic and sexual nature of the murders and that there were child victims was, in all likelihood, more than members of Stumpp's community could conceive a fellow human being capable of at the time. In his book examining the archetype of the werewolf throughout literature, *The Modern Literary Werewolf*, Brent Stypczynski points out that thinking of killers as supernatural in some way enables us to 'separate humanity from excessive violence': it may have been easier for the people of Stumpp's time to attribute such brutality and wickedness to some supernatural being or state, rather than to acknowledge its existence in human nature, making it all the more tempting to accept and believe in his werewolfism.

If we examine the more popular belief that Stumpp was indeed guilty of the charges levelled at him, then his story opens up an equally sobering line of discussion. Public opinion of the time, as reflected in the pamphlet, was that Stumpp indulged in maiming and killing for the pleasure and thrill of it. In the Holmes and DeBurger model, this would have placed him well in the category of the Hedonistic serial killer.

By the time Holmes and DeBurger developed their classification model in 1988, however, a deeper and more complex understanding of human and criminal psychology was available. A third explanation of Stumpp's crimes, which occurs naturally to us today but was likely to have been overlooked in his time – and much less admissable as a legal defence – was that Stumpp may have indeed been guilty, but living in the grip of a serious mental illness requiring treatment. Transposed into the 21st century and given a psychiatric assessment today, Stumpp may well have qualified as a Visionary serial killer. His case is similar to that of Gilles Garnier and of the Werewolves of Poligny: all these men may have had serious mental illnesses prompting the delusional belief that they had the ability to shape-shift into werewolves. As discussed in previous chapters, they may have suffered from psychosis-triggering conditions as far-ranging as schizophrenia, dementia, brain tumours or infection, epilepsy or clinical lycanthropy, a rare psychiatric syndrome with psychotic episodes involving a delusional belief that one has transformed into an animal.

If Stumpp had lived today, his werewolfism may well have been attributed to such a delusion: the Werewolf of Bedburg might have had the benefit of necessary psychiatric or medical assessment and treatment, rather than being faced with the pain of torture and brutal execution, and being immortalized as a supernatural killer.

CHAPTER FOUR

Countess Erzsebét (Elizabeth) Báthory de Ecsed – The Blood Countess/The Tigress of Čachtice

'Elizabeth rose up on her bed, and, like a bulldog, the Countess opened her mouth and bit the girl first on the cheek. Then she went for the girl's shoulders where she ripped out a piece of flesh with her teeth. After that, Elizabeth proceeded to bite the girl's breasts.' Aldo César das Neves Rodrigues, *The Worst People in History*

Introduction

A book dedicated to the exploration of the lives and crimes of supernatural serial killers would not be complete without Báthory, the infamous Hungarian countess and mass murderer who has become a staple character of vampire lore for many followers of the genre. An abundance of accounts exist (reliable and otherwise) of her regular habits of cannibalism and bloody torture. With her legendary beauty, alleged obsession with blood and eternal life and terrible misdeeds leading to her eventual fall from grace, her story is undoubtedly a gripping one.

Elizabeth Báthory

Báthory has been called the most prolific female serial killer that has ever lived, with academics from King's College London referring to her as 'one of the most infamous figures in history'.

The stories that many are familiar with in relation to Báthory involve her killing virgins in order to drink – and bathe in – their blood, thereby regaining and preserving her youth and good looks. These tales of her vampire-like proclivities were all recorded years after her death, and different sources almost unilaterally agree that they are likely to be untrue or, at least, poorly substantiated. Interest in her and her legend continues unabated, however, with stories written about her since the 18th century and films produced based on her life and crimes capturing the imagination of millions. The 1971 film *Daughters of Darkness* depicts her as a Hungarian countess and modern-day vampire. In the 2006 horror movie *Stay Alive*, the villain is a character in a video game named Elizabeth Bathory, who murders her victims in a similar way to her infamous namesake. The films *Bathory* (2008) and *The Countess* (2009) were both based on Bathory's life. In the 2013 sequel film, *Fright Night 2: New Blood*, a character named Báthory is an ancient vampire residing in Romania. Popular culture and society's fascination with Bathory, having lasted for centuries, is still very much alive and well.

This book covers a wide range of heinous killers, all of whom well deserve their place in history for the crimes they committed. In the course of our research we were frequently presented with a dearth of information; where Báthory is concerned, however, we found the opposite to be true. So much has been written about Báthory, her life, her crimes and the legends that surround her that a great number of contradictions and inconsistencies exist between the different accounts. This may be due in part to the fact that her crimes occurred centuries ago, or that information may have been withheld by the nobility of the time in order to avoid even greater shame than was already caused by the facts being made public. Over time, some historians have come forward to dispute that she was a serial killer at all. In this chapter we shall delve into the stories and folklore in order to present the most likely events in the life of Elizabeth Báthory.

Most of the information we have today regarding her life and crimes comes from documents at the National Archives of Hungary in Budapest. She was accused of killing hundreds of girls between the years of 1585 and 1610, with some sources claiming a victim count of over 600. Though the exact (and even estimated) number of girls who died at her hand is a topic often debated, church records at the time certainly reflect the fact that there were an inordinate number of deaths of young girls in the area where she lived.

In order to more objectively understand Báthory's story, we must first draw a distinction between the person and her crimes, and so attempt to better understand the woman behind the legend. Unlike many women of her time, Báthory was very well-educated and, by all accounts, highly accomplished and possessed of a great intellect. She was fluent in Hungarian, Latin and Greek and able to read and write in each of these languages. She was a skilled negotiator with a strong grasp of military matters, often exercising these abilities when her husband was away at war, leaving her to run his vast estates. She was, furthermore, a woman of great ambition and wanted to be the next Queen of Poland, which was not such a far-fetched notion as she was, in fact, next in line to be crowned the reigning monarch.

Accounts of her life and depictions of her in fiction often focus on her extreme good looks. Most sources agree that she was a beautiful woman, with delicate features and long, raven black hair that contrasted with her milky complexion. She had large, cat-like amber eyes and a figure that has been referred to as 'slender' by some and 'voluptuous' by others. A surviving portrait of her certainly reflects this beauty; however, it is very possible that these reports overstated the truth. She was certainly a woman of great power, and most people of her acquaintance would have been likely to sing her praises in this regard.

Báthory has been connected to Vlad III, or Vlad the Impaler, who is more widely known by the name Dracula. In 1476, the commander-in-chief of the expedition that eventually returned Vlad III to his throne was Prince Stephen Báthory. Some experts claim that the Hungarian branch of Dracula's family may have been related to the Báthory family. In addition, a fiefdom that once belonged to Dracula eventually fell under Báthory's possession.

Dracula was not Báthory's only unsavoury family connection. She was known to have had a devil-worshipping uncle and her brother was considered a famous drunkard and lecher, a danger to both women and children. Her aunt Klara was bisexual – which, although hardly worthy of note today, was deeply shocking at the time Elizabeth lived – and well-known for her sexual adventures.

Báthory was born on 7 August 1560 in Hungary, into a

time of brutal and relentless battles between the Catholics and Protestants, as well as the Christians and the Ottoman Empire. Although she was born at Ecsed Castle, into incredible wealth, power and privilege, the violence surrounding her and the extent to which she experienced it may have had a significant impact on her character.

Báthory was the daughter of George and Anna Báthory; her father was a soldier and her mother was the sister of the King of Poland. During the 16th century, there was a significant history of incest among the European nobility and royalty in order to preserve a 'pure' bloodline and to keep inheritances and property in the family. The inevitable genetic issues that arise from generations of incest may well have been responsible for the fits of epilepsy and violent behaviour that members of Báthory's family were prone to. The countess herself suffered from extreme epilepsy from infancy. Some sources also hint at the fact that Báthory suffered from mental instability in her childhood, which persisted and was amplified in adulthood, suggesting that her ensuing crimes were more attributable to psychiatric illness rather than a psychopathic desire to commit evil deeds.

She spent her childhood, such as it was, at her family estate at Ecsed. Back then, childhood did not last long, and her time with her parents was short-lived and not particularly pleasant. According to one source, at the age of six, Báthory witnessed an extreme act of violence by her father, who was exacting punishment on a gypsy. A horse was flayed open and the gypsy was sewn into its stomach and left to die. The long, slow process of the gypsy's death and subsequent decaying flesh was allegedly witnessed by the six-year-old Báthory, an event which may well have had an impact on her mental state at such a tender age. It is not hard to imagine, given this story, the atmosphere of violence and bloodshed in which the young countess grew up, and the other grisly incidents that she must have been privy to.

She was engaged at the age of ten to a Count Ferenc Nádasdy, the result of an arranged marriage, and moved out of her family home to live with him at the age of eleven. Despite her tender years, Báthory was far from chaste in the years before her marriage. She was something of a tomboy and ran around and socialized with the local peasant boys, eventually becoming pregnant at 13 years of age. When her pregnancy became noticeable, she was taken away by her mother to a secluded Báthory castle in 1574, so that the baby could be delivered in secrecy. Once born, her daughter, Anastasiá Báthory, was sent out of the country, although some believe that Nádasdy had the infant killed. Afterwards, Nádasdy had Báthory's lover, László Bende, castrated, killed and thrown to the dogs. However, this in no way curbed her habit of extramarital sexual dalliances, which continued well into her marriage, even resulting in her running away with one of her lovers for a short time before reconciling with her husband.

On 8 May 1575, shortly before her 15th birthday, Báthory was married to twenty-one-year-old Nádasdy (who would later earn the nickname 'The Black Knight'), uniting the two most important clans of the region. The ceremony took place at Varannó Castle and 4,500 guests were invited. Báthory did not take her husband's name, as her family outranked his; instead he took hers, becoming Ferencz Báthory Nádasdy.

According to surviving letters, Báthory was a loving wife. Other sources suggest that while she was a good wife, particularly in Nádasdy's presence, she did not especially care for him. Due to the demands of his military career, the two barely saw one another for the first ten years of their marriage.

They did appear to share at least one common passion, however: they both had an interest in torture. When he was home, Nádasdy spent his spare time torturing Turkish captives. Báthory allegedly learned some new techniques from her husband, such as 'star kicking', where oil-soaked rags were placed between the toes of the person being tortured and set on fire. This would prompt the victim to begin kicking and eventually see stars due to the pain. Báthory would later enact this method of torture on her servants. She also took to sticking needles into their flesh, or under their fingernails, and to pressing scalding hot coins or keys into the palms of their hands. Her husband, too, abused their servants, reportedly having covered one in honey and made her stand outside, naked, for over a day, all the while being stung and bitten by wasps and ants. Although a certain amount of mistreatment from their masters was the unfortunate norm for servants at the time, this level of abuse evidently went above and beyond normal behaviour. A local minister felt the need to write a letter to the pair complaining about the amount of violence being carried out; it must have been terrible indeed for him to have seen fit to stand up to such a powerful couple.

Bathory and Nádasdy had five children: Anna, Katalin, Orsika, András and Paul. On 4 January 1604, after 29 years of marriage, Nádasdy died at the age of 48, following an illness that had reportedly begun in 1601, ultimately leaving him permanently disabled. Though many claim that she was a loving mother, some accounts state that following the death of her husband, Báthory sent her children away to live with relatives so that she could fully indulge her steadily growing sadistic whims. The widowed countess was immensely powerful and in control of ten castles and estates and had land that stretched across Hungary and Transylvania. However, she was becoming increasingly uncontrollable in her cruelty. She settled in Čachtice Castle, where, bored and frustrated, she committed the majority of her gruesome crimes.

Crimes

Although to most outsiders Báthory appeared to run an efficient and sophisticated court, the girls who served her were privy to an entirely different – and much darker – side to the countess.

The majority of the existing information concerning Báthory's crimes comes from her original trial records and the written depositions accumulated by Count György Thurzó, then Palatine of Hungary and the man who would bring Báthory to account for her evil deeds.

Four individuals, named Dorottya Szentes, Ilona Jó, Katalin Benická and János Ujvári, allegedly aided Báthory, both in selecting servant girls from surrounding areas and in executing her crimes. The parents of the local girls would have been extremely happy, even honoured, for their daughters to serve in Báthory's court, even after the rumours about the goings-on within the walls had begun to spread. The power of masters over their servants was absolute and uncompromising: Báthory's servant victims led miserable lives, entirely at the mercy of her obsession with sadism and blood.

Initially Báthory's preferred victims were the adolescent daughters of local peasants. The girls were usually those with more robust or sturdy body types, as they would be more likely to survive long periods of torture. The torture was varied and extreme, including severe beatings, burns and mutilation of the hands. It is believed that Báthory allowed her victims to freeze or starve to death. She also abused them sexually, demonstrating the nature of a true sexual sadist: she would burn the pubic hair of her victims with candle flames and focused a great deal of her torture on the genital area, before allegedly experiencing orgasm as her victims died. Sources also claim that Báthory forced her seamstresses to work naked.

Unsurprisingly, many claim that Báthory had a terrifying temper and little patience for imperfection, and her cruelty was often the result of fits of sudden and extreme anger. According to many sources, one such outburst occurred after an item was ironed incorrectly, after which she ordered that the burning hot iron be pressed to the servant's face, resulting in a permanent and terrible disfiguring scar. One servant reportedly had her lower jaw ripped from her face, as Báthory, enraged by some perceived slight, seized the lower part of her mouth, broke her jaw and tore it off with her bare hands.

There are, however, certain devices that Báthory is said to have possessed that also betray a significant degree of premeditation. She reportedly owned an iron maiden: a torture device consisting of an iron cabinet with a spike-lined interior which, when activated, pulled the victim within it and slowly forced spikes into his or her body, resulting in a slow and agonizing death. She also owned a clockwork-based cage, containing springs that would shoot out blades in time with the clockwork mechanism. In some instances, the torture she inflicted is said to have gone on for weeks on end.

Among the other allegations were accusations of cannibalism, which is the most likely element of her story from which the supernatural associations to her developed. She reportedly had a taste for flesh, biting the skin off her servants from areas such as the face and the arms. Famously, in one incident when she was too weak to go downstairs to inflict her routine torture, she gave instructions for a servant girl to be brought up to her bedside, whereupon Báthory leaned out of bed and bit at the girl's neck, ripping out chunks of flesh. She also enjoyed manipulating or forcing others to partake in this particular gruesome pastime: she forced servants that she was torturing to consume parts of their own skin and, apparently, tricked her own soldiers on occasion into eating human meat. As the bodies were not eaten entirely, parts of corpses were left to rot inside her castle.

Her crimes were not limited to Hungary. On occasion, she would travel to Vienna, where she had a mansion on Augustinian Street, Lobkowitz Square. Here, she instructed a blacksmith to construct an iron cage to contain her torture victims. The trial that took place in 1611 would reveal that on one occasion in Vienna, such screams were elicited from her victims that they aroused the attention of the monks in the old monastery across the street. They attempted to help, hurling pots against the windows to get her attention, but to no avail. There was little that they could really do, given the fact that Báthory was such a powerful woman.

Over time, as is the pattern with many serial killers, Báthory became less careful. She changed her victim type, which ultimately led to her discovery. As long as she focused her cruelty and murderous intentions solely on peasants, her crimes went unnoticed – even as they were noticed, it was easier for people who knew of her crimes to turn a blind eye to them. It was only when Báthory began to kill girls of a more noble background, the ladies of the lesser gentry, that the deaths began to draw greater attention and concern. These girls were sent to her by their parents to learn etiquette. In 1610, following complaints from István Magyari, a Lutheran minister, King Matthias II assigned György Thurzó, Báthory's cousin, to investigate.

On 29 December 1610, Thurzó led a party of soldiers to Čachtice Castle and, upon their arrival (according to a surviving letter from Thurzó to his wife, dated 30 December), were met with a horrifying series of sights. They discovered the lifeless body of a girl in the main room, drained of blood, and another girl who was alive but whose body had been pierced multiple times. In the dungeon they found several more girls, alive; some of them had also been pierced several times all over their bodies. They unearthed the bodies of some 50 more girls who had presumably been murdered at the castle. Báthory and four of her servants, who were accused of being accomplices, were arrested.

Trial and Sentence

Thurzó had begun assembling evidence against Báthory as early as March 1610. In total, his team of interrogators interviewed 289 witnesses. Of this number, 229 stated that they knew nothing but hearsay, while 29 claimed to know nothing at all. Only four claimed to have had first-hand knowledge of Báthory's crimes, but as the nature of these crimes was not recorded, it is likely that the information was not regarded as worthy enough to note. However, 25 of the witnesses stated that they had seen a number of dead or badly wounded bodies on the property but did not know how the deceased or dying girls had acquired their injuries. A local doctor said that he had examined a servant girl who had had flesh ripped out of her shoulder and buttocks, along with cuts on her hands, but a link to Báthory could not be validated. Some witnesses pointed the interrogator in the direction of Báthory's accomplices.

The decision was made to not allow Báthory to be present at her own trial. Thurzó himself, together with Báthory's son and two of her sons-in-law, argued that having Báthory attend the trial would seriously harm the good name and honour of both the Nádasdy and Báthory families, causing damage to the Hungarian nobility. This was reportedly contrary to the wishes of the king, who wanted to see Báthory brought to trial and sentenced to death for her crimes. The church officials were bribed to waive their rights to interrogate the accused, despite the fact that such an interrogation would have been the norm at the time when allegations of witchcraft were involved.

The first trial began on 2 January 1611, five days after the arrest, and was presided over by Royal Supreme Court Judge Theodosious Syrmiensis de Szulo, along with 20 associate judges. The servants were put on trial at Bytca, and during the proceedings 17 testimonies were heard, including four from Báthory's accomplices. Torture, in some cases in the extreme, was used to extract confessions from her accomplices. Ironically, these torture methods were very similar to those Báthory was accused of employing herself: their limbs were pulled, they were burned and forced to suffer a tremendous amount of pain until they admitted to the crimes of which they were accused. This, of course, always presents the possibility that the confessions were not reliable, as they might have been given to avoid further agony.

There was no real consistency between the accounts of Báthory's accomplices when it came to the number of girls killed. Ujvári claimed that it was 37 in 16 years, while Szentes claimed the number to be 36 in five. The other two suggested that the number was 50 or higher. None of them, however, was able to give any useful identifying information, such as first names or surnames. Other castle personnel attested that the bodies removed from the castle had, in fact, numbered between one and 200. While on trial, one witness by the name of Susannah spoke of a book she had discovered in the castle, which belonged to Báthory and detailed the murders of over 650 victims – a number which, although unverified, is commonly recited today as Báthory's real victim count. Officially, the number of murdered girls rested at 80.

The trial became a strange and eventful affair, full of colourful and sometimes bizarre accounts by witnesses, with one claiming to have seen Báthory having sex with the Devil himself. Another spoke of cannibalism, having seen Báthory torturing a servant girl on one occasion, describing how she 'rose up like a bulldog and tore the flesh from her shoulders, and bit her breast'.

The second trial was held on 7 January, when three of Báthory's accomplices were found guilty. They were sentenced to death on the same day. Before being executed, Szentes and Jó had their fingers ripped off with a pair of pincers. Then, still alive, the two were thrown into a fire. Ujvári, who was considered less culpable than the others, was beheaded. Benická was exonerated.

With justice already seemingly carried out, the decision was made to spare Báthory from a death sentence or even extreme punishment, but instead to imprison her in solitary confinement in Čachtice Castle for the rest of her life. She was locked in one set of rooms, with the only gaps being small slits to deliver food and ventilation. This decision, in fact, was recorded in a letter from a local pastor on 1 January 1611, which means that her life sentence had been decided even before the trial had begun.

On 21 August 1614, a curious guard was overwhelmed with the desire to look upon the woman who had been described by some as being one of the most beautiful women in Europe. He discovered the 54-year-old Báthory lying dead inside her prison of rooms.

Báthory was buried in the cemetery of the church in Čachtice, but following an uproar from the villagers who were unhappy about having her body so close by, it was moved to her home at Ecsed, and interred in the family crypt. The current location of her body is unknown. Not long after her death, King Matthias II of Hungary banned the mention of her name, adding to the mystery and enigma of her life and crimes.

Discussion

Discussions about Báthory's story tend to focus, at least in part, on the fact that she was a woman. With such adjectives as the 'kinder', 'softer' or 'fairer' sex attached to the female gender, women are often thought to be less likely to be violent or aggressive than men, and a woman's murderous impulses are often perceived as more shocking than those of a man. Throughout history, however, there have been a significant number of women who have been turned into great icons or symbols of evil, and Báthory certainly is an exemplary case.

Interestingly, there have been many attempts down the years by authors and historians to exonerate or defend her behaviour. Two noteworthy authors who argue her innocence are Dr Irma Szádeczky-Kardoss and László Nagy. They state that the countess was most likely a victim of a political conspiracy, and that the physical evidence at the time was greatly exaggerated. Thurzò, they argue, was a political rival and it would have therefore been in his best interests to frame Báthory.

Once again, this may be an example of the unwillingness of the human mind to accept the possibility that anyone, and particularly a woman, could be capable of these grotesque murders and on such a substantial scale. Some historians go so far as to claim that she was actually attempting to help her victims: they state that the torture devices found at her castle were actually primitive instruments designed to heal, such as long metal items that could have been heated up and used to cauterize wounds. There has also been talk of illegal abortions taking place at the castle, where Báthory is said to have been helping women desperate to get rid of unwanted pregnancies. Arguments in favour of her innocence usually stem from the fact that the people who took control of her castle and land following her confinement all had ties to Thurzó and, therefore, something to gain from framing and disgracing her and forcing her into imprisonment.

If we assume that Báthory was, in fact, a serial killer who ruthlessly butchered young girls in their dozens, her reasons for doing so would have been either that she truly believed she was disciplining these servants, as was customary at the time (but the punishments regularly got out of hand), or that she did it for her own sadistic pleasure, which is a more likely alternative. Some claim, given the cases of genital mutilation and burning of pubic hair, that this pleasure was of a sexual nature. Later, others would argue that she was jealous of her servants' youth and beauty, and murdered them for this reason, using their life's essence to renew her own. Despite the fact that there is not a great deal of evidence to substantiate this myth, it makes for a compelling story, which is the likely reason why it has persisted for so long, strengthening her ties with the supernatural and vampirism in particular.

It we were to categorize Báthory using the Holmes and DeBurger typology, she would sit quite comfortably in the Hedonistic type, like many of the killers included in this book. The general consensus among those who have studied her crimes is that she killed for the thrill of it, which certainly fits that category. It is true, however, that she took extreme advantage of the power she had over her subjects. She tortured and mutilated them simply because she was in a position of absolute superiority to them and did not have to answer to any other authority. This kind of power is likely to have been exciting and satisfying for Bathory, and for this reason she might also fit into the Power/Control type. However, the murders themselves did not give Báthory her sole sense of power; she was powerful in life outside of her crimes, regardless of the lives she took.

The case of Elizabeth Báthory is both fascinating and frustrating. There are shelves of information dedicated to this complicated, terrifying woman, and yet there remain massive gaps in our knowledge that will never be filled. The information we have today is frequently contradictory and baffling and we know very little for certain, as the majority of the records about her crimes come from a court case that utilized severe torture in order to obtain the relevant confessions, which are thus rendered questionable at best. This, added to the fact that Báthory herself was never able to testify in court, means that we have no first-hand account of the alleged murders, and that facts have a habit of changing over time with the result that there will always be questions relating to her story that we will never be able to answer. Inevitably, where these gaps exist, especially in a story as intriguing as that of the 'Blood Countess', they are regularly filled with conjecture, speculation and fanciful myths.

CHAPTER FIVE

Friedrich Heinrich Karl 'Fritz' Haarmann – The Vampire of Hanover/The Werewolf of Hanover/The Butcher of Hanover

'I always hated doing this, but I couldn't help it – my passion was so much stronger than the horror of the cutting and chopping.'
                                                    Fritz Haarmann

Friedrich Heinrich Karl 'Fritz' Haarman flanked by policemen.

Introduction

As the First World War drew to a close, Hanover was a city struggling with hyperinflation, food shortages and deprivation. Its people were hungry and desperate; social unrest and discontent were rampant and opportunities for a variety of criminal activity lay around every corner. Fritz Haarmann, the 'Butcher of Hanover', was to take advantage of this miserable state of affairs and commit one of the most unspeakable and gruesome series of crimes of the 20th century.

Haarmann gained infamy throughout Germany and the world not only for the grisly nature of his murders but also for the sheer number of his victims: he claimed that his victim count was in excess of 50, although he was eventually only convicted of 24 murders. He preyed on young men, mainly runaways and prostitutes, earning the titles of 'Butcher', 'Vampire' and *'Wolfsmensch'* (The Wolf Man) due to his method of killing: a violent bite to the throat, often during the throes of passion and at the point of sexual climax. With the assistance of a young male live-in lover, he would profit from his killings by selling the clothing and personal belongings of his victims. He was also alleged to have sold flesh from his victims' bodies on the black market in the guise of animal meat, though he never confessed to this.

Friedrich Heinrich Karl 'Fritz' Haarmann was born on 25 October 1879, the youngest of six children. Haarmann's parents were an unlikely couple. His mother, Johanna Claudius, was 41 years old at the time of his birth and his father, Ollie Haarmann, was seven years her junior. Ollie Haarmann, a locomotive stoker, was infamous locally for his bad temper and unpleasant disposition. He had precious little inclination to spend time with his children, preferring instead to frequent seedy local bars, and was a well-known and open womanizer who even brought his mistress home. Johanna Claudius, by contrast, was a mild-mannered woman who was wealthy in her own right and brought a small fortune in property to the marriage. Johanna was either blissfully ignorant of her husband's drunken, cheating habits or chose to continually look the other way. Following Haarmann's birth, she fell ill and spent the majority of her last 12 years bedbound; she was, however, a doting mother who pampered her son and provided for all of his needs.

Haarmann was a quiet child who was often alone. He had few friends his own age and rarely interacted with children other than his siblings. From a young age, Haarmann's behaviour was visibly effeminate. He shunned activities traditionally associated with boys at the time, such as sports, and enjoyed dressing in his sisters' clothes and playing with their toys and dolls. He also had a talent for needlework and cooking, which were considered exclusively feminine pastimes at that time.

Haarmann did not get on with his two brothers and three sisters and had an antagonistic relationship with his father, who openly disliked him, perhaps for his gentle and effeminate manner. They frequently quarrelled, and on numerous occasions his father threatened to have him committed to an asylum. With his mother, on the other hand, Haarmann always felt a deep bond. Throughout his childhood he was loved and spoiled by her and until the end of his trial and long after her death, she remained the only person he spoke of with warmth and emotion.

At home, he demonstrated an early sadistic streak by tormenting his sisters. On some occasions he would tie them up against their will so they looked like dead bodies; on others he would sneak outside in the middle of the night, creep up to their windows and knock on the glass panes, pretending to be a ghost or werewolf – which is particularly fitting, considering the moniker he would later acquire.

In 1886, Haarmann started school. Although he was reported by his teachers to be well-behaved, his academic performance was poor: a habit of constant daydreaming and limited attention span meant that he had to repeat two school years. When he left school in 1894 aged 15, he enrolled in a military school in Breisach where his training began in April of 1895. Haarmann performed well in the military school and was highly regarded as a trainee soldier. After only five months, however, he began to suffer from fainting spells with periods of unconsciousness. In October 1895, he was diagnosed as having a condition 'equivalent to epilepsy' and discharged himself from the military.

A post-mortem examination of his head later revealed that his brain was swollen in several places, to the point that it was in contact with his skull, a likely result of childhood meningitis. Haarmann himself also blamed a head injury acquired during bar exercises at the school gymnasium for his fainting spells. These two incidents are thought to be the most likely reason for them.

Returning to Hanover, he started work in a cigar factory. It was around this time, when he was only 16 years old, that Haarmann committed his first series of sexual offences. From the account of Theodore Lessing, a psychologist who interviewed Haarmann in prison, the sum of Haarmann's sexual experiences up till this point consisted of being sexually molested at school when he was only seven years old and then, at the age of 16, and just before committing his own sexual offences, having a sexual experience with a 'mannish woman'. Colin Wilson, in his book *A Plague of Murder*, suggests that it is possible the latter experience convinced Haarmann that he was, in fact, homosexual, and that 'the attempts to seduce children resulted from a kind of revulsion', a feeling he had towards his own sexuality, which was illegal and generally socially unacceptable in Germany at the time.

Haarmann's victims were invariably young boys. He would persuade them to follow him to isolated places, such as doorways or underground cellars, before abusing them. He was first arrested for child molestation in July 1896. These repeated offences came to the attention of the Division for Criminal Matters, which placed Haarmann in a mental asylum in Hildesheim in 1897. There were concerns that he might be mentally deranged, and therefore a threat to those around him. He was put under observation to try to determine a psychological diagnosis. Haarmann hated his time in the asylum; it generated in him an intense fear of such institutions, which caused him later to say, during his trial: 'Hang me, do anything you like to me, but don't take me back to the loony bin.'

During his time in the asylum, Haarmann was brought to Hanover hospital for a psychiatric evaluation. There he was certified as 'incurably deranged' and unfit to stand trial, by psychologist Gurt Schmalfuss, who further recommended that he be returned to the asylum and held there permanently. But Haarmann had other plans: only seven months after his committal, he escaped and fled to

Zurich in Switzerland, where he lived for 16 months before returning to Hanover in April 1899.

The following year, at the age of 20, Haarmann married a woman named Erna Loewart. The couple were soon expecting their first child, but before the baby was born, Haarmann received his notice for compulsory military service and left his wife in October 1900 to serve his country. While he was away his wife arranged to have an abortion.

Haarmann was deployed to Alsace in north-eastern France, where he was reportedly an excellent soldier and a skilled marksman, 'full of obedience and esprit de corps'. Haarmann would later describe this period as 'the happiest of his life'. His stint in the military came to an end, however, only one year after it began. In October 1901, during a company exercise, Haarmann collapsed and was admitted to the military hospital, where he remained for more than four months. He was diagnosed with a mental deficiency and continued to suffer dizzy spells. He was subsequently deemed unsuitable for service.

Following his discharge in July of 1902, Haarmann was given a full military pension, which he would continue to receive until his arrest for murder in 1924. His mother had died while he had been away but he returned to live with Erna Loewart in Hanover, briefly working for his father, before the relationship between father and son took a turn for the worse. The following year, a violent fight between the two resulted in Haarmann's father unsuccessfully filing a lawsuit against his son for alleged death threats and blackmail and appealing to have his son returned to a mental institution. These charges against Haarmann were dropped due to a lack of evidence; nonetheless, Haarmann was ordered by the court to undertake a psychiatric evaluation in May 1903. The findings showed although 'morally inferior, of low intelligence, idle, coarse, irritable and totally egotistical', Haarmann was 'not mentally ill'.

Haarmann and Erna set up a fishmonger's business, with financial aid from his father. In 1904, Haarmann was officially classified by the military as disabled and unable to work and his monthly military pension was increased. The same year, Haarmann accused his wife – then pregnant for the second time – of having an affair. Erna had had enough of Haarmann's unreasonable and often paranoid behaviour and ended their relationship. As the fishmonger business was registered in her name, she ordered Haarmann to leave the premises and never return.

Haarmann spent a third of the following 20 years either in custody or in prison having been involved in burglary, theft, embezzlement, assault, smuggling and confidence scams. Although he did find a job every now and again, he stole from his employers or customers and also took to burgling homes and grave robbing, digging up recently buried bodies to steal clothing and possessions. In 1904, still in his twenties, Haarmann visited a fair and met a man named Adolf Meil, who invited him to his lodgings.

'He kissed me,' Haarmann later told psychiatrist Theodore Lessing, 'I was shy. He said, "It's late . . . stay with me." I did. He did things I'd never imagined.' The affair was Haarmann's first consensual homosexual encounter and the relationship was to last for a number of years.

In late 1913, Haarmann was arrested for burglary. A police search of his home turned up various pieces of property reported stolen in numerous other thefts and Haarmann was convicted of several instances of burglary and fraud and sentenced to five years' imprisonment. He spent the First World War in prison. When he was finally released in April 1918, he returned to Hanover, finding himself in a post-war Germany stricken with poverty and rising inflation. The country was bankrupt and Haarmann took advantage of this to return to a life of crime. He began to trade in stolen property at Hanover Central Station, which he quickly discovered was the headquarters of the black market. Through this he managed to establish a good number of criminal contacts with whom he could trade in illegal or stolen goods.

Germany's poverty at the end of the First World War meant that basic commodities were limited and inflated in price, promoting higher incidences of crimes, such as theft, assault, illegal trade and murder. Furthermore, under the terms of the Treaty of Versailles signed in 1919, Germany was forbidden to have an army or to trade in arms, and the police forces, who were overworked, poorly paid and had extremely limited resources, were eager for assistance from civilians. This worked greatly to Haarmann's advantage: it provided him with even more opportunities for criminal activity and, interestingly, gave him the opportunity to begin his life as a police informant. Haarmann joined a smuggling ring and began a thriving career as a smuggler and thief. For a man struggling with a history of psychological issues, Haarmann demonstrated impressive signs of preparation and organization in his crimes: he used his role as a police informant to help deflect police attention away from his own criminal activities. Although the Hanover police were aware that Haarmann was both a known criminal and a known homosexual – then illegal and punishable by imprisonment in

Germany – he managed to establish a relationship with them, and they began to regard him as a dependable source of information on Hanover's criminal scene. With the co-operation of police officials, he came up with a scheme to offer his apartment to thieves as a place to store their stolen property, then pass this information on to the police, who would raid his apartment at an agreed time and arrest the perpetrators of the theft. He also often placed commuters under citizen's arrest for offences such as travelling on forged papers.

Haarmann's physical appearance as an adult did nothing to betray his potential for the terrible deeds he committed. He was someone who would not have stood out in a crowd, with an average-looking, even friendly, face. He was of average height, unthreatening and modest, described as having a 'courteous nature' and an 'open expression'; someone even a stranger might feel they could trust. There was also something feminine about his manner, with his nervous gestures – licking of the lips, stroking of his own fingers, the constant blinking of his eyes – and his speech 'like the querulous voice of an old woman'.

Officers would later attest to his contradictory personality: he could at times be talkative and eager to communicate, at other times distant and guarded. He was calculating and devious, but simultaneously he seemed to desire attention and sympathy. His appearance was, as the Hanover police stated, 'far from evil'.

Crimes

Haarmann's infamous killing spree spanned the years of 1918 to 1924, during which time he is known to have killed at least 24 people and possibly more than 50. Each person Haarmann killed was male and between the ages of 10 and 22, with most of them in their mid to late teens. Haarmann preyed on the transient and less visible members of society: commuters, runaways and male prostitutes, perhaps realizing that there would be less risk of a concerned family initiating a manhunt. The initial encounter with his victims would, more often than not, be in or around Hanover Central Station.

Haarmann's role as a police informant also worked to facilitate his contact with potential young male victims. The Hanover police began to rely on Haarmann as a valuable source of information about the criminal network in Hanover and, by 1919, he was often found patrolling the railway station as he pleased.

For a man of Haarmann's specific sexual appetites, the station presented plenty of ideal potential targets. Young male prostitutes and runaways would come to the station, looking for customers or an opportunity to travel out of the city and, at this time, young men were flocking to Hanover from the countryside seeking employment. Haarmann would demand to see their papers and sometimes even bring them to the stationmaster's office for questioning.

The young men that he took a liking to would be invited back to his apartment. Sometimes he would offer them food or accommodation as an incentive, sometimes work or assistance in general, and at other times he would pretend to be a policeman and place them under 'arrest'. This, in fact, happened so often that one guard at the railway station believed Haarmann to be a real police detective.

Once at the apartment, Haarmann would approach

them sexually: he claimed to be impotent and was disinclined towards sodomy, but would force or convince the young men to engage in mutual oral sex with him until he reached orgasm. At this point, he would experience the desire to bite down on the throat of his sexual partner and did so sometimes so aggressively and so violently that their tracheas would be ripped out entirely. Haarmann would later say that he referred to this act as a 'love bite'. The last moments of the victims' lives were often spent desperately gasping for air before they asphyxiated to death.

Following the murders, Haarmann would dismember the boys and dispose of their bodies. His earliest victim was buried, but the bodies of his subsequent murders were typically thrown into the Leine River. The bodies were stripped of all their possessions, which were either kept for his personal use, given to his lover Hans Grans (whom he would meet a year into his murderous crime spree), sold on the black market or given to friends as gifts.

An even more disturbing aspect of his disposal of the bodies was to surface later, when his case came to trial and witnesses came forward with their accounts. One commodity that was in great shortage in Germany at the time was that of meat, and Haarmann himself was a known trader in the meat of horses and other contraband meat. His landlady often heard the sounds of chopping and banging coming from his room and assumed it was to do with the meat trade – once she even met him on the stairs, holding a bucket filled with blood. Following his capture, there were assertions by neighbours and acquaintances that his victims' flesh had been given away or sold as horse, pork or minced meat. His landlady and her family claimed to have fallen ill after eating some sausages she had received from him and suspected they were possibly made from humans. Haarmann, however, never confessed to these accusations of selling or making gifts of human flesh.

Haarmann's murders were so numerous that we will probably never know their true scope – the killer himself claimed to be unsure of the exact number of his victims. When asked during his trial how many he had murdered, Haarmann said, 'I forget. Maybe 30, maybe 40'; at other times he claimed to have killed as many as 50 or 70. He would only ever confess to murders that the police produced evidence for, never willingly providing supplementary information. A search of Haarmann's apartment revealed 400 items of clothing, but only 100 of these items were ever associated with his known victims.

To the best of our knowledge, Haarman's terrible killing spree began with 17-year-old runaway Friedel Rothe, who disappeared on 27 September 1918. Haarmann was inexperienced in these early days, and made the mistake of being observed by Rothe's friends, who told the police that the victim had last been seen with him. In October, the police acted on this information and raided Haarmann's single-room apartment at 27 Cellerstraße.

On arrival, they were confronted by the sight of Haarmann, naked and engaged in sexual behaviour with a 13-year-old boy. He was immediately arrested and charged with the sexual assault and battery of a minor. As a result of the unexpected scene that they had witnessed, the police completely overlooked the grisly evidence of Rothe's murder, which was hidden right under their noses. Behind Haarmann's stove, wrapped in newspaper, was the dismembered head of the unfortunate young runaway. Haarmann was sentenced to nine months in prison, but was not charged with the murder at the time as the police failed to find Rothe's head. For that reason, he would be a suspect in the future for sexually related crimes, particularly those involving young boys, but not a suspect for murder.

One year after this first killing, in October 1919, Haarmann met a 'pretty' youth named Hans Grans, who had recently run away from his Berlin home after an argument with his father and who had established a career of petty crime. A friend of Grans had told him, pointing to Haarmann, that 'that queer over there gave a pretty young boy 20 marks the other day'. Although Grans claimed to be heterosexual, he was prostituting himself to men in order to bring in money and saw Haarmann to be as good a customer as any. He approached Haarmann, who was selling old clothes around Hanover station at the time.

Something about Grans failed to incite Haarmann's murderous inclinations. Despite the significant age difference, the two men became lovers and close friends, and Grans moved in with Haarmann soon after their first meeting. Haarmann began to recruit Grans into his career in illegal trade, giving him meat to sell and gifts of money, which Grans often spent trying to attract girls.

Their relationship was complex: Haarmann would later claim that he regarded Grans 'like a son', claiming that he 'pulled him out of the ditch and tried to make sure he didn't go to the dogs'. They had frequent and violent quarrels, which regularly resulted in Haarmann kicking Grans out, after which Haarmann would always chase after the younger man and beg him to return. Haarmann would reveal, during police questioning, that he needed Grans and his affections, claiming that he 'had to have someone [he] meant everything to'.

Haarmann and Grans eventually moved into an apartment together, at 8 Neue Strasse, near the Leine River. They funded their lifestyle through stealing and working in the black market, in addition to Haarmann's military pension. Grans became aware of Haarmann's sexual preferences for young boys and often found or pointed out potential sexual targets for him.

Haarmann's second known murder took place on 12 February 1923. The victim was Fritz Franke, a 17-year-old pianist. Haarmann encountered Franke at the train station, where the young man had been travelling with a friend. As Franke was the more attractive of the two, Haarmann decided to dismiss the other boy and take Franke home. Until this murder, it is difficult to say for certain whether or not Grans was aware of Haarmann's murderous tendencies, but he was left in no doubt when he came home that evening and saw Franke lying naked and dead on the bed. According to Haarmann's testimony, Grans entered their home, saw the body on the bed, and asked his lover, simply, 'When shall I come back again?'

This saw the true beginning of Haarmann and Grans' murderous career together. The murders became more frequent after this, but there was little variation in the way in which the victims were chosen and killed. The two had an efficient and reliable system, which enabled them to evade capture for some time. The third murder took place on 20 March: the victim was 17-year-old Wilhelm Schulze. As no remains of Schulze were ever found, the only evidence that linked him to Haarmann was his clothing, which was found in the possession of Elisabeth Engel, the couple's landlady. After this, 16-year-old Roland Huch and 19-year-old Hans Sonnenfeld were murdered on 23 May and approximately 31 May respectively. Haarmann allegedly kept Sonnenfeld's yellow coat and often wore it after his death.

Haarmann and Grans then continued their spate of murders unabated. On 25 June, 13-year-old Ernest Ehrenberg went missing, followed by 18-year-old Heinrich Struß on 24 August, 17-year-old Paul Bronischewski exactly one month later and Richard Gräf on 30 September. From this point on, the killings were regular and unrelenting. Widespread fear had begun to take hold of the city of Hanover. A huge manhunt was launched and citizens lived in fear of boys and young men falling prey to the unidentified murderer among them, who was now being referred to as the 'Werewolf of Hanover'.

It all came to an end on 14 June 1924, when Haarmann killed his final victim, a 17-year-old by the name of Erich de Vries. The tide had begun to turn for Haarmann and Grans a month earlier, on 17 May 1924, thanks to two children who were playing near the Leine River. The children discovered a human skull, which was identified as belonging to a young male. At the time, however, it was unclear whether or not a murder had taken place. The police thought it was possible that the skull had been discarded by grave robbers or planted as a prank by medical students from the anatomical institute in Göttingen.

When a second skull was discovered on 29 May, however, the authorities began to take things more seriously. From then on, the evidence began to pile up. On 8

June, hundreds of Hanover locals congregated in a search of the Leine River and its surrounding area. Two more skulls were discovered on 13 June, as well as a sack of human bones. When the police dragged the river, 500 more human bones were discovered. Medical examiners determined that they belonged to at least 22 different people.

It was not long before suspicion fell upon Haarmann. The police were well acquainted with him and knew that he had a significant criminal career, was a homosexual and had, in the past, committed crimes involving acts of indecency with children. Surveillance on Haarmann began on 18 June. Then, four days later, police witnessed an argument between Haarmann and a 15-year-old boy, Karl Fromm. Haarmann approached the police, claiming that the youth was travelling under forged documents. After his arrest, Fromm revealed that he had been living with Haarmann for four days, during which time he had been repeatedly raped. Haarmann was arrested the following morning, charged with sexual assault, and a search was promptly carried out on his apartment.

Incriminating evidence was discovered; clothes and possessions belonging to a number of the victims were found among those of Grans and Haarmann. Bloodstains were present on the walls, floors and bedding; Haarmann tried to explain these away by saying that it was animal blood from his contraband meat. Past and present neighbours were interviewed, many of whom claimed to have witnessed many teenage boys entering Haarmann's home who were rarely seen leaving. They also stated that he sometimes left his property at odd hours with sacks that he tried to conceal. Critically, two of these witnesses claimed to have followed Haarmann and seen him throwing one of these sacks into the Leine River.

The Hanover police confiscated the items of clothing and personal effects that they suspected belonged to the missing youths. They then invited family members of the missing teenage boys to come to Hanover Police Station and, each day, more and more items were identified. Haarmann maintained that this proved nothing, saying that the items had come into his possession through his business or been left behind by youths who had come to his apartment for sex.

By 29 June, however, Haarmann was unable to deny the increasingly damning evidence piling up before him. Clothes, boots and keys discovered at his apartment were identified as belonging to Robert Witzel, a missing 18-year-old boy. Witzel's jacket was found among the belongings of Haarmann's landlady. Then a skull, which had been found in a garden on 20 May, was identified as Witzel's. Finally, a friend of Witzel's identified Haarmann as the 'police officer' he had seen Witzel with the day before he had disappeared.

After seven days in custody and in the face of such evidence, Haarmann broke down and made a full confession to the superintendent and examining magistrate, stating that he had raped, killed and dismembered 'somewhere between 50 and 70' people with a 'rabid sexual passion' – although the official tally was to be 24 victims. Grans also was arrested once Haarmann detailed their joint activities, and was charged with being an accessory to at least one murder.

Haarmann insisted that he had never really intended to murder, but that during the throes of passion, he would be overtaken by an extraordinary desire: 'I never intended to hurt those youngsters, but I knew that if I got going something would happen and that made me cry . . . I would throw myself on top of those boys and bite through the Adam's apple, throttling them at the same time.'

He also stated that he hated the dismembering process, which would typically take him up to two days. In order to prepare himself to take his victims apart, Haarmann would make himself a black coffee and place the victim's lifeless body on the floor, its face covered with a cloth so that 'it wouldn't be looking at me'. He described his ensuing, morbid routine as follows: 'I'd make two cuts in the abdomen and put the intestines in a bucket, then soak up the blood and crush the bones until the shoulders broke. Now I could get the heart, lungs and kidneys and chop them up and put them in my bucket. I'd take the flesh off the bones and put it in my waxcloth bag. It would take me five or six trips to take everything and throw it down the toilet or into the river. I always hated doing this, but I couldn't help it — my passion was so much stronger than the horror of the cutting and chopping.'

For a man who claimed to hate this process, he displayed remarkable attention to detail in its execution, taking great pains to carefully remove flesh from bone using a small kitchen knife, often flushing smaller pieces of flesh or skin down the toilet. He would also crush the skulls of his victims to tiny pieces with an axe to aid their disposal. Despite his supposed disgust for this post-mortem ritual and the time it took to complete it, his lust for blood was so great that he felt compelled to kill again and again.

After the confession, Haarmann proved to be very

co-operative and aided the police in finding additional body parts in the Leine River. His demeanour changed: he became friendly, almost child-like, and more than willing to answer questions posed to him by the authorities. Some believe that he found a sort of cathartic relief in being able to reveal and discuss his crimes. This co-operation, however, extended only to the police. When the victims' family members approached him with questions, he became reticent and guarded.

Haarmann remained in police custody until 16 August, at which time he was sent to Göttingen medical school for a psychiatric examination. The findings from this examination revealed that he was competent to stand trial.

Trial and Sentence

Haarmann's two-week trial began on 4 December 1924 at the Hanover Assizes, during which over 100 witnesses were brought forward to give their accounts. He was charged with the murder of 27 boys and young men who had disappeared between 1918 and June 1924. The trial was one of the first in Germany to provoke widespread media coverage.

Understandably, given the number and average age of his victims, Haarmann and his crimes dominated the media in Germany but also aroused significant interest from the international press. The case was described as being 'the most revolting in German criminal history'. The term 'serial killer' had not yet been coined and the terminology did not yet exist to describe Haarmann's extensive and bloody criminal repertoire. Dramatic but not entirely inappropriate names, such as 'vampire' and 'werewolf', were often given to him, and, in the headlines, Haarmann was often referred to as the 'Wolf Man' or the 'Vampire of Hanover'.

Haarmann was charged with 27 counts of murder. He freely admitted to 14 of them, but claimed that he could not say for sure whether or not he had killed most of the others, as he was unable to identify them from photographs provided to him. When he was told that incriminating evidence belonging to the victims, such as clothing, had been found in his apartment, he would simply shrug and agree that chances were, he was responsible for their deaths, with comments such as, 'I probably killed him.' Some he flatly denied murdering: when he was shown, for example, the photograph of a boy named Hermann Wolf, he declared that Wolf was far too ugly to have interested him and, as such, the boy could not have been one of his victims.

During the opening days of the trial, 285 bones, including skulls, were presented as evidence, as well as Haarmann's bloodstained bed and the bucket he had used to store and dispose of the victim's remains. Although he freely admitted to multiple counts of murder, he claimed that the skulls in question could not possibly have belonged to his victims, due to his method of disposing of the bodies: smashing the skulls to pieces before throwing whatever remained into the river.

The hearing was unique from the outset. Haarmann was allowed an unconventional degree of freedom and adopted a casual and almost jovial manner in court, showing no indication that he understood the severity of the charges levelled at him. His conduct was consistent with that of a man who had lost touch with reality. He would regularly joke or make light of the situation and frequently interrupt court proceedings. He protested at the large number of women in court, whereupon the judge responded regretfully that he had no power to deny them entrance.

Haarmann went on to accuse Grans of taking part in a number of the murders. For his part, Grans pleaded not guilty to being an accessory to murder. Compared to Haarmann, the younger man was solemn and took the court case very seriously.

Some witnesses implied, under oath, that the meat Haarmann sold or gave to his friends and acquaintances might well have been human. However, throughout the trial, Haarmann repeatedly denied eating or selling human flesh, a statement that was supported by a medical expert. This expert stated that a search of Haarmann's apartment following his arrest revealed that none of the meat found was human. Other expert witnesses stated that, despite the fact that Haarmann had a 'pathological personality', he was in control of his actions and able to exercise his free will and did not have 'manic depressive insanity'.

Apart from the cruelty of what Haarmann had done, even more scandalous – shaking German society to the core – was the involvement of the police in the case: Haarmann was a police informant who had frequently given up other criminals to investigators. Until Haarmann was arrested, it had never occurred to police that the serial killer they had been looking for was right under their noses and so well known to them.

At the end of the trial, Haarmann requested of the jury

to 'keep it short. I want to spend Christmas in heaven with Mother.'

On 19 December, the court reconvened to deliver verdicts. Both Haarmann and Grans were deemed sane enough to understand the nature and consequences of their actions and were sentenced to death by beheading. Haarmann was found guilty of 24 of the 27 murders; he was acquitted of three murders that he denied. At the end of the trial, Haarmann stated that he '[accepted] the verdict fully and freely' and admitted that if he were ever released, he would more than likely kill again. He also agreed that he was perfectly sane, stating: 'I'm not ill – it's only that I occasionally have funny turns.'

Grans' reaction to his fate was in stark contrast to Haarmann's. Grans was indignant and frantic at being found guilty of enticement to murder and sentenced to death, and reportedly fainted after being returned to jail.

Of his own death Haarmann made the following requests: 'I want to be executed on the marketplace. On the tombstone must be put this inscription: "Here Lies Mass-Murderer Haarmann".' Neither of these demands was adhered to. Haarmann was not made aware of the date of his execution until the night before it was to happen, pursuant to German legal procedure at the time. Upon receiving the news, Haarmann prayed with his pastor and ordered expensive cigars and Brazilian coffee as his last earthly requests. He was beheaded via guillotine in Hanover Prison at 6 am on 15 April 1925.

Despite the fact that witnesses claimed he appeared pale and scared, Haarmann's final words were, 'I repent, but I do not fear death.' Following his decapitation, his head was set aside and preserved in a jar in order for scientists to carry out forensic analysis on slices of his brain. The head was held at the Göttingen Medical School for decades until 2014, when it was finally cremated.

What remained of the bodies of Haarmann's victims was buried in Stöckener Cemetery in February 1925. A large granite triptych on which the names and ages of the victims were engraved was later built to mark the communal grave and to act as a memorial for those who had lost their lives.

The story, however, was not to end there: a letter was found on the streets of Hanover addressed to an Albert Grans – Hans Grans' father. This letter made its way to its intended recipient, who handed it into the police after reading its message. The letter comprised a four-page message from Fritz Haarmann, dated 5 February, and had been penned – and likely dropped – as Haarmann had been on his way to the police station by car. In the letter Haarmann insisted that Grans was innocent of his charges. He wrote that, during the trial, he had been angry with Grans, believing that the younger man had seen him simply as a 'meal ticket' throughout their relationship. He wrote: 'Hans Grans has been sentenced unjustly and that's the fault of the police and also because I wanted revenge . . . May Hans Grans forgive me for my revenge and humanity.' He added that Grans 'had absolutely no idea that I killed' and claimed that he had falsely confessed that Grans had taken part in the murders under extreme duress and pressure from the police.

Some believe that Haarmann wrote the letter in order to absolve himself of guilt, or in order to extend his own life with further legal proceedings. Others suggest that incriminating Grans in the first place and procuring his lover a death sentence was a way for Haarmann to take revenge upon the Hanover police, as another letter written by him was found years later, in which he wrote:

'You won't kill me; I'll be back – yes, I shall be among you for all eternity. And now you yourselves have also killed. You should know it: Hans Grans was innocent! Well? How's your conscience now?'

Whatever the case, the discovery of the first letter was sufficient evidence to merit a second trial for Grans. He was retried in January 1926, with charges of aiding and abetting two murders. On 19 January, he was found guilty on both counts and sentenced to two concurrent 12-year sentences. Following the completion of his prison sentence, Grans remained in Hanover until his death in 1975.

Discussion

Although the end point of Haarmann's crimes was murder, they invariably had their roots in his sadistic sexual appetite. He would repeatedly coerce his victims into non-consensual or reluctant sexual activity and subsequently expose them to unfathomable agony and a terrible, undignified death. The fact that he could do this again and again, perfecting a modus operandi that allowed him to go unnoticed for years while routinely working as an informant for the police, betrays not only a particular kind of viciousness and a lack of human compassion, but also a marked capacity for careful planning, premeditation and compartmentalization of the different aspects of his life. Although he might have appeared odd to his acquaintances or neighbours, he was not outwardly a blatantly violent or abusive individual, perpetually slipping under the radar as a round-faced, respectable looking man.

It is clear that Haarmann was not a complete sociopath entirely devoid of empathy or sympathy. His story occasionally demonstrates elements of both. He was able to maintain a relatively lasting – albeit unstable – relationship with not only Hans Grans, but also Adolf Meil before him. Haarmann was aware that Grans was most likely using him as a means of self-preservation, yet he took the younger man in, continued to live with him and provided for him. He gave gifts of sausages and clothing to his landlady, and had a caring relationship with his mother, whom he apparently regarded warmly up until his death, indicating that he was capable of some degree of love and affection.

Throughout his life, Haarmann was the subject of a number of psychiatric and psychological evaluations, all of which had slightly different results. At various times in his life he was diagnosed as 'incurably deranged', suffering from a 'mental deficiency', 'morally inferior, of low intelligence, idle, coarse, irritable and totally egotistical' and having a 'pathological personality'. It was arguably a failure of the healthcare system at the time that, as a young boy and a man, he never received the help he needed. Had he received appropriate psychological care and treatment, he might not have gone on to commit the brutal murders for which he was put to death, and the senseless loss of at least 24 – and possibly in excess of 50 – innocent young lives could have been prevented.

We will probably never now know the truth about Haarmann's psychiatric conditions, if any, or his psychological issues. It is likely that, as expert witnesses in his trial attested, Haarmann was 'sane' in that he knew what he was doing at all times and retained insight about and responsibility for his actions. It is equally possible that, alongside whatever other psychological issues he may have had, he may have suffered from an impulse control disorder, or a condition featuring impulse control issues. On inviting his victims back to his apartment, he claimed he 'never intended to hurt those youngsters', yet, at the point of sexual climax, was unable to help himself from '[throwing himself] on top of those boys and [biting] through the Adam's apple, throttling them at the same time' – suggesting that when the murderous impulse overtook him he lacked behavioural self-control.

Haarmann's early life and upbringing are important to consider when discussing his influences. He was often made to feel insignificant and unimportant by his father, who showed more of an interest in womanizing than spending time with his family. Haarmann was, on the other hand, very close to his mother, who coddled him, praised him and attempted to make life as easy as possible for her beloved son. This dichotomy may have played a role in Haarmann's rejection of 'traditional' male pastimes and toys in his youth, causing him to grow up very much influenced by the tastes and hobbies of his sisters and mother, while lacking a strong, respected or loved father figure. His mother's coddling and indulgence may have contributed to a sense of self-entitlement that remained with him into adulthood, extending, along the way, to the desire for constant sexual gratification on his own terms.

Many serial killers are known to have sustained traumatic head injuries in their time, and Haarmann was no exception: he suffered from meningitis, head injuries and epileptic fits that may well have had a contributory effect on his criminal and violent behaviour. In a study published in 2003, in *The Journal of Neuropsychiatry and Clinical Neurosciences* by Tateno et al, post-traumatic aggression was found to be significantly more frequent among patients with traumatic brain injury than those without. In addition, numerous neuropsychiatric studies have demonstrated that injury to parts of the brain, such as the hypothalamus and the temporal lobe – via, for example, trauma, epilepsy or dementia – could result in violent or aggressive behaviour. The hypothalamus, a pearl-sized piece of grey matter that sits approximately in the middle of the brain, is involved in the regulation of emotions and hormones. Altered behaviour in the form of episodic rage and increased emotional disregulation has been observed in cases of hypothalamic damage. The temporal lobe, on the other hand, one of the main lobes of the brain, is involved in sensory input, memory and emotion. In patients with epilepsy affecting the temporal lobe, episodic aggression is a well-recognized – albeit rare – problem, so much so that it has been given the term 'intermittent explosive disorder'. Haarmann was diagnosed as having a condition very similar to epilepsy, and his 'love bite' was certainly an act of violence and extreme aggression.

Of course, a brain injury in itself would not result in the creation of a serial murderer. Myriad other environmental and psychological factors also come into play. The existence of a correlation between head injury and the subsequent development of murderous urges, however, has often been propagated in criminological literature. A 2014 study conducted in Glasgow reinforced this link: in its investigations of 239 killers, 21 per cent of them had suffered 'a definite or suspected' head injury.

Haarmann's own criminal tendencies began at a young age, after sustaining these head injuries, but we can never know to what extent these biological influences may have interacted with environmental factors to create the most prolific German serial killer of all time. Had he been able to remain at the military school, for example, this might have provided an outlet for his violent impulses and given him the opportunity to learn strict discipline and boundaries, something his life of crime never afforded him, and his life might have turned out very differently despite his head injuries and other predisposing risk factors.

One of the most interesting aspects of Haarmann's case is the relationship between Haarmann and Grans. Alhough it was Haarmann who provided financially for them, the power balance in the relationship leaned very much in Grans' favour. Grans was reportedly sometimes openly hostile towards Haarmann, laughing at him and mocking him, knowing that he had an emotional hold on the older man, who was unable to bring himself to sever their relationship. This power imbalance was likely heightened when Grans discovered Haarmann's murderous crimes and both knew that, at any moment, Grans could turn him in to the police. Although Grans was not the primary driving force behind the killings, we know, at the very least, that he allowed them to continue without reporting them and benefited from them in the form of gifts of the victims' clothing and possessions, whilst simultaneously using his knowledge of them to his advantage in the relationship.

Psychology was not as evolved in 1925 as it is now and, as a result, we may never fully appreciate the complexities of this spectacularly twisted criminal mind. It is difficult to adequately place him within the Holmes and DeBurger typology, although he is, arguably, best suited to the Hedonistic type, specifically as a Hedonistic Lust killer. Haarmann was not necessarily driven by his need to kill, but his murders were certainly the result of seeking sexual satisfaction. During a fit of 'rabid sexual passion', Haarmann would sink his teeth into his victim's throat and rip it open, often with his fingers wrapped around their neck. Regardless of the fact that he experienced remorse afterwards and that he wished he could refrain from them beforehand, he enjoyed his killings. He also fits well within the Comfort-oriented subtype of this category, meaning that his quality of life benefited from his murders. Selling his victims' possessions brought him a degree of material gain from which he and his lover certainly benefited.

The case was a sensation in Germany, not only for its gruesome facts but also for the subsequent controversy it generated about various issues, such as the legitimacy of the death penalty, the appropriate approach towards mentally ill criminals and police investigation procedures. The most intense discussions generated by Haarmann's crimes, however, were those relating to the topic of homosexuality, which was already illegal in Germany at the time; the discovery of the murders stirred a further wave of homophobia throughout the country. Historian Richard Plant, in his book *The Pink Triangle*, noted that the case 'split the [gay rights] movement irreparably, fed every prejudice against homosexuality, and provided new fodder for conservative adversaries of legal sex reform'.

Along with the other biological and environmental

factors discussed in his chapter, it is possible that Haarmann may have struggled with the legal and social prejudice against his sexual preferences. Having to repress and hide his strong sexual needs may well have aided in the development of his sexual crimes and even his murderous ones, which had a deeply sexual nature.

CHAPTER SIX

Hamilton Howard 'Albert' Fish: The Werewolf of Wysteria/The Brooklyn Vampire

'I have always had a desire to inflict pain on others and to have others inflict pain on me. I have always seemed to enjoy anything that hurt.'   Albert Fish

Introduction

With violence and murder ceaselessly reported in the news media and depicted gratuitously in books and magazines, on screen and in various forms of entertainment, we have as a society built a high threshold of tolerance for stories of brutality. Every so often, however, a murderer surfaces whose actions are so vicious and cruel that they shock even professionals within the field of criminology.

Albert Fish – child molester, rapist and cannibal – is one such man. This is a sentiment echoed by Dr Joel Feinberg (Regents Professor Emeritus of Philosophy and Law at the University of Arizona), who lists Fish as a candidate for committing 'the century's most revolting crime' and Colin Wilson, author of *A Plague of Murder*,

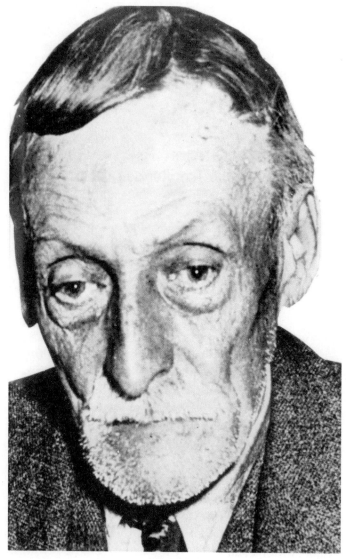

'Albert' Fish

who considers Fish to be one of the most unique and spectacular examples of polymorphous perversity in the entire history of sexual abnormality. Wilson also points out the fact that Fish was at large for a significant length of time, which makes him stand out from the average serial killer. We cannot know for certain precisely how many murders Fish committed, but what we do know is that he was psychologically extremely unstable and held a firm belief that whatever murders or evils he committed were upon instruction from God.

Fish had a long and varied criminal career and has been described as being 'one of the strangest [cases] in the bizarre history of serial murder'. His crimes range from obscene letters he wrote to women, whose information he acquired from classified advertisements, to perverse forms of rape, murder and cannibalism. Dr Fredric Wertham, psychiatrist and author of *Seduction of the Innocent*, who had the opportunity to analyse Fish during his detention and who would eventually evaluate Fish's mental state for his trial, suggested that his compulsion to write these letters was not typical and was not based on fantasy, but were genuine offers to practise and share his inclinations with others. Fish was born at a time when sex crimes were practically non-existent; so much so that when his crimes became public, the horror and shock would have been far more significant than today. Jack the Ripper, whose criminal activities took place primarily in the year 1888, was considered by many to be the first sex-related serial killer and would have been the only other person with whom the public could draw a comparison.

Albert Fish was born Hamilton Howard Fish, but his extensive criminal repertoire gained him a great number of aliases. By the time of his arrest and trial, his nicknames included 'The Werewolf of Wysteria', the 'Brooklyn Vampire', the 'Grey Man' and the 'Boogeyman'. The youngest of four children, he was born in Washington DC on 19 May 1870 and had a difficult childhood. His uncle suffered from religious mania – characterized by periods of extreme hyperactivity and agitation associated with hallucinations experienced by religious adherents; he had a brother who was permanently confined to a mental institution, a sister who also suffered from mental afflictions and another brother who died from hydrocephalus. At the time of Fish's birth, his father was 75 years old – 43 years older than his mother. When Fish was just five years of age, his father suffered a fatal heart attack; unable to cope with being the sole provider for her children, Fish's mother placed him in Saint John's Orphanage in Washington DC.

Fish was far from happy at the orphanage and regularly attempted to run away. The institution was extremely religious and unflinchingly strict with regard to enforcing rules and discipline, responding to even the slightest infraction with physical punishment. This punishment took a form that would be unimaginable in our childcare systems today – children would be stripped naked and beaten, in full view of the other children and residents of the orphanage. According to the available records about Fish, he was punished in this way many times and eventually came to enjoy the pain that was inflicted upon him. This was to become the root of the sadomasochistic tendencies that formed the basis for the majority of his crimes. It was also in the orphanage that Fish suffered from bullying from his peers: he was, among other things, teased with the nickname 'ham and eggs', adapted from his given name of

Hamilton, which led him to adopt the name of his dead brother, Albert, to stop this, and thus the serial killer we now know as Albert Fish was born.

In 1880, Fish's mother obtained a job with the government, so he was taken out of the orphanage to live once again under her care. His years at the orphanage, however, had taken their toll and his psychological problems were already beginning to take hold. They were, unhappily, to develop much further. By the tender age of 12, Fish had met and begun a romantic relationship with a telegraph boy. The pair would hold conversations in which Fish's new partner would describe graphic sexual scenes he had witnessed in brothels. The telegraph boy also introduced Fish to coprophagia – the ingestion of faeces – and urophagia – the drinking of urine. Feinberg hypothesizes that these were self-punishing behaviours, which would eventually become an attempt by Fish to 'atone for his sins and free himself of obsessive guilt'. These acts of self-punishment would later escalate to involve placing alcohol-drenched rags or pieces of cotton wool inside his rectum and setting them alight, along with inserting needles between his fingers and inside his rectum. Fish would later perform these practices on others, as well, especially young children. When he eventually confessed this behaviour during his mental state evaluation, Wertham was unconvinced and believed him to be lying. Subsequent X-rays, however, showed at least 29 needles in Fish's pelvic region that he had been unable to extract. Several must have been in his body for a long time: the erosion observed on the needles would have taken at least seven years to occur. In addition to this, the erosion resulted in fragments of the needles embedding themselves in Fish's tissue.

Fish began to visit public baths at the weekends, where he was able to observe other boys undress. When the time came for him to earn a living, he decided to become a house painter, a profession he continued for the rest of his life. This would prove integral to his future crimes, as it gave him access to children as well as an excuse to spend time in the cellars and basements of other people's homes. In his book, Wilson describes how Fish would dress in nothing but his painter's overalls in the morning, so that if an opportunity for sexual assault arose, he would be able to undress at a moment's notice.

In his late teens, Fish was already possessed of and tortured by a violent and all-consuming sexual appetite that would never leave him, even in his later years. At 20 years of age, Fish moved to New York City and became a male prostitute. According to the transcripts that exist of the dialogue between Fish and Wertham, this is when he began raping small boys, usually under the age of six. Fish also continued to molest and rape children throughout his marriages.

In 1898, when Fish was 28, he married for the first time, an arranged marriage set up by his mother. He was far from faithful, and took a male lover who habitually took him to a waxworks museum. It was at this time that he became fascinated by a bisection of a penis and developed a strong and morbid interest in castration. He would later perform the procedure on selected victims. He became a frequenter of brothels, where he could pay to be beaten, continuing and strengthening his mental association between sex and pain.

Fish's first marriage ended unhappily in January 1917, when his wife ran away with their lodger, a handyman named John Straube. Fish went on to have three more marriages, all of which were bigamous and none of which were happy or lasting. He fathered six children and also had grandchildren. Fish remained completely devoted to them all, thus providing us with a paradox when trying to reconcile the terrible and unthinkable acts he committed against his child victims with the warm, caring father and grandfather that he was. In the course of their conversations, Wertham noted that Fish's face 'lit up' when he spoke of his 12-year-old grandchild. Fish is reported to have said, 'I love children and was always soft-hearted.' He claimed, furthermore, to be a deeply religious, God-fearing man who read the Bible constantly. With this context in mind, the fact that he was able to commit the crimes discussed in the following section is all the more disturbing.

Crimes

In 1903, Fish was arrested for embezzlement and sentenced to a stay in Sing Sing Correctional Facility in New York. His criminal career took off in earnest following his release: in 1910 Fish committed his first murder, or so he claimed, though the police at the time could find no record of the incident. It took place in Delaware, and the victim was a child named Thomas Bedden: little information exists about this killing. Following his wife's desertion, Fish began to demonstrate further signs of deeper psychological disturbance, including hearing voices and religious delusions. His subsequent victims were mentally challenged, from extremely poor families or African Americans, whom he targeted as he was aware of the racial bias that existed within the police force at the time. Fish understood that if an urban black child came to harm or went missing, the police would most probably either ignore the crime or take it far less seriously than if the victim had been white. This allowed Fish to quite literally get away with murder for much longer than he otherwise would have, as the lack of thorough investigation meant that the police did not make the link between the murders or attribute them to the work of a serial killer. He often lured his victims with bribery in the form of treats or small sums of money. Later, following his imprisonment, Fish claimed that at one point he 'hired' a young African American girl and would pay her five dollars to bring him African American boys to be his victims.

On 13 July 1924, a notably grisly murder occurred in the Charlton Woods area of Staten Island. The victim was eight-year-old Francis McDonnell, who had been reported missing by his parents after he had failed to come home after a day out playing with his friends. A search party was organized and it was not long before his body was found in a nearby wood, hanging from a tree. An investigation revealed that the boy had been sexually assaulted, beaten and strangled with his own braces. The autopsy also revealed lacerations to his abdomen and legs, with his left hamstring almost completely stripped of its flesh. The extent of McDonnell's injuries was, in fact, so drastic that the police at the time were convinced that the killer must have had an accomplice. This murder was not attributed to Fish until after his capture. He initially denied responsibility for McDonnell's murder, while at the same time freely admitting that he had seen the child and had intended to castrate him, but had fled the scene before he had had the opportunity. It was not until March 1935, at the conclusion of his trial, that he finally confessed to raping and murdering McDonnell, which led a journalist from the *New York Daily Mirror* to describe Fish as 'the most vicious child-slayer in criminal history'.

This murder was followed, three years later, by that of four-year-old Billy Gaffney. On 11 February 1927, Gaffney was playing with a friend outside his home. This was the last time he was seen alive. His friend, who was three years old, also went missing but was found not long after, on the roof of the apartment building where they lived. When the boy was asked about the whereabouts of Gaffney, he responded that the 'boogeyman' had taken him. When the police failed to find Gaffney's body, it was widely assumed that the boy had fallen into the river. It was not until after Fish's arrest and the subsequent media frenzy surrounding it that a man named Joseph Meehan was able to identify Fish as the man he had seen, around the time of Gaffney's disappearance, trying to quieten a young boy who was crying for his mother.

Gaffney's mother would later visit Fish in Sing Sing to ask for details of her son's death. Fish freely confessed to the murder to her, describing that he had brought her young son to a desolate house, stripped him naked, tied him up and gagged him with a dirty rag. Fish had then gone home, leaving the child alone until the following day. He had burned the child's clothes and thrown his shoes in the dump. Upon his return, he had beaten the child until blood had run down his legs. He had then cut off Gaffney's ears and nose before he had 'slit his mouth from ear to ear' and gouged out his eyes, which had finally killed him. This may have been the incident that prompted Fish's interest in cannibalism, as he admitted to Gaffney's mother that he had drunk blood from the boy's body before cutting him up and putting the pieces in old potato sacks to later cook and eat with 'onions, carrots, turnips, celery, salt and pepper'.

Throughout his criminal career, Fish is known to have travelled over 28 states. He claimed to have killed a child in each one. Wertham would later attest that 15 murders would be a believable number, but that it was possible that Fish had assaulted and mutilated about a hundred. Fish was 58 when, on 28 May 1928, in Manhattan, he committed the crime that would ultimately lead to his execution.

On this day, Fish, under the assumed name of Frank Howard, knocked on the door of the family of Albert Budd. Albert's 18-year-old son, Edward, had recently placed an advertisement in the local newspaper asking for a job. Fish told the family that he owned a 20-acre farm on Long Island and that he desperately required a farmhand. Edward, Fish's intended victim, readily accepted the job offer and invited him into his home for lunch. Fish's initial plan deviated when Grace, Edward's ten-year-old sister, returned home from church and joined the family at the dinner table. Fish took an instant liking to Grace and could not help but be taken by her charm. She sat on his lap at dinner and, in that instant, Fish decided that she, rather than Edward, would be his next victim. He told the family that he had to leave, as he had to attend a party for one of his sister's children, but said that Grace would be more than welcome to come with him. Grace left hand-in-hand with Fish. He promised to bring her home by nine that night, but Grace never returned.

The next morning, Edward sent for the police and filed a missing persons report. It was only then that Edward

Grace Budd, one of Albert Fish's victims, with her family.

discovered, through the police, that 'Frank Howard' did
not exist and neither did his farm. Fish clearly had not
anticipated the extent of the publicity this case would

provoke, however, as the media coverage concerning Grace was intense. The police received and investigated hundreds of tips, without success. When the case arrived at the desk of Detective William F. King, from the Missing Persons Bureau, he developed a particular interest in it and invested a substantial amount of time and resources in tracking down the fictitious Frank Howard. It was not until six years after Grace went missing – when the Budds received an unsigned letter from Grace's kidnapper – that King finally uncovered the necessary proof to break the case. The letter detailed how the kidnapper had taken Grace to an empty house in Westchester. He had left her outside, picking flowers, while he had gone inside to strip himself naked. He had leaned out of the window and called her inside. The letter described how, when he had confronted her, unclothed, she had begun to cry and tried to run away. He had grabbed her to prevent her from leaving and then strangled her, immediately killing her. He had then cut her body in half and taken it home to eat. According to the letter, it had taken nine days to eat the entire body. He was left with only the bones, so he had returned with them to the empty house and buried them in the garden.

The clue to unravelling the case was in the inked-out logo on the envelope, which read 'N.Y.P.C.B.A' – the initials of a private chauffeur's association. This led King to the relevant association, where a janitor confessed to King that he had, in the past, taken some of the stationery from the office to a room he used to rent on 200 East 52nd Street. His landlord had been none other than Albert Fish. King compared Fish's handwriting on the boarding house register to the handwriting on the letter. They were a definite match.

When Fish was caught, he was initially unhesitant and

compliant when asked to go to headquarters for questioning. Once he reached the door of the police station, however, he attempted to attack King with a razor. King managed to subdue Fish, handcuff and arrest him. Fish made no attempt to cover up his murder of Grace and, ultimately, his confession led to the unearthing of her bones from the garden.

Trial and Sentence

Fish was apprehended in 1934, whereupon he underwent intensive questioning, during the course of which he admitted to having killed approximately 400 children since 1910. This figure was never confirmed and the judge involved later estimated a realistic figure to be 16. It became clear to King that Fish was the killer who had been known up till then as 'The Brooklyn Vampire' and who had killed four children in the years 1933 and 1934 by luring them into a basement and garrotting them with a rope. Interestingly, however, King was advised not to introduce these murders into evidence, as the District Attorney was intent on prosecuting Fish as a sane man and an excessive number of murders would have called his sanity into question.

Following his arrest, Fish was visited by Wertham, who would eventually testify to Fish's insanity for the defence. Wertham claimed that Fish 'looked like a meek and innocuous little old man, gentle and benevolent, friendly and polite.' He also claimed that, by all appearances, 'if you wanted someone to entrust your children to, he would be the one you would choose'. Ultimately, Wertham's examination of Fish revealed that he was an 'extreme pathological case' and he suffered from advanced paranoid schizophrenia, which manifested itself in delusions, as well as acts of paedophilia, masochism and mutilation. His case was so extreme that Wertham was completely unable to establish a parallel to Fish in the available psychiatric or criminal literature. In fact, in his own words, Wertham stated that:

'Fish's sexual life was of unparalleled perversity . . . I found no published case that would even nearly compare with this . . . There was no known perversion that he did not practise and practise frequently. Sadomasochism directed against children, particularly boys, took the lead in his sexual regressive development.'

Fish's trial began on 11 March 1935, in White Plains, New York. It lasted ten days, with the defence plea being that Fish was not guilty by reason of insanity. Fish claimed that he regularly heard God's voice instructing him to commit crimes and kill children. A number of psychiatrists were brought in to testify regarding Fish's propensities for masochism, paedophilia, coprophagia and urophagia. James Dempsey, Fish's defence attorney, described him as a 'psychiatric phenomenon', echoing Wertham's findings that Fish had so many sexual abnormalities that he actually had no existing legal or medical equivalent.

As the defence's chief expert witness, Wertham delivered over two days of testimony in which he described Fish as introverted, 'extremely infantalistic' and suffering from 'paranoid psychosis'. He explained Fish's innate obsession with religion, which began in his youth. He specifically detailed his fixation with the biblical story of Abraham and Isaac, where God asked Abraham to sacrifice his son. Wertham claimed that Fish identified with the tale and believed that if he sacrificed a boy, it would be penance for his sins – and, furthermore, that if the act were innately wrong, there would have been divine intervention. Wertham went on to explain Fish's fascination with cannibalism, which he had associated with Holy Communion. Wertham was adamant and insisted that Fish was insane, stating that 'however you define the medical and legal borders of sanity, this [case] certainly is beyond that border'.

When the prosecution cross-examined Wertham, they asked whether Fish, when committing his crimes, knew the difference between right and wrong. Wertham claimed that yes, Fish knew the difference, but that this knowledge was perverted as it was distorted by his views on religion, atonement and sin. Due to this, his knowledge was an 'insane knowledge'. The defence called a further two psychiatrists, who corroborated Wertham's findings.

When the time came to call the witnesses for the prosecution, there were four professionals who were ready to label Fish as mentally fit. The first witness was Dr Menas Gregory, who testified that, although Fish was certainly abnormal, he was legally sane, citing that coprophagia and urophagia were 'common perversions' that were 'socially perfectly alright' and also claiming that, in this respect, Fish was no different to millions of others. The second witness was Dr Perry Lichtenstein, a prison doctor, who attested that he did not believe Fish even suffered from masochism as a mental condition. The defence objected to this statement as the doctor had no psychiatric training and therefore did not have the qualifications to determine whether an individual was sane or insane. This objection was overruled by the judge, who said that the jury was free to decide how much weight they should give to the doctor's opinion. The third witness was Dr Charles Lambert, who argued that coprophagia was relatively commonplace and that cannibalism itself was not evidence of a psychosis. This opinion was echoed by the fourth and final witness, Dr James Vavasour.

It has since been argued that both the prosecution and the judge knew that Fish was legally insane, but felt that it would benefit society more not to be burdened with a man who was capable of such atrocities, no matter his mental state. In addition, the fact that the criminal responsible for so many murders had finally been apprehended and tried would have been a massive relief to the public at the time. The execution of such a criminal would further serve a ritual function, in which the public feels justice or morality has been upheld when a killer receives the same punishment he has meted out to his victims. It is a conclusion that serves, as Wilson points out, the purpose of 'exorcising the horror'.

Fish was found sane and guilty by a jury and was sentenced by the judge to death by the electric chair. Far from giving up, Wertham tried to get Fish's sentence commuted. He claimed at the time that 'to execute a sick man is like burning witches'. His efforts were to no avail; this, however, seemed not to bother Fish, who appeared almost excited with his fate. Speaking of the prospect of his execution, he said it would be 'the supreme thrill of my life' – bizarre and yet unsurprising words from a man who so savoured pain. However, on the day of his execution he seemed less pleased and more confused, and is recorded to have mumbled, 'I don't know why I'm here.' On Thursday, 16 January 1936, aged 65, Albert Fish was finally put to death. He entered the chamber at 11:06 pm and was pronounced dead three minutes later. He was buried in the prison cemetery.

Years later, Wertham criticized the court proceedings and the psychiatrists involved in the prosecution, saying that they had served a 'black eye to psychiatry'. He remained insistent that society would have benefited far more had we gained an understanding of Fish, his mental state and what prompted him to do what he had done, rather than simply executing him.

Discussion

Under the Holmes and DeBurger (1985) typology for serial killers, Fish would be a mixture of the Visionary and the Hedonistic type. He claimed to have heard God's voice, instructing him to commit murder and castrate young boys, which puts him comfortably in the Visionary category. Fish was consumed with religious imagery: it was a constant refrain throughout his life and one that became entwined with his love for receiving as well as inflicting pain. He also fits into the category of the Hedonistic killer, as the act of murder itself, together with the pain involved and the cannibalism that often followed, also brought him pleasure. We know as much from records of his in-depth conversations with Wertham.

Fish himself stated that he had always had an interest in pain. As he told Wertham, 'I have always had a desire to inflict pain on others and to have others inflict pain on me. I have always seemed to enjoy anything that hurt.' Fish's early life throws up some interesting clues to the root of this desire. He was an introverted child who was often ill. He wet the bed for a time, and was taunted by his peers as a result. According to Wertham, Fish then withdrew into his own world of daydreams. At one point in his childhood, he had fallen from a cherry tree and received a serious blow to the head, resulting in a concussion. Afterwards he had a tendency to develop severe headaches and have convulsive fits. He also experienced dizzy spells and developed a stutter. This head injury could be significant, as much research has examined – and found evidence of – the link between brain injuries or defects and violent behaviour (as examined in the discussion of Fritz Haarmann in the previous chapter). Furthermore, Fish experienced the trauma of his father dying, his mother's perceived abandonment and the corporal punishment at the orphanage within quick succession, at a very delicate age. He was only five years old when he entered the orphanage; he left when he was nearly nine. Psychological research has demonstrated that a person's personality is established when they are young and that by the time they are seven, traits that define an individual for the rest of their lives are established. The fact that Fish spent these integral years being beaten, physically abused and, in all likelihood, emotionally neglected are very telling.

Fish's propensity towards violence may have begun during his time at the orphanage, where the discipline and corporal punishment he experienced were severe. The matron would require the children to pray for hours every day and learn chapters of the Bible by rote. This was also likely to be a significant contributing factor to his obsession with religion; at one time he even harboured an ambition to become a priest. This deep-seated interest, together with the regular floggings he and his peers received for disciplinary or religious trespasses, may have caused violence and sexual and religious fantasy to fuse. Punitive acts, such as whipping inflicted on him in his early years, ultimately brought him a sense of spiritual release and of sexual gratification.

Another early contributing factor might have been that when Fish's brother, Walter, returned from the navy, he told Fish gory stories of cannibalism that he had reportedly witnessed while overseas. At such a young age, this might well have captured Fish's imagination and factored into the development of his sadomasochistic and cannibalistic inclinations. Fish also spent a lot of time reading about real-life murder cases, snipping the stories out of the newspapers whenever one surfaced. At the time he was apprehended, Fish was carrying around an article about Fritz Haarmann, the 'Butcher of Hanover', examined in the previous chapter.

Despite the issues that overwhelmed his childhood, it seems that it was not until later in life that Fish began to suffer extreme hallucinations and delusions. At the age of 55, he began to develop a religious psychosis wherein he identified with God and believed that he should sacrifice his own son. He had visions of Christ and his angels. He also experienced auditory hallucinations, in which he was convinced angels spoke seemingly random words and phrases to him, such as 'stripes', to which he would attribute meaning. Fish told Wertham during their meetings that 'stripes means to lash them, you know'. On one occasion Fish's children witnessed him beating himself, nude, with a nail-studded paddle until he was covered in his own blood. The self-harm he inflicted was, in some measure, a way of atoning and of symbolically purging himself of his sins.

Because Fish lived comparatively recently and Wertham

invested a great amount of time and energy in studying him, we are fortunate to have a considerable amount of information available about his life, crimes and mental state. As Fish was mentally unbalanced, he was an arguably unreliable historian and it is possible that he embellished his stories or admitted to crimes that he did not commit. There are things we shall never know, such as his exact number of victims, but the pages of detail that we do have concerning his crimes paint a vivid and startling enough portrait. It is clear that he committed unthinkable crimes, which have been understandably described as 'evil'. Similarly understandably, society has and will continue to judge Fish for his actions. His crimes were committed against children, the most innocent and defenceless members of our society and those we instinctively feel the greatest need to protect.

It can also be argued, however, that to label Fish as 'evil', as a 'werewolf', 'vampire' or as a 'monster' does psychology, criminology and indeed society at large a disservice, as labels such as these can be unhelpfully reductive. Frederic Wertham was an advocate of an entirely different point of view: that it is much more beneficial for us to embrace the complexity of Fish's psychology and his case, to look into how and why he ended up committing the crimes he did. Considering his mental state and psychotic symptoms, many believe it was an injustice and a failure of the criminal justice system that Fish was found to be legally sane. Experts believe that in the current climate, he would have in fact been judged legally insane and sentenced to spend his years in a relevant institution, where he would have received psychiatric treatment – and we would have gained a better, more comprehensive insight into one of the most dysfunctional and psychologically complex criminal minds of the time.

CHAPTER SEVEN

Peter Kürten - The Vampire of Dusseldorf/ The Dusseldorf Monster

'The man Kürten is a riddle to me. I cannot solve it. The criminal Haarman only killed men, Landru and Grossman only women, but Peter killed men, women, children and animals; killed anything he found.'　　　Dr Wehner

Introduction

Between the months of February and November 1929, a series of grisly murders and sexual assaults occurred in the city of Düsseldorf that sent shockwaves of horror through Germany and the international community. These crimes are among the clearest cases of sexually driven murder and sadism on record. Behind them was Peter Kürten, a softly spoken, well-dressed man with neatly parted hair and a pleasant face, known alternately as 'The Vampire of Düsseldorf' and the 'Düsseldorf Monster'.

As a result of his crimes, Kürten became the focus of intense examination, both judicial and scientific, not only for the purpose of seeking justice for his crimes but also

Peter Kürten

to study the psychology and physiological make-up of such an outrageous and enigmatic criminal mind. This has resulted in advances in our understanding of psycho-pathological crime – and established Peter Kürten as one of the most infamous serial killers of our time. Following his death, Kürten's head was dissected, mummified and placed on display at the *Ripley's Believe It Or Not!* museum in Wisconsin. References throughout popular culture followed, including mentions in novels, such as Stephen King's *Salem's Lot* and Philip Kerr's *The Pale Criminal*. Kürten has also been alluded to in a number of films, a play and even in music.

The man who would come to be known as the 'Vampire of Düsseldorf' was born on 26 May 1883 in Mülheim am Rhein, formerly a town in Cologne, Germany. Kürten was born into poverty, brought up in a one-room apartment housing his parents and 13 children, of which he was the eldest. His father, a brutal alcoholic, frequently came home drunk and repeatedly sexually assaulted his mother. His father was later sentenced to three years imprisonment for committing incest with one of Kürten's sisters, aged 13 at the time. Living in such close quarters with such a large family, Kürten was often a witness to these assaults. He describes their effect upon him in interviews with his prison doctor, Dr Karl Berg[1], following his capture:

'The whole family suffered through his drinking, for when he was in drink, my father was terrible.

---

1   Dr Berg would go on to write and publish his book, Der Sadist, perhaps one of the most comprehensive accounts of Kürten's crimes available to us today, as confessed and described to him with extraordinary frankness and in great detail by Kürten himself during his detainment.

I, being the eldest, had to suffer most. As you may well imagine, we suffered terrible poverty, all because the wages went on drink. We all lived in one room and you will appreciate what effect that had on me sexually.'

The seed had been planted for the sadistic nature of Kürten's sexual urges and fantasies. In 1894, Kürten relocated with his family to Düsseldorf, where he found work with a local dogcatcher who taught him how to torture animals, especially dogs, and to masturbate them. Kürten's aggressive sexual urges were developing at an alarming pace and he was soon committing bestiality on sheep and goats in the nearby stables. It was in the course of this that he discovered something that would eventually come to motivate and characterize the crimes for which he would gain infamy: in his own words, 'the pleasure of the sight of blood'. He also learned that his orgasms were the most powerful when he stabbed an animal as he had intercourse with it, an act that he performed with increasing frequency.

By the age of 16, Kürten had run away from home and received the first of many prison sentences that would take up more than 20 years of his life. Initially his crimes were petty ones, including the theft of food and clothing for his own survival, which earned him short stays in Düsseldorf prisons. His first lengthy sentence was for two years as punishment for theft, which left him bitter and angry at the conditions within prisons at the time, particularly for young prisoners.

During this period he also discovered a new sadistic pursuit: indulging in fantasies where he could bring himself to orgasm by imagining brutal sexual acts. This grew to be such an obsession that he would intentionally commit minor infractions while in prison in order to be placed in solitary confinement – the ideal environment to engage in sadistic fantasies.

In 1899, Kürten began living with a prostitute twice his age who had an inclination towards masochism and enjoyed being abused and ill-treated. They lived together for two years, a period which greatly reinforced Kürten's own sadistic urges. For the first time, he was allowed to enact them not merely on animals, but on a person.

The prison sentences that followed, for crimes such as assault and theft, only served to intensify Kürten's feelings of injustice and anger towards the prison system. His fantasies, previously of a sadistic sexual nature, grew to revolve around the theme of revenge upon society – which also seemed to provoke a sexual pleasure in him.

'I thought of myself causing accidents affecting thousands of people and invented a number of crazy fantasies such as smashing bridges and boring through bridge piers,' Kürten described, at his trial. 'Then I spun a number of fantasies with regard to bacilli which I might be able to introduce into the drinking water and so cause a great calamity. I imagined myself using schools or orphanages for the purpose, where I could carry out murders by giving away chocolate samples containing arsenic, which I could have obtained through housebreaking. I derived the sort of pleasure from these visions that other people would get from thinking about a naked woman.'

Crimes

Kürten's murderous career was to span at least 16 years, during which he committed at least nine murders, for which he was eventually charged, though he was suspected to have committed more than 60. He was also charged with seven attempted murders, and admitted to 79 offences in total, including attempted murder, sexual assault, arson and petty theft.

Kürten committed his first officially recorded murder in 1913[1]. It was only much later, in 1929, when he would begin what came to be known as his 'Year of Terror' – a nine-month long spree of murder and sexual outrages that would culminate in his eventual capture.

In the spring of 1913, while living in Düsseldorf, Kürten frequented the nearby town of Köln, where he took to committing a series of thefts. His own account of his first murder was frankly and graphically delivered during his trial:

'It was on May 25, 1913. I had been stealing, special-izing in public bars or inns where the owner lived on the floor above. In a room above an inn at Köln-Mülheim, I discovered a child of 13 asleep. Her head was facing the window. I seized it with my left hand and strangled her for about a minute and a half. The child woke up and struggled but lost consciousness.

---

1   Kurten would, however, later claim that his first murders were committed much earlier. At the age of nine, he said, he drowned a schoolmate while playing on a raft in the Rhine. When the boy's friend dived in to rescue him, he, too, was pushed under the raft by Kürten and held down until he drowned.

'I had a small but sharp pocketknife with me and I held the child's head and cut her throat. I heard the blood spurt and drip on the mat beside the bed. It spurted in an arch, right over my hand. The whole thing lasted about three minutes. Then I locked the door again and went back home to Düsseldorf.

'Next day I went back to Mülheim,' Kürten continued, in court. 'There is a cafe opposite the Klein's place and I sat there and drank a glass of beer and read all about the murder in the papers. People were talking about it all round me. All this amount of indignation and horror did me good.'

Kürten's first victim had been Christine Klein, a 13-year-old schoolgirl from Köln. Her father, Peter Klein, owned the inn in which the killing took place. It so happened that on the day before the murder, Peter Klein had refused his brother, Otto, a loan. In a fit of anger, Otto had threatened to do something Peter 'would remember all his life'. At the murder scene, the police discovered a handkerchief with the initials 'P.K.' on it – and, in another stroke of sheer luck for Kürten, they surmized that Otto had borrowed it from his brother, Peter Klein. Otto Klein thus became the primary suspect in Christine's murder. He was eventually charged, but the jury decided that there was insufficient evidence against him and he was rightly acquitted.

With all the attention focused on Otto Klein, Kürten had managed to evade capture. His bloodthirsty, murderous urges had finally been executed and fully awakened. His crimes, however, were put on hold until 1921 while he served an eight-year prison sentence for deserting from the army. Upon his release, he moved to Altenburg. There he met his future wife, a former prostitute who herself had served a prison sentence of four years, for shooting her fiancé for jilting her.

Following their marriage, the couple lived in Altenburg until 1925, with Kürten gaining permanent employment as a moulder in a factory. He also became an active trade unionist and seems to have lived a peaceful and respectable life for the first four years of marriage.

However, in 1925, the couple moved to Düsseldorf to find work and Kürten found his self-control slowly diminishing. For the second time, something about the town had the effect of drawing out his aberrant, criminal impulses. He noted that 'the sunset was blood-red on my return', interpreting this as symbolic of his murderous destiny. In the four years between 1925 and 1928, he attacked four women in Dusseldorf, choking them to the point of unconsciousness, often during sex. He took up arson, which gave him sexual pleasure, and he also derived sexual satisfaction from imagining that a tramp was burning alive in a barn he had just torched.

These crimes, however, were to be a mere prelude to the terrible events that occurred in Düsseldorf in 1929: the infamous 'Year of Terror'.

The Düsseldorf police were first made aware of the existence of a depraved murderer in the community on 9 February 1929, when the body of an eight-year-old girl by the name of Rosa Ohliger was found stashed under a hedge. Ohliger had been stabbed 13 times and an attempt had been made to burn the body with petrol. The murderer had stabbed her in the vagina and semen found on her underwear indicated that he had ejaculated. Kürten, who had tried to dispose of his victim's body by setting it alight, later recalled to a shocked courtroom that 'when that morning [he] poured petrol over the child Ohliger and set fire to her, [he] had an orgasm at the height of the fire'.

Six days earlier, Kürten had attacked a woman by the name of Kühn, whom he had singled out at random and stabbed 24 times with a knife before fleeing the scene. His sadistic sexual appetite, however, had been nowhere near sated and he described at his trial how he had derived sexual enjoyment from returning to the scene of the crime. 'The place where I attacked Frau Kühn I visited again that same evening twice and later several times,' he said. 'In doing so, I sometimes had an orgasm.'

Only five days after the murder of Ohliger, the body of a 45-year-old mechanic named Scheer was found, on a road in Flingern. He had sustained 20 knife wounds, including several in the head. The day after the murder, Kürten once again returned to the crime scene and boldly initiated a conversation with a policeman at the site, asking about the murder – an incident confirmed during the trial by the policeman in question.

On 21 August, in the suburb of Lierenfeld, Kürten stabbed three people who were walking home at night. These three random victims were all politely bidden a good evening by their assailant before being stabbed with a knife in their chests and backs.

Two nights later, an annual fair took place in the town of Flehe, an event attended by hundreds of people, including Kürten. At around half past ten at night, Kürten followed two children as they left the fair and began walking home. The two girls were five-year-old Gertrude Hamacher and 14-year-old Louise Lenzen. Kürten stopped them and asked the older child if she 'would be very kind and get some cigarettes for [him]', adding that he would 'look after the little girl'. Louise took the money Kürten offered her and ran back towards the fairground. Once she was gone, Kürten picked up Gertrude in his arms and strangled her, then slit her throat with a clasp knife. When Louise returned from her errand, Kürten dragged her off the footpath before strangling and then decapitating her.

The next day, Gertrude Schulte, a servant girl, was attacked by a man who attempted to have sexual intercourse with her. When she responded that she 'would rather die', he answered, 'Die then!' and stabbed her. But Schulte survived the attack and was afterwards able to describe her attacker as a pleasant-looking, nondescript man of about 40 years of age.

In September, a young girl named Ida Reuter was raped and battered to death. On 12 October, another servant girl by the name of Elizabeth Dorrier was beaten to death. This was followed by attacks with a hammer on two women by the names of Frau Meurer and Frau Wanders, both on 25 October. On 7 November, five-year-old Gertrude Albermann disappeared and, two days later, the newspaper *Freedom* received a letter from the killer with a map enclosed, stating that the child's body would be found near a factory wall. The body was found where the letter had described, among a mass of bricks and rubble. Albermann had been strangled and stabbed 35 times.

The increasing rate and viciousness of Kürten's attacks during this period led medical and forensic experts to believe that the 'Vampire of Dusseldorf' had lost all control of his cruel impulses and was working himself into a sexual and sadistic frenzy. Düsseldorf was thrown into a panic as the murder toll continued to mount. The methods employed by the elusive Kürten in his attacks were constantly changing and, as such, provided no clear pattern for the investigating detectives. Despite the best efforts of the police and the massive manhunt that was in operation, Kürten remained elusive and unidentified. Between February and May 1930 further strangulation and hammer attacks occurred, although none with fatal consequences. By May 1930, sheer terror had gripped the people of Düsseldorf and the perpetrator was still on the loose.

On 14 May 1930, however, Kürten's luck was about to change. A woman named Maria Budlick arrived in Düsseldorf, having travelled from Köln in search of employment as a domestic servant. On the platform at the Düsseldorf train station, she was approached by a stranger, who offered to show her the way to a hostel. She followed him for a while down a few well-lit streets, but when he turned to enter a park she recalled the stories of the Düsseldorf murderer she had read about in the newspapers and refused to go any further. An argument ensued between the two, during which a second man appeared and enquired as to whether everything was all right. Intimidated by the newcomer's arrival, the man from the railway station left. Budlick was left alone with her rescuer: none other than Peter Kürten himself.

Kürten later said of the meeting: 'The girl told me that she was out of work and had nowhere to go. She agreed to come with me to my room on the Mettmanner Strasse and then she suddenly said she did not want sexual intercourse and asked me whether I could find her somewhere else to sleep.'

Kürten took Budlick into the Grafenberger Woods, where he seized her by the neck and demanded sexual intercourse with her. 'I thought that under the circumstances she would agree and my opinion was right. Afterwards I took her back to the tram, but I did not accompany her right to it because I was afraid she might inform the police officer who was standing there. I had no intention of killing Budlick as she had offered no resistance. I did not think that Budlick would be able to find her way back to my apartment in the rather obscure Mettmanner Strasse. So much the more was I surprised when on Wednesday, the 21 of May, I saw her again in my house.'

Contrary to Kürten's belief, Budlick clearly remembered the sign 'Mettmanner Strasse' from her encounter with Kürten. She wrote a letter to a female acquaintance detailing the incident – but the letter was misdirected and never reached its intended recipient. It was opened instead by a woman named Frau Brugmann, who read it and, alarmed by its contents, called the police.

Budlick was immediately called in and questioned intensively by the police. She led Chief Inspector Gennat to 71 Mettmanner Strasse. Kürten happened to be returning home at the time of their visit and met them as he was on his way upstairs. He was startled, but continued calmly to his room and shut the door. A few moments later he left the building with his hat pulled low over his face, passed two plainclothes policemen standing in the street and disappeared around a corner.

Realizing that his capture and exposure were imminent and inevitable, Kürten rented lodgings away from his own flat, in which his wife still lived, and spent some time thinking about what to do next. He came to a surprising decision: to explain the incident with Budlick to his wife.

As it could have been considered a rape, taken together with his previous convictions, Kürten realized the attack could be enough to earn him 15 years in prison. Nothing yet linked Kürten with the assaults by the infamous vampire killer. His only suspected crime up to this point was rape, but he knew now that there was no longer any hope of escaping capture and imprisonment.

Kürten himself described the subsequent events of 23 May 1930 in writing: 'Today, the 23rd, in the morning, I told my wife that I was also responsible for the Schulte affair, adding my usual remark that it would mean ten years or more separation for us — probably forever. At that, my wife was inconsolable. She spoke of unemployment, lack of means and starvation in old age. She raved that I should take my life, then she would do the same, since her future was completely without hope. Then, in the late afternoon, I told my wife that I could help her.'

Kurten decided to reveal all to his wife. He told her that he was the Düsseldorf Vampire and revealed the details of all his murders to her. A large reward had been offered for the capture or discovery of the vampire, he told her – and she would earn it if she reported his confession to the police. Kürten's account continues:

'Of course, it wasn't easy for me to convince her that this ought not to be considered as treason, but that, on the contrary, she was doing a good deed to humanity as well as to justice. It was not until late in the evening that she promised to carry out my request and also that she would not commit suicide.

It was 11 o'clock when we separated. Back in my lodging, I went to bed and fell asleep at once.'

The next day, Kürten's wife told the story to the police. She also informed them that her husband had arranged to meet her outside St Rochus church at three o'clock that afternoon. By the time of the arranged meeting, the area around the church had been completely surrounded. The moment Kürten appeared, four officers rushed forward with loaded revolvers pointed at him. He reportedly smiled, offered no resistance, and said with remarkable calm, 'There is no need to be afraid.'

Trial and Sentence

Under arrest, Kürten confessed his crimes with aston- ishing frankness to Professor Karl Berg, who was later to write the most comprehensive guide to the career of the Vampire of Dusseldorf in his book *The Sadist*. At the time, Berg was a professor of forensic medicine at the Düsseldorf Medical Academy and the medical director and founder of the Düsseldorf Institute of Legal and Social Medicine. He was also a medico-legal officer in the Düsseldorf Criminal Court, making him well placed to interview and assess Kürten. Berg was successful in winning Kürten's confidence and, consequently, in providing a fascinating insight into the mind of a killer.

The way in which Kürten provided the details of his crimes was extraordinary: he was not accused of the offences one by one and made to respond to the charges, but described them all of his own volition, beginning with the first murder and ending with number 79. His vibrant

A dummy dressed in the clothes of one of Kürten's victims that was taken around Dusseldorf's dance halls and cabarets to try to jog people's memories and find witnesses.

and incredibly detailed recollection of his crimes was unusual and led some to doubt that he was telling the truth. As the questioning continued, however, and he went on to give the same, unwavering accounts of the murders and attacks in interviews with Dr Berg as well as during pre-trial questioning and in court, it became clear that Kürten was telling the truth and was, in fact, the infamous 'Vampire'.

It was also evident that the motivation behind his confessions was not one of guilt or remorse, but rather to provide for his wife. It is this dedication to his wife during the trial that some argue is the most intriguing aspect of the case: throughout his marriage, Kürten had committed a great number of infidelities, showing no visible consideration to her. His speech and actions during his trial, however, were in complete contrast to this established behaviour and made it clear that he wanted to secure a comfortable future for his wife: 'I had already finished with my life when I first knew the police were on my track,' he said. 'I wanted to fix up for my wife a carefree old age, for she is entitled to at least a part of the reward. That is why I entered a plea of guilty to all the crimes.'

Kürten's trial began on 13 April 1932. The Düsseldorf Vampire was charged with nine murders and seven attempted murders. The case was unique in that it demanded the construction of a special, shoulder-high cage inside the courtroom, which would eliminate any chance of the defendant's escape. Behind this cage lay evidence of his crimes in the form of the victims' skulls, together with various body parts, which displayed the injuries that he had inflicted. As an illustration to the jury, weapons that he had used were also on exhibit, including ropes, knives, scissors and a hammer. A spade he had used to bury one of his victims was also shown, as well as some pieces of clothing that had belonged to the victims – all culminating in a terrifying and damning exhibition of guilt.

The jury and crowd were puzzled by the visual incongruence between the gruesome exhibits and the alleged perpetrator who was presented to them. Kürten came to court looking well-dressed and presentable, in a respectable suit and neatly parted hair that made him look completely normal, even pleasant. The trial would see many bemused people professing that they knew Kürten to be polite and well-mannered. Neighbours denied the possibility that he could have committed the crimes and former employers insisted that Kürten had always been a reliable and honest man. The only slightly negative aspect of his reputation was the fact that the locals knew him as a 'Casanova', able to charm and seduce women easily. His reputation had otherwise been so pristine, in fact, that years earlier a former girlfriend had suggested that Kürten might be the Vampire, but the police had actually fined her for making damaging and malicious accusations.

To further complicate matters, Kürten went on to calmly deny his original confession, presenting a plea of not guilty to the examining magistrate. He asserted that his initial confession was fabricated in order to obtain a generous reward for his wife. It took two long months before he was finally backed into a corner and admitted to the veracity of his original confession.

Doctors called to the stand as expert witnesses testified

that Kürten was not legally insane and 'perfectly responsible for his actions at all times'. The motive for his canon of terrible crimes was evident to most involved in the investigation: Kürten committed these acts in an attempt to revenge himself on society. He had suffered what he perceived as extreme inequity in prison and he was exacting his own brand of justice. During the trial, the judge asked Kürten whether or not he possessed a conscience. This was Kürten's reply:

> 'I have none. Never have I felt any misgiving in my soul; never did I think to myself that what I did was bad, even though human society condemns it. My blood and the blood of my victims will be on the heads of my torturers. There must be a Higher Being who gave in the first place the first vital spark to life. That Higher Being would deem my actions good since I revenged injustice. The punishments I have suffered have destroyed all my feelings as a human being. That was why I had no pity for my victims.'

This speech is completely in line with the remorseless nature of a psychopath, who knows right from wrong but does not feel necessarily compelled to act within moral parameters and who rarely accepts responsibility for his actions, attributing them instead to be the fault of someone or something else. In this case, the people behind the German penal system, in Kürten's view, were the real murderers. These words were delivered in a voice that was described as 'flat' and 'unemotional', displaying a chilling lack of empathy.

Kürten, during his trial, went on to describe his life

and to attempt to deflect any trace of responsibility for his actions. He blamed not only the men of the prison who made his life miserable, but the environment he had lived in throughout his life and his unfortunate family background. According to his own account, all these factors combined to amplify a latent and terrible sadistic streak that he had been born with. The court listened as Kürten described how he was sexually gratified by the sight of his victims' blood and how, on occasion, he would drink blood directly from their bodies, once straight from a throat and once from an open wound on a temple. Once, he claimed, he drank so much that he became physically sick. He also recalled how he once licked the blood from a victim's hands.

With all these shocking confessions, the prosecution had little work to do in securing a conviction. The only real option for Dr Wehner, the defence counsel representing Kürten, was to argue legal insanity, despite the fact that a number of reputable psychiatrists had argued that Kürten did not qualify for that defence. Wehner asked a Professor Sioli during his testimony to reconsider his appraisal of Kürten's sanity, claiming that 'Kürten is the king of sexual delinquents . . . he unites nearly all perversions in one person.' His efforts, however, were in vain: the consensus that this was a legally sane man stood. The jury took an hour and 30 minutes to reach a unanimous guilty verdict and Kürten was sentenced to death nine times by the presiding judge, Dr Rose.

Kürten's execution was set for 2 July 1932. In the last moments before his beheading at the guillotine, Kürten asked the prison psychiatrist:

'After my head has been chopped off, will I still be able

to hear, at least for a moment, the sound of my own blood gushing from the stump of my neck? That would be the pleasure to end all pleasures.'

Discussion

Under the Holmes and DeBurger (1985) typology for serial killers, Kürten undoubtedly belongs to the Hedonistic type. He killed because killing brought him pleasure. He can be further subcategorized as a Hedonistic Lust killer, as the pleasure he derived from his murders was clearly of a sexual nature. Many sources claim that Kürten was a psychopath, and an over-sexed one. He was self-involved, egocentric and regarded those around him as pawns that he might use, depending on his desires, his mood and what his immediate situation called for.

It is impossible to discuss the case of Kurten without also discussing Renfield's Syndrome, a condition otherwise known as clinical vampirism. The syndrome presents itself as an obsession with blood or, more specifically, the drinking of blood. Someone suffering from Renfield's Syndrome will derive a sexual pleasure from the sight or the ingestion of blood. Psychologist Richard Noll, author of *Bizarre Diseases of the Mind*, attests that cases of clinical vampirism have features that are in line with the behaviour of a character from Bram Stoker's novel *Dracula*, named Renfield, which explains the eponymous origin of the name.[1]

Noll suggests that clinical vampirism originates from

---

1   In the novel, Renfield is an inmate at a lunatic asylum suffering from delusions, which compel him to eat creatures, such as flies, spiders and birds, in an attempt to obtain their life-force for himself.

'some event that happens before puberty where the child is excited in a sexual way by some event that involves blood injury or the ingestion of blood. At puberty it becomes fused with sexual fantasies, and the typical person with Renfield Syndrome begins with autovampirism. That is, they begin to drink their own blood and then move on to other living creatures. That's what we know from the few cases we have on record. It has fetishistic and compulsive components.'

The condition is thought to emerge in three distinct stages. The first stage is called, as Noll describes, *autovampirism*, where the individual will drink their own blood, usually through self-harm. The second stage is known as *zoophagia*, and involves either eating or drinking the blood of animals. The final stage, *true vampirism*, is when the individual turns their bloodlust upon other human beings. This can take the form of stealing blood from blood banks or hospitals, or the more violent form where the individual attacks and drinks blood directly from another person.

It is worth noting, however, that clinical vampirism has not been given official recognition by the psychiatric profession and is not found in any edition of the *International Classification of Diseases* (ICD) or the *Diagnostic and Statistical Manual of Mental Disorders* (DSM), the medical texts which set out diagnostic criteria for all medical conditions and for mental health conditions, respectively. Clinical vampirism comes from an older era of psychiatry, predating the onset in the 1980s of categorized mental illness with standardized diagnostic criteria contained in the *DSM* and *ICD*. In those days, the field of psychiatry abounded with case studies of 'uncommon psychiatric syndromes' or 'extraordinary disorders of human behaviour' that included not only clinical vampirism, but also lycanthropy (as discussed in the earlier chapter on Peter Stumpp, the Werewolf of Bedburg), demonic or spiritual possession, stigmata and other supernaturally associated phenomena.

Kürten admitted, time and again, that he experienced orgasm either during or shortly after he executed a terrible crime. Experts attest that the attacks were therefore sexually motivated; they were planned events that he carried out in order to achieve sexual satisfaction. This flagrant disregard for the welfare of others in favour of his own gratification is perfectly demonstrative of his advanced egotism – he believed wholeheartedly that he deserved what he wanted and that he would get it, regardless of the cost. In an interview, Kürten discussed his sadistic sexual proclivity: 'I committed my acts of arson for the same reasons – sadistic propensity. I got pleasure from the glow of the fire, the cries for help.'

The most fascinating element of the case of Peter Kürten might arguably be his attitude toward his wife throughout his trial, which contradicts the nature of most psychopaths. Although he was unfaithful to her on countless occasions during their marriage, he certainly appeared to be deeply concerned about her future once he had been captured. Kürten said of this relationship, 'My relations with my wife were always good. I did not love her in the sensual way, but because of my admiration for her fine character.'

It is a trademark of psychopathy to never accept responsibility for one's own faults, but when Kürten reflected on his childhood and misspent time in prison, noting how poorly he was treated and how these factors led to his eventual crimes, he may have been somewhat justified in his reasoning. He certainly possessed a degree of insight and understood where his life began to go awry. The mistreatment he suffered in prison might have seriously hampered his ability to sublimate his more violent urges. George Godwin, author of *Peter Kurten, A Study in Sadism*, wrote of Kürten that, 'if he did become a victimizer of the innocent, it must be remembered that he began life as an innocent victimized'.

Our legal and penal systems do not forgive transgressions simply because their perpetrator was moulded by society into a person capable of committing violent acts. Equally, however, cases like Kürten's remind us that violent criminals and serial killers are not made in a vacuum. These violent or sadistic urges do not materialize out of thin air or, for a large number, deliberate choice, but are created by a combination of genetics, nurture, societal injustices, life events and triggers, physiology and psychology. In this case, the product of these factors was a man with such a desperate need for vengeance that he was filled with conviction that by executing violent acts on others, he was somehow carrying out justice for the wrongs done to himself, even perceiving the murders as a 'mission'. He claimed never to feel any remorse for his crimes. As he said, 'How could I do so? After all, I had to fulfil my mission.'

Kürten did monstrous things and fully deserves his place in the annals of criminal history. Yet there were aspects of him, such as his tormented upbringing and incarceration, which cast him in an almost sympathetic light. Other traits, such as his deep concern for his wife or even his neat, pleasant appearance were incongruous with what we know to be his sadistic nature. For many it is this strange dichotomy that keeps us, as a society, captivated by serial killers such as Kürten. It is fascinating to attempt to reconcile such disparate elements in one individual – and indeed to attempt to reconcile his terrible crimes with his mild manner, agreeable appearance and such eloquence as he possessed:

'As I now see the crimes committed by me, they are so ghastly that I do not want to attempt any sort of excuse for them. I am prepared to bear the consequences of my misdeeds and hope that thus I will atone for a large part of what I have done. And when you consider my execution and recognize my goodwill to atone for all my crimes, I should think that the terrible desire for revenge and hatred against me cannot endure. And I want to ask you to forgive me.'

CHAPTER EIGHT

John George Haigh – The Vampire Killer/ The Acid Bath Murderer

'If I told you the truth, you would not believe me. It sounds too fantastic to believe . . . Mrs Durand-Deacon no longer exists. She has disappeared completely and no trace of her can ever be found again. I have destroyed her with acid . . . Every trace has gone. How can you prove murder if there is no body?'

John George Haigh

Introduction

John George Haigh is quite possibly one of Britain's most cold-blooded serial killers. Commonly known as 'The Acid Bath Murderer' and touted by the press as a vampire due to his alleged propensity to drink the blood of his victims, Haigh is a terrifying example of what excessive greed can do to a person. His story was eagerly covered by the newspapers of the day and horrified the nation, which was shocked by the fact that this seemingly respectable, charming man with intense, sparkling blue eyes was capable of killing six people in cold blood.

John George Haigh

Haigh was born in Stamford, Lincolnshire on 24 July 1909 before moving to Outwood, in the West Riding of Yorkshire, where he grew up. His parents, John Robert (a power station foreman) and Emily were members of the Plymouth Brethren, a puritanical, anticlerical Protestant sect that advocates an austere lifestyle. The sect believes in foregoing traditional entertainments, considering them sinful indulgences, meaning that as a young boy Haigh was forbidden from taking part in any form of sport or activity that might have been described as 'fun' for a growing child, with the exception of the reading of bible stories. Christmas was not celebrated in the Haigh household, which opted instead to attend sermons about Satan, Hell and eternal damnation. Haigh's father eventually erected a 3 m (10 ft) fence around the perimeter of their home: an attempt to keep harmful, evil influences of the outside world at bay. Haigh would later testify that such extreme surroundings caused him to have recurring nightmares as a child, which he described in detail:

'I saw before me a forest of crucifixes which gradually turned into trees. At first, there appeared to be dew or rain, dripping from the branches, but as I approached I realized it was blood. The whole forest began to writhe and the trees, dark and erect, to ooze blood . . . . A man went from each tree catching the blood . . . . When the cup was full, he approached me. "Drink," he said, but I was unable to move.'

Growing up, Haigh was taught that God kept a strict eye on each and every person on earth, monitoring their sins. The restrictions this placed on Haigh meant that he had a very insular and deprived upbringing. He described that he was largely friendless for most of his formative years and extremely lonely, his only friends being his pets and his neighbour's dog. His father would routinely remind him that the world at large was evil and corrupt, and that it was best to avoid temptation altogether. As an example of how he himself had once been lured in by sin, he showed Haigh a blemish on his head, claiming it was a 'sign of the Devil', the result of an indiscretion he had committed against God as a child. His wife, on the other hand, did not have a blemish because she was an 'angel'. Haigh was terrified at the prospect of acquiring a similar mark and tried to be on his best behaviour.

When Haigh did misbehave, however, as children will, after minor misdemeanours and indiscretions, he noticed that no blemish or mark of the devil appeared on his own skin. Some believe that this was a vital turning point for the young Haigh, who felt suddenly liberated, invincible and capable of getting away with anything. He began to test his boundaries, seeing whether he would get caught or if he was simply too clever to be detected.

Although his life was sheltered, Haigh spent his time at home becoming a gifted pianist, which ultimately earned him a scholarship to Queen Elizabeth Grammar School in Wakefield and another to Wakefield Cathedral, where he would become a choirboy. As a young boy, he was described by his teachers as 'mischievous'; it was during this time that he became skilled at forgery, sometimes forging the signatures of his teachers. He stayed in education until the age of 17, when he left school to become an apprentice at a firm of motor engineers, due to his enthusiasm for cars. Like most of his later attempts at an honest career, however, this period did not last long. A distaste for dirt that bordered on phobia meant that he could not stand having to be in constant contact with the grime and oil in his workplace. After only a year, he abandoned the apprenticeship.

Haigh became bored easily or broke too many rules at the places in which he found employment and so hopped from one job to another for most of his life. Following his apprenticeship, he worked as a clerk at the Wakefield Education Community for a year before becoming an advertising copywriter. He was quite successful in this post, earning a decent amount of money, with which he managed to purchase an Alfa Romeo. Haigh's life seemed to be going from strength to strength: his success in this job was followed shortly by success in his personal life. He met 23-year-old Beatrice 'Betty' Hammer, whom he married on 6 July 1934. The union was doomed from the start: the couple hardly knew each other, but Hammer was quickly seduced by Haigh's charm and agreed to marry him.

Although Haigh's new wife did not agree with his parents' strict religious beliefs and they disapproved of her, Haigh's parents allowed the newlyweds to move into their home. The marriage lasted only four short months, however, before Haigh was arrested for stealing money from his company, and received a 15-month prison sentence. During Haigh's time in prison, Hammer gave birth to a baby girl and decided to leave him. The baby was quickly given up for adoption. This outraged Haigh's puritanical parents, who shunned him from that point on.

Haigh's first stay in prison was the beginning of a steady series of incarcerations. His crimes all related to money and illegal ways of obtaining it. His experiences in prison did nothing to rehabilitate him. On the contrary, they instilled in him a determination to perfect his 'craft' and to be a better criminal. He was once quoted as saying:

'When I discovered there were easier ways of making a living than to work long hours in an office, I did not ask myself whether I was doing right or wrong. That seemed to me to be irrelevant. I merely said "That is what I want to do."'

After his release from prison, he tried his best to run a legitimate and honest business, starting up a dry cleaning company with a partner. The business went well until his partner unfortunately died in a motorcycle incident. This coincided with the outbreak of the Second World War, when, out of necessity, people began to cut back on luxuries of which dry cleaning was one. As a result, Haigh's business collapsed, further convincing him that honest, legitimate ventures were not the way to go if one genuinely wanted to succeed and make money.

Haigh decided to move to London in 1936, landing a job at an amusement arcade, where he worked as a chauffeur to a Mr William McSwan, the owner. He was even able to put his mechanical skills to good use, maintaining some of McSwan's arcade machines. Haigh and his employer appeared to develop a good friendship. The two would spend time together outside of work, merrily drinking their way around many of the pubs in London. Though Haigh did well in this role, he decided to move on after a year, determined to make more money. This decision ultimately led to him setting up a solicitor's office, despite the fact that he, of course, had no legal qualifications whatsoever. He made money selling shares, which he did not possess, at below market prices. He was eventually discovered by a client who received a letter from his office, on headed paper, containing a misspelling of the name Guildford. Suspicious and knowing how unlikely it would have been for a real solicitor to make such a glaring error, the client contacted the police. This time, a charge of fraud saw Haigh sentenced to prison for four years.

Haigh spent his time in prison trying to craft the 'perfect crime', one that would make him rich. He spoke to other inmates about his ideas, describing what he believed to be a legal loophole but which was, in fact, a legal concept that he had severely misinterpreted. He had learned the term 'corpus delicti' and believed that it meant that, in cases of murder, if the police were unable to find a physical body, there was no way for the murderer to be convicted[1]. Haigh became preoccupied with this concept to such an extent that his fellow inmates gave him the nickname of 'Ol' Corpus Delicti'. He eventually decided that the most efficient, foolproof way for a murderer to dispose of a victim's body, so that no evidence of it remained, would be to dissolve it in acid.

Working in the prison tin shop, Haigh performed experiments using sulphuric acid and dead mice. He made notes regarding how acid affected animal tissue, recording that it took only half an hour for a mouse to completely dissolve in the solution.

---

1   In fact, the term means that a crime has to be proven to have been committed in order for someone to be convicted of it. There needs to be a sufficient 'body of evidence'.

By 1944, Haigh was free and able to begin crafting his perfect murder. He found a job as an accountant at an engineering firm and met a man named George Stephens, who took a liking to him, finding him a 'bright boy', despite knowing vaguely that he had been in some trouble with the law. Stephens decided to sponsor Haigh, inviting him to stay at his home in Crawley, with the rest of his family. Barbara Stephens, George Stephens' daughter, 20 years Haigh's junior, became enamoured with Haigh and dreamt of marrying him one day, despite the fact that, unbeknownst to her, he was still legally married at the time. The two began a relationship that lasted throughout his killing spree.

Notably, it was also during this year that Haigh suffered a serious car accident, which resulted in an injury to his head. Haigh would later reflect on this incident, stating that it was more than likely the event that prompted his bloodlust: the blood that dripped into his mouth from his wound reminded him of the blood-filled nightmares of his youth – and retriggered them. Not long after this, Haigh rented a basement 'workshop' at 79 Gloucester Road and purchased a 180-litre vat of sulphuric acid, ready to carry out his murderous plans.

Crimes

Haigh's first victim was no stranger to him, but someone who believed Haigh to be a good friend. On a night out at the Goat Pub in Kensington, Haigh bumped into McSwan, his former employer. The two had a happy reunion; McSwan was delighted to see Haigh again, and they caught up over drinks. McSwan took Haigh to see his parents, Donald and Amy McSwan, and in the course of the evening it was revealed that the family had recently made a lucrative investment in property. The opportunistic Haigh devised out a plan that would be sure to bring in money.

Several weeks later, on 9 September 1944, Haigh invited McSwan over to his Gloucester Road workshop. McSwan believed that he was going over to help his friend in repairing some pinball machines. Haigh's diary would later reveal that, when the two met again, he was suddenly overcome with a fierce desire for blood and was driven to pummel his friend over the head with a heavy metal pole, before slitting his throat. 'I got a mug and took some blood, from his neck, in the mug, and drank it,' Haigh stated later. This desire for the taste of blood is something that is largely disbelieved by experts on the case, who assert that it was simply a convoluted attempt to make a bid for insanity seem plausible and that the motive for his crime was much more likely to have been financial gain.

Whatever the case, Haigh immersed McSwan's body in the vat of sulphuric acid. During his later confession, Haigh stated that once the body was completely submerged in the acid, the fumes emanating from the barrel affected him so much that he had to go outside. He returned not long afterwards to cover the drum before going home to sleep, while McSwan's body was left to slowly dissolve. When the body was finally reduced to a pool of sludge, Haigh simply tipped the remains down a drain.

Of course, the fact that McSwan had a family meant that his disappearance was not going to go unnoticed. This was something that Haigh was prepared for and something that he diligently handled to ensure that he would not be caught. McSwan's parents were initially frightened and confused over the disappearance of their son, but Haigh visited them and managed to convince them that McSwan had decided to run away to Scotland, rather than risk being called up to fight in the war. Haigh went to great lengths to make sure that his story rang true, including travelling up to Edinburgh so that he could send the McSwans a postcard that they believed was from their son. McSwan had previously made threats to leave the country, rather than face the Germans, and his parents therefore believed the story. When the war ended, however, and McSwan did not return, Donald and Amy began to grow suspicious that something had happened to him. Haigh knew that he had to act to prevent the couple from alerting the authorities.

Some time after his last murder, Haigh had purchased a range of new equipment to facilitate his killings, including a stirrup-pump and a steel bathtub. To protect himself from the acid, Haigh had also bought rubber gloves, a large rubber raincoat, a butcher's apron, wader boots and a tin wartime mask. On 2 July 1945, Haigh lured Amy and Donald to his workshop, telling them that their son was planning to pay them a surprise visit. He first killed Donald with a swift blow to the head with an iron bar, followed by Amy, in an identical fashion.

Haigh later claimed to have also drunk their blood prior to dissolving their bodies. After pouring the remains of the McSwans down the drain and into the Thames, Haigh followed through on his plans for financial gain by forging William McSwan's signature, giving himself power of attorney, which meant that he was able to sell the McSwan estate. Haigh had all of their mail, including their pensions, forwarded on to himself. After selling all their possessions and capitalizing on whatever he was able to, Haigh had gained a total of roughly £100,000, in today's money. Along with his substantial fortune came a liberating sense of invincibility: he had managed to get away with three murders and was not even a suspect. Just as when he had been a child and able to commit sins without receiving the mark of the devil, he was confident in his ability to continue his criminal behaviour without any repercussions.

Haigh lived a life of luxury for the next three years, with a new residence at the Onslow Court Hotel in Kensington, but his persistent gambling habit meant that his fortune soon dwindled and he felt compelled to seek out another source of money.

He knew that his next victim had to be wealthy, preferably without any close friends or family who might notice their disappearance. He was becoming skilled at finding appropriate victims and patiently awaited the next opportunity. Eventually, in the summer of 1947 he replied to an advertisement to buy a house, claiming that he wanted to buy the property so much that he would pay above the asking price, insisting that it was undervalued. The house belonged to a middle-aged couple, Dr Archibald Henderson and his wife, Rosalie. They were in possession of a small fortune, a block of flats and a toyshop known as the 'Dolls Hospital'. The deal for the house fell through as Haigh had no money, but he remained in contact with the Hendersons, building a trusting relationship with them over a matter of months. They bonded over their interest in music and the Hendersons gradually revealed more and more to Haigh regarding their financial situation. Haigh eventually proposed a joint venture with them, involving a fictional engineering company that Haigh claimed to own in Crawley, West Sussex. What he actually owned there was yet another workshop, where he had transported his various pieces of equipment. On 12 February 1948, Haigh invited Dr Henderson to come to the workshop on the pretext of business and, within seconds of entering, Henderson was shot in the head with his own .38 Webley service revolver, which Haigh had earlier stolen from the doctor's house. Haigh left Henderson's body in his workshop and went to see Rosalie Henderson. He told her that her husband was ill and needed her help. She followed Haigh back to the workshop willingly, only to be shot by the same gun. Again, Haigh later claimed to have drunk blood from each victim before dissolving their bodies in acid and leaving them overnight.

After disposing of the remains of their bodies the following morning, Haigh set to work forging a letter of authority from the Hendersons, allowing him to take possession of their fortune. He sold their entire estate, with the exception of the family dog, which he kept, and a few items of clothing, which he gave to his girlfriend, Barbara. In total, Haigh made roughly the equivalent of £200,000 from the Hendersons, allowing him to pay off his growing hotel bills and maintain his flashy lifestyle. As before, Haigh went to great lengths to ensure that there would be no suspicion regarding the Henderson's absence. He wrote a 15-page letter to Arnold Burlin, Rosalie's brother, explaining that the couple had run away to South Africa due to an illegal abortion that her husband had carried out.

The substantial amount of money Haigh pocketed from

Dr and Mrs Archibald Henderson, two of Haigh's victims.

his second set of victims lasted only a few months. Soon he was on the lookout for yet another target. His sixth and final victim, Henrietta Helen Olive Robarts Durand-Deacon, was 69 years old and known simply as Olive to her friends. Haigh befriended Durand-Deacon and told her that he was interested in her proposition for a new business involving artificial fingernails. On 18 February 1949, she accompanied him to his workshop, where she was promptly shot in the back of the head with a .38 Enfield revolver. Haigh then removed her jewellery and fur coat before dumping her body in the vat of acid.

This time, however, Haigh had made a fatal error. He had not accounted for the fact that Durand-Deacon would be missed. Two days following the murder, Durand-Deacon's friend, Constance Lee, also a resident of the Onslow Court Hotel, reported Durand-Deacon missing at the Chelsea police station. Lee stated that her friend had been missing since her meeting with Haigh. However, when questioned, Haigh claimed that he was just as worried about the lady because she had failed to turn up for their meeting. Thankfully, the detectives who were investigating decided to run background checks on Haigh and uncovered his history of fraud and theft. This prompted the detectives to obtain a search warrant. The workshop revealed evidence that Durand-Deacon had been there, leading to Haigh's arrest.

Trial and Sentence

Following his arrest, Haigh was taken to Horsham Police Station, where officers set to work to procure a confession. At first, Haigh tried to lie and use his skills of manipulation and deception to extricate himself from the situation, but he was repeatedly caught out by the officers as a result of the inconsistencies in his story. Eventually, Haigh told Detective Inspector Albert Webb:

'If I told you the truth, you would not believe me. It sounds too fantastic to believe . . . I will tell you all about it. Mrs Durand-Deacon no longer exists. She has disappeared completely and no trace of her can ever be found again. I have destroyed her with acid. You will find the sludge which remains at Leopold Road. Every trace has gone. How can you prove murder if there is no body?'

Haigh then fully confessed to Webb, Detective Inspector Symes and Superintendent Barratt, shocking them with the true extent of his criminal and murderous repertoire. He peppered his recollections with details giving the impression of insanity, such as instances of vampirism and dreams that drove him to kill. The confession took two and a half hours, during which time Haigh admitted to the six murders recounted in this chapter, in addition to a further three that he was never charged for, as no evidence existed to prove that these crimes ever took place. The three additional victims were, allegedly, a man named 'Max' from Kensington, a woman named 'Mary' from Eastbourne and an unnamed woman from Hammersmith.

The investigating officers quickly set about compiling evidence to ensure that they would be able to convict Haigh and that he would receive the sentence he deserved. Led by Detective Inspector Pat Heslin, the team discovered a wealth of incriminating evidence. Inside an attaché case with Haigh's initials was a dry cleaner's receipt for Mrs Durand-Deacon's expensive Persian lambskin coat, together with forged papers pertaining to the McSwans' and Hendersons' property.

In addition, the team found the sludge within Haigh's workshop, the contents of which betrayed a great deal of information. Technicians, working under Home Office pathologist Keith Simpson, clad themselves in protective rubber cloves and Vaseline to protect themselves from the acid. They found Dr Henderson's partially eroded foot, a gall bladder, three gallstones, 28 pounds of human fat, 18 miscellaneous fragments of bone, a set of false teeth belonging to Mrs Durand-Deacon and a lipstick container. Simpson described examining one of the 'many small pebbles' outside Haigh's workshop: 'I picked up one and examined it through a lens. It was about the size of a cherry and looked very much like the other stones, except it had polished facets.' Further examination at the laboratory later revealed that the pebbles were in fact human gallstones.

Of the evidence, Simpson wrote: 'Haigh's labours had been in vain. The remains of Mrs Durand-Deacon were identified as surely as if her body had never been in an acid bath.' A jeweller from Horsham also revealed that someone had pawned Mrs Durand-Deacon's jewellery at his shop after her disappearance. The jeweller later identified this customer as Haigh.

There was more than enough incriminating evidence to formally charge Haigh with murder. His parents were, understandably, completely shocked and bewildered, as was Barbara Stephens, the girl who loved him and whom he had planned to marry. After his arrest, Stephens visited Haigh regularly in Lewes Prison, trying to come to grips with what she now knew about the man she loved. On 4 March 1949, Haigh sent Stephens a letter, a copy of which exists on the National Archives website, in which he addresses her with great tenderness:

'Barbara Darling,
Many, many thanks for coming to see me yesterday. It grieves me that it was such a shocking ordeal for you. I suppose no one knows better than you do how difficult it is to upset my calm; but I can assure you that irrespective of superficial appearance I was very badly shaken. I have never in my life seen a face so utterly convulsed in sheer agony of sorrow. And what could I do about it with a large sheet of glass between us. Darling, if only I could have met you normally I would have left no doubt in your mind as to whether the last 5 years have meant anything to me or not. Surely you must know that I have loved you intensely during that time.

How foolish of you to ask why I hadn't murdered you. Of course I had millions of opportunities, I know that. But the idea never even crossed my mind. I wouldn't have hurt a hair on your head.

The other business is something entirely separate and different. There was no affection involved there. I know the papers talked of 6 victims but they haven't got the whole story yet. There were men as well as women, how many I don't know. Probably a dozen more, and it was not their money but their blood that I wanted. You were very perceptive yesterday. You did really sum up the position rightly. These two things had to go on together.

It was so kind of you to ask if you should write to my mother. Yes, I think you should. I'd like you to and the greater kindness would be to explain what you told me yesterday. Not that you thought it was her fault but about the people at who I used to laugh. She'd take that better than anything else.'

The build up to the trial, the trial itself and the sentence that followed were covered extensively by the media at the time, which loved the extraordinary and salacious case of the respectable young man turned vampiric killer. Newspapers christened Haigh the 'Vampire Killer' and 'Acid Bath Murderer'. The *Daily Mirror*, capitalizing on this aspect of the case, was found in contempt of court for depicting Haigh as a vampire while the trial was still ongoing. Silvester Bolam, the editor, was sentenced to three months in prison and the newspaper was forced to pay £10,000 in court costs. Haigh took great pride in the vast press coverage, which endured until after his sentence was carried out, and expressed little or no remorse.

Whether or not Haigh had committed the murders was not in dispute, thanks to his lengthy confession and to fairly conclusive evidence. The talking point was the question of whether or not Haigh was in fact mentally ill. Did he truly feel a vampiric compulsion to consume human blood, or was it a tall tale, designed to make him appear insane and thereby avoid the hangman's noose? For his own part, Haigh was as committed to ensuring that people regarded him as insane as he had been to covering up his murders. He seemed absolutely intent on pleading insanity from the outset, even asking Webb, 'Tell me, frankly, what are the chances of anybody being released from Broadmoor[1]?'

Haigh's first hearing was on 1 April 1949 at the Sussex magistrates' court. E.G. Robey opened the prosecution's case, portraying a perpetrator who had determinedly, deliberately and with premeditation killed six people for his own personal financial gain. He insisted that the actions taken by Haigh were not those of someone with diminished responsibility. During the hearing, Haigh appeared confident and calm, seemingly unaware of the gravity of his situation. He talked through the proceedings and showed no regret for his crimes.

Haigh pleaded not guilty to the charges levelled at him. He had no means to pay for his defence and so accepted a deal with the newspaper the *News of the World*, which included an offer to pay all his legal expenses in return for an exclusive story. The trial began in the Lewes Assizes on 18 July, with over 4,000 people visiting Lewes in the hopes of getting a seat. It was a short but fascinating trial, lasting only two days. Attorney-General Sir Hartley Shawcross led the prosecution and urged the jury to ignore Haigh's defence of insanity, as there was more than enough evidence to prove that he had acted with self-awareness, coldly and with malice aforethought[2].

The trial called on 33 witnesses and a dozen medical experts, who were consulted to determine whether or not Haigh satisfied the legal requirements for insanity. Although most agreed that Haigh suffered from certain mental health issues, he was not insane, as he was and

---

1 A well-known high-security psychiatric hospital in Crowthorne, Berkshire.
2 A largely historical legal term meaning premeditation or mens rea – the intention to kill, evidence of which is required for a murder conviction.

had been very much aware of his actions, as was clear by the lengths he had gone to in order to cover up his crimes.

The defence, led by Sir David Maxwell Fyfe, called forward witnesses to attest to Haigh's mental incapacity, including Dr Henry Yellowlees[1]. Yellowlees argued that Haigh had a paranoid constitution (which Hitler is known to have suffered from) – the equivalent of which, in modern-day psychiatry, would most likely be paranoid personality disorder. He added that 'the absolute callous, cheerful, bland and almost friendly indifference of the accused to the crimes which he freely admits having committed is unique in my experience'. What the experts were not aware of, however, was the fact that, years ago, Haigh had befriended an employee of the Sussex Psychiatric Hospital and learned a great deal about mental illness, which meant that it would be easy for him to replicate the symptoms of certain illnesses he wished to affect.

Ultimately, it was clear to the jury that Haigh was feigning mental illness and that he was not legally insane. It took them only 17 minutes to return with a guilty verdict. Haigh was then sentenced by the judge, Sir Travers Humphreys, to death. The judge asked Haigh if he had anything that he wanted to say. Haigh, seemingly unaffected, replied, 'Nothing at all.'

Haigh awaited his sentence in Wandsworth Prison, during which time he completed his exclusive story for *News of the World*, wrote letters to his parents and girl-friend, and was fitted for a death mask that was to be displayed at Madame Tussauds, the famous wax museum

---

1   Dr Yellowlees was later to rise to prominence as the Chief Medical Officer of the United Kingdom, 1973–84.

in London. He kept up his show of insanity until the end, even drinking his own urine in an effort to showcase his unbalanced mind. In a letter to his solicitor, Haigh wrote that he had been bored by his trial, and was glad that he had brought a crossword with him to the proceedings. He also said that madness was simply a label that was liberally applied to the most distinguished of men; ones brave enough to think differently. Haigh told his solicitor that one day he would reincarnate and return to Earth, build a church and continue his 'spiritual sacrifices'. Haigh appeared unfazed by the prospect of death, writing that he 'laughed at it', never once mentioning regret or remorse for the lives he had taken. Haigh was finally executed on 10 August 1949 at 40 years of age, when he was hanged by Albert Pierrepoint.

Following his death, Madame Tussauds erected his wax statue, dressed in his own clothes, something Haigh had agreed to on the understanding that his wax figure would always be kept pristine, with attention paid to any creases and his hair perfectly parted.

Discussion

John George Haigh is an interesting case study and unique in this book for a number of reasons. The other serial killers examined here strongly identified with the supernatural, were accused of being supernatural entities, or were labelled as such by the media due to the manner in which they carried out their crimes. Haigh, on the other hand, attempted to use vampirism and the supernatural as a part of his legal defence, in order to be identified under the law as insane. He also began his murderous lifestyle at the relatively late age of 35; serial killers usually claim their first victim in their twenties.

Haigh also varies from the other serial killers discussed in the way in which he killed. The act of killing itself was not very personal to Haigh; he did not feel the need to be *close* to his victims at the time of their deaths. Most serial killers we have examined here did not use guns as Haigh did. Instead, they preferred short-range weapons so that they could be up close and personal with their victims, often looking into their eyes or watching intently as they passed away. Haigh shot a number of his victims in the back of the head: he seemed to have felt no great need to prolong their suffering, because witnessing a slow death would have neither benefited him nor brought him any pleasure.

Interestingly, killing for Haigh appears to have been merely a means to an end – a lucrative, financial end. He demonstrated no real signs of enjoyment or fascination when it came to the actual act of murder; he committed it clinically, as a practical method of getting his victims out of the way so that he could appropriate and enjoy their substantial fortunes. If we set aside his claim to bloodlust, which was most likely false, it is possible to argue that motivation for Haigh was largely extrinsic. Unlike many of the other killers examined in this book, Haigh did not kill to satisfy a need arising from psychological dysfunction – there was no sexual motive, for example, no enjoyment of bloodlust or a need for power and control over his victims. He was simply a greedy and determined individual who murdered to sustain the lifestyle he wanted. He regarded his victims as obstacles to be removed and spared them little to no thought or consideration, demonstrating his clear lack of empathy.

Haigh had a pronounced ability to compartmentalize and to emotionally separate his everyday life from his criminal one. Outwardly, he was charming and likable, which enabled him to draw in his victims and even to charm the people he met, male and female alike, such as Hammer and Stephens. As with many psychopathic serial killers, however, this was superficial: once he had charmed someone into his trap, he was able to kill them without hesitation and do away with their bodies. The average person, possessed of a healthy amount of empathy, simply would not have been able to watch as a fellow human being slowly dissolved in acid. Haigh, however, not only did this, but also then returned to his hotel and resumed normal human interaction with other people. Then, later, while the gruesome details of his crimes were enumerated during his trial, he displayed no remorse.

Haigh experienced a massive criminal career shift when he took the life of his first victim. Although he was no stranger to the wrong side of the law, his crimes were, up to this point, limited to fraud, theft and other such minor misdemeanours. Committing murder was on a completely different level, yet it seemed to be one that Haigh embraced with little hesitation. He carefully planned his first kill from his prison cell and proceeded to execute it once he was free. Having taken his first life, taking another, and then others after that, meant little to him. If he had not been caught, it is very likely that he would have continued killing to maintain his lifestyle, especially given the fact that he believed himself to be above suspicion.

Haigh very clearly fits within Holmes and DeBurger's Hedonistic Comfort – or Profit – type of serial killer, for whom murder is a means to a personal, usually financial, gain: he killed for the money he required to enjoy the better things in life. The lavish lifestyle was something that very much appealed to Haigh and was something that contrasted greatly with his solemn, reserved upbringing, where indulgences of any kind were considered sinful.

If Haigh knew that his story was still being discussed today, decades after his execution, it would, most likely, appeal to his ego and delight him to know that he had gone down in history and that his name was still remembered. As long as we are discussing Haigh, however, we are also discussing his victims, who deserve to be remembered. Only by studying Haigh and his fellow serial killers and getting to grips with their mental processes can we understand what causes people like them to kill and kill again. This in turn gives us the knowledge to help prevent such occurrences in the future. Raising his story for discussion and remembering him are, to this end, a necessary evil.

CHAPTER NINE

Richard Trenton Chase –
The Vampire of Sacramento/The Dracula Killer/
The Vampire Killer

'He wants to explore the body. He wants to drink her blood. He wants to engage with the body in a sexual way, and the longer he's able to stay with the victim, the longer he's able to sustain some feeling of sexual satisfaction.'

Professor David Wilson

Introduction

Richard Trenton Chase, born 23 May 1950, was to become one of the most feared schizophrenic serial killers in American history. His story has been retold and referenced in, or been the inspiration for, films, documentaries and even popular television programmes, such as *CSI: Crime Scene Investigation* and *Criminal Minds*. As a result of his barbaric method of killing and the randomness with which he selected his victims, Chase would eventually be given the title 'The Vampire of Sacramento': after killing his victims, he would often drink their blood or cannibalize

Robert Ressler, who headed the FBI investigation into Chase's crimes.

their remains. Chase suffered from psychological issues that stretched far back into his youth and resulted, ultimately, in the murder of six innocent people.

As is common with the early lives of serial killers, Chase did not have a loving childhood. He was born in Santa Clara County, California, to a mother with mental health issues, while his father was an alcoholic who believed in physically disciplining his son. In addition to the beatings Chase suffered from his father, he also witnessed the unhappy relationship between his parents, who were constantly at odds with one another. Many sources claim that there were relentless arguments between the two. Chase's mother believed that her husband was being unfaithful to her and was trying to poison her; this theme was to echo in Chase's own adulthood, when he became paranoid about poisoning later in life.

By the age of ten, Chase demonstrated evidence of the three characteristics that constitute the 'homicidal trial[1], which has proven useful in predicting violent, criminal behaviour. These characteristics included persistent bedwetting after the age of five, finding satisfaction in inflicting cruelty upon animals and pyromania.

When Chase was 12 years old, his mother began to see two psychiatrists for treatment for paranoia. When he was 13, his family began to suffer financially and eventually lost their home. By the time Chase was in high school, his reckless behaviour was fast escalating out of control. He was drinking heavily and abusing drugs, most notably marijuana. He got into trouble for his behaviour but never

---

1 This homicidal triad has been utilized by psychologists since 1963, when the term was coined by the forensic psychiatrist John Marshall Macdonald.

seemed to show any signs of shame or remorse. During his sophomore year, Chase was arrested for possession of marijuana and ordered by the juvenile court to work at weekends. It was around this time that his delusions began – delusions that would, ultimately, form the motivation behind his bloodlust and murderous impulses.

Chase managed to complete high school albeit with mediocre success. He eventually graduated from Mira Loma High School with grades ranging from Cs to Fs. His IQ was later revealed to be 95. In his teenage years, Chase was described to have been 'clean-cut and unassuming'; beneath this normal exterior, however, lay a much darker and more complex inner world. The damage that had already been done to his psyche at this early stage of his life, through his early trauma and chronic drug abuse, was well-established. Chase dated a few girls in his teens, but was unable to form any lasting or meaningful relationships. These girls later reported that their relationships had never been sexual, due to the fact that Chase was completely unable to perform sexually.

At the age of 18, a consultation with a psychiatrist revealed that Chase's sexual impotence was likely a result of repressed anger and 'potential mental illness'. At this time, however, the specific mental problem remained undiagnosed and Chase was not committed to an institution. It was only later, in his twenties, that he would be diagnosed with schizophrenia. Chase came to believe that his erectile dysfunction and resulting sexual performance issues were due to restricted blood flow to his genitals, the root of, or perhaps reinforcement for, his pervasive belief that his blood was evaporating. This was a delusion that resulted from his as yet undiagnosed schizophrenia. The chilling solution that he came up with was later to earn him his vampire moniker: Chase believed that he needed to replenish his blood to compensate for the deficit and to survive, and that drinking blood would help him to do so.

As the years went by, Chase developed a severe hypochondria, examples of which included a belief that his pulmonary artery had been removed, that bones were protruding through the back of his head and that his heart would occasionally stop beating. He also developed the bizarre belief that bones in his head were moving around and so shaved his hair to better observe it. Chase also came to believe that his mother was attempting to poison him and moved out of his family home to live in shared accommodation. His housemates were, however, unnerved by his odd behaviour and his drug use, which included marijuana and LSD. This led to friction in the house and Chase was asked to leave. When he moved back in with his mother, his behaviour began to spiral out of control.

In 1975, Chase was rushed to hospital with blood poisoning. He had injected himself with blood he had procured from a rabbit that he had killed. Chase had blood smeared across his face and, when questioned, insisted that he had cut himself shaving and that the blood was his own. It later emerged, however, that he had in fact been biting the heads off birds and sucking the blood from their bodies. It was here that he was given the nickname 'Dracula', a term which the hospital staff used to refer to him. Psychiatric observation revealed Chase to be a paranoid schizophrenic suffering from somatic delusions. The usual drug regimen for schizophrenia was utilized, but unfortunately this yielded no results. Doctors at the hospital concluded that this was because Chase's psychosis was brought about by his heavy abuse of drugs, rather than schizophrenia.

Chase's symptoms earned him a stay at a mental institution named Beverly Manor. During his time here he frightened many of the other patients with his alarming behaviour. He later claimed to have drawn blood from a therapy dog while at the institution, in order to feed his need for blood. To attain the blood, he stole syringes and needles from the doctor's office. He was also reported to have soiled himself and decorated the walls with his faeces.

After being placed on a regimen of psychotropic drugs for a number of months, Chase was, in 1976, deemed healthy enough to be released back into the care of his mother, who was now divorced from his father. This situation was ideal for neither mother nor son, and a great deal of tension developed between them resulting in many arguments, which on occasion turned physical: during one particularly heated argument, Chase slapped his mother and knocked her to the floor.

Not long after his release, Chase's mother made the decision to wean her son off the drugs prescribed at Beverly Manor. She also decided to get Chase his own apartment, paying his rent and shopping bills. Unsurprisingly, the fact that Chase was now isolated, without any medication or psychiatric support, meant that his multitude of complex mental issues escalated rapidly. He was able to fully exercise his compulsion to capture and kill animals, disembowel them and eat them raw. On occasion, Chase would blend the disembowelled remains with Cola to drink. His paranoid obsession with his various perceived bodily maladies deepened, sometimes resulting in emergency trips to the hospital to ask for help and treatment for imagined illnesses.

On 3 August 1977, Chase was found naked and covered in blood near Pyramid Lake in Nevada. A bucket of blood was also found in his truck. He was immediately arrested, though he initially claimed that the blood covering his body was his own. It was revealed in the subsequent investigation that the blood in fact belonged to a cow, so the incident was reported but no charges were filed. It was shortly after this that his homicidal crimes began.

Crimes

The killing spree that would ultimately become one of the most infamous in American criminal history began in 1977. On 27 December, Chase's psychosis pushed him over the edge and he attempted a drive-by shooting, which was unsuccessful. Two days later, he attempted another such shooting and this time secured his first victim.

Chase killed Ambrose Griffin, a 51-year-old engineer and father of two, with a .22 automatic handgun. Chase shot him once in the chest, killing him instantly. As will become evident, this method of killing was rare for Chase, as his murders were normally committed within the victim's home. The afternoon following Chase's first murder, he attempted a third drive-by shooting, this time of a 12-year-old boy. Fortunately, the boy was unharmed and lived to report that the shooter had been a man in his mid-twenties with brown hair, driving a Pontiac Trans Am. The police, however, were unable to follow up this lead successfully and Chase remained free of suspicion.

Chase's crimes continued into 1978. On 23 January, on

Burnece Street, Barbara and Robert Edwards were met with a bizarre state of affairs when they returned from a shopping trip. Upon entering their home, they heard a window slam at the back of the house. A man whom they described as 'dishevelled' ran towards them and, although Robert attempted to stop the intruder, he was able to make an escape. A police investigation would later reveal that the intruder had defecated on their child's bed and that a drawer of baby clothes had been urinated into. The Edwards family was extremely lucky to have suffered only that, as it was on that same day that Chase found his next victims.

Chase walked down Tioga Way, trying the door handles to the houses as he went. Chase would later tell FBI agent Robert Ressler that this was the method he adopted to select his victims: when he tested a door and found it locked, he moved on to the next house as he took it as a sign that he was not welcome. If the door was unlocked, he saw it as permission to enter.

On this particular day, Chase encountered Teresa Wallin, who was 22 years old and three months pregnant. Teresa came upon Chase when she stepped out of her house to take out the rubbish, at which point he shot her twice: one bullet entered her palm, travelled up her arm and exited at her elbow. The second bullet went through her skull. Once she had fallen down, Chase approached and shot her once more in the head. He dragged her body into her bedroom, leaving a bloody mess in his wake. When her body was found, it was discovered that her left nipple had been removed and that her abdomen had been cut open. Her intestines had been removed from her body, as had her spleen. Stab marks were found in her lungs, left breast, diaphragm and liver. During the act, Chase had covered his face with the victim's blood and ingested some, presumably using the blood-stained yoghurt container that was found near the murder scene. On top of this horrendous display, the victim was found with animal waste shoved in her mouth and down her throat, which was discovered to be dog faeces from the garden.

The time span between victims was diminishing. On 27 January, Chase committed his next series of crimes only a mile away from the location of the Wallin murder. There was a massacre that day, involving Evelyn Miroth and her family. The crime scene was horribly gruesome. Evelyn, aged 38, was found naked on her bed with her legs spread wide. She had suffered a gunshot wound to her head, her abdomen had been cut open and her intestines removed. Nearby, the police found two carving knives, each one stained with blood. The police hypothesized that Evelyn had been caught unawares in the bath and attacked there, as the tub was also stained with blood. She had then been dragged to her bed and sodomized. The police also found a substantial amount of semen in her vagina. She was stabbed through the anus into her uterus six times. Her body had been sliced across the neck several times and the murderer had clearly tried to extract one of her eyes. Nearby, there were small, perfectly circular stains of blood – the police deduced that they had been left by a container, such as the yoghurt pot found at the previous murder scene. This, obviously, had been used to collect the blood. The body had been stabbed in a number of organs, in a manner that (according to the coroner) would have caused blood to pool in the abdomen. On top of all of the terrible wounds already described, Evelyn had been partially eaten.

Next to Evelyn on the bed was Jason, her six-year-old son. He had been shot twice in the head at close range. Within the same house, a friend named Daniel Meredith, aged 51, was found with a gunshot wound to his head. The neighbours reported that Daniel had parked his car nearby, but it was now gone, obviously stolen.

As devastating and gory as these events were, they did not mark the end of the story. The police could not account for the whereabouts of a 22-month-old baby named David. David's mother, Karen, had placed the baby in her sister-in-law Evelyn's care for a short while. Upon the discovery of a bullet hole in a blood-soaked pillow in David's playpen, the police were not optimistic about his survival. David's whereabouts would not to be revealed until Chase's capture, when he admitted to murdering the baby. He claimed to have mutilated the baby's body in the family's bathroom. He described how he had forced open the baby's skull, spilling out small pieces of brain into the bath. At this point he had been spooked by a noise and had run, taking the little body with him. He had stolen a car and returned to his own home. Chase admitted to having severed the child's head from his body and eaten the organs that he removed from it. The police later found the small, beheaded remains of David's body in a box outside a church.

Trial and Sentence

The chase was now on to find the serial murderer responsible for these terrible crimes and to bring him to justice. The police had linked all the attacks mentioned due to their relative proximity, the short time frame between murders, the elements of necrophilia and cannibalism and, of course, the fact that the same type of gun had been used in all the cases.

The FBI began the search by compiling an extensive profile of the killer. On the team were Russ Vorpagel and Robert Ressler, who believed the murderer to be a disorganized killer. The murders in no way seemed carefully planned or thought-out, and the killer did nothing to destroy evidence, leaving footprints and handprints in plain view. In addition, they assumed that, following the bloody murders, the killer likely exited the home in broad daylight with blood-smeared clothing – hardly the actions of a rational, organized criminal. All this demonstrated that the murderer was unpredictable and gave little thought to covering his tracks at the scenes of his crimes.

With this in mind, the FBI reasoned that his living space would be likewise disorganized and messy. They believed that the killer walked to all the crime scenes (as they were all quite close to one another), that he lived nearby and did not own a car. They were positive that the killer would strike again and would continue to do so until he was finally caught. They believed him to be a man, white, in his mid-twenties and thin. He was most likely a loner. It was also likely that the culprit had a history of mental illness, was abusing drugs, or a combination of the two. Considering this, the killer was either unemployed or had an extremely menial job.

Police began to question people in the neighbourhood, hoping for potential witnesses. Many people reported seeing a Caucasian man driving a red station wagon, which was likely to have been Daniel Meredith's missing car. The police then began to create an official identity sketch based on the descriptions the public gave of this man.

The manhunt, however, did not look promising until the police questioned a woman by the name of Nancy Holden and showed her the sketch. Nancy recalled a very strange encounter she had on the day of the Wallin murder. She was shopping when a man approached her; he had been gaunt, nervous and wearing blood-stained clothing. He asked her a completely unexpected question: whether or not she had been on the motorcycle with Kurt when he had been killed.

Nancy's ex-boyfriend by the name of Kurt had been killed in a motorcycle accident, and the question took her completely by surprise. Nancy felt sure that this strange man was familiar, but she was not able to place his face. She asked him who he was, to which he replied 'Rick Chase', her high school schoolmate. This surprised her even more as he looked so different from the boy she had known in high school. This older Rick was so thin (only 65 kg/10 st 3 lb at 1.8 m/6 ft tall) and unkempt. Nancy told the police that, at the time, he appeared to be confused, agitated and dirty. While Chase paid at the shop counter, Nancy escaped to the car park. He followed her outside, but before he could talk to her again, she had rolled up the windows and driven away. It had been rude, she admitted, but there was something about him that had made her nervous. The clincher was the fact that she distinctly recollected the orange ski parka that the dishevelled man wore in the sketch – Chase had been wearing the same parka the day she had seen him.

Following this tip, the authorities did some investigating. They discovered that in December 1977, a .22 calibre semi-automatic handgun had been sold to a Richard Chase. This was followed up on 10 January by a purchase of ammunition. A background check revealed that Chase did, in fact, have a history of mental illness, as well as a concealed weapons charge and a record of an escape from hospital.

One Saturday afternoon after the Miroth massacre, a team of detectives went to Chase's place of residence to investigate, led by Lieutenant Ray Biondi. Chase refused them entry. The police pretended to give up and leave. When Chase finally left his home, however, the police attempted to arrest him, but Chase struggled. At the time, he was wearing the infamous orange parka, which was smeared with dark brown stains. His shoes were also stained with blood and he was in possession of a .22 semi-automatic. As if all this was not incriminating enough, Chase was also found with Daniel Meredith's wallet in his pocket, together with a pair of latex gloves.

Chase was taken to the police station, where he insisted that, although he had killed a number of dogs, he was not a murderer. Unconvinced, the police searched his apartment for the body of the missing baby. His home was, as expected, filthy and chaotic. It was covered with blood stains, pieces of bone and various body parts. Some brain tissue was found and his blender stank of rotting flesh. Chillingly, Chase had a calendar with the word 'today' written on it a number of times – the first marked the date of the Wallin murder and the second the date of the Miroth massacre. There were 44 more dates marked with the same word: all murders planned out for the rest of the year.

Back at the police station, the staff took hair samples from Chase and collected his blood-stained clothes. They attempted to extract a blood sample, but Chase reacted so violently that he had to be restrained. The police, of course, did not know about his intense paranoia and phobia concerning blood loss.

Chase was assigned a public defence attorney by the name of Farris Salamy. In a statement made in Salamy's obituary, Salamy's younger brother claimed that he had taken the case because he 'didn't want to saddle one of the younger attorneys with [it]'. Salamy instantly took to his role and removed Chase from the station, where he might have given an incriminating confession. Police officers, meanwhile, continued their search for the missing baby David, using a bloodhound. The baby was eventually found by a church caretaker who instantly notified the police. The body had been decapitated, with the head placed under the body. The head had a gunshot wound, and there were several stab wounds to the body as well as several broken ribs.

The prosecutor for the case was Ronald W. Tochterman, who was determined that Chase would receive the death penalty. Despite the fact that the defence was entering a plea of not guilty by reason of insanity, Tochterman put a case together with the aim of demonstrating that Chase certainly knew the difference between right and wrong, meaning that he did not qualify as being legally insane. Before the trial began, the defence requested a change of venue due to the fact that Chase and his crimes were already notorious in the area. The trial was relocated 193 km (120 miles) south to Santa Clara County.

The trial began on 2 January 1979 and stretched on for four months. Chase was charged with six counts of murder. On exhibit were 250 items of evidence from the prosecution, including Chase's gun and Daniel Meredith's wallet, which had been found in Chase's pocket at the point of his arrest. The prosecution maintained throughout that Chase had a choice in the commission of his murders and the fact that he had brought rubber gloves along with him to the houses of his victims was clear evidence of premeditation. David Wallin was a witness for the prosecution and he gave full details of the scene he had encountered when he came home to find his pregnant wife butchered.

Numerous psychiatrists who had examined Chase also gave witness. One psychiatrist found him to be suffering from antisocial personality disorder and not schizophrenia. Chase had admitted that he feared that his victims would return from the dead to exact revenge upon him. However, the general consensus among the psychiatrists was that there was no evidence that Chase had felt compelled by a mental disorder to murder – only that he believed the blood to be therapeutic. His thought processes were not disrupted, he was aware of his crimes and he was aware, furthermore, that they had been wrong.

When Chase took the stand in his own defence, he was even more emaciated than he had once been, weighing less than 50 kg (7 st 12 lb). On the stand, he claimed that he had been only semi-conscious during the Wallin murder. Chase went on to describe his childhood mistreatment and his growing obsession with blood. He admitted to drinking the blood of, and partially cannibalizing, some of his victims. He said that he did not even remember the events of the Miroth murders, but did remember the baby. He also described how he had decapitated the baby, believing that it had been 'something else' at the time, although he did not elaborate further. He blamed most of his psychological issues on the fact that he had been unable to have normal sex with girls and form functional sexual relationships during his teenage years.

Given his psychological problems, the defence asked for a judgement of second degree murder, which would mean a sentence of life imprisonment rather than the death sentence. The prosecution was adamant that this should not be allowed, that Chase had known exactly what he was doing at all times and should pay the price. The jury took five hours to deliberate and, on 8 May, Chase was found legally sane and convicted of six counts of first degree murder. He was sentenced to die in a gas chamber at San Quentin Penitentiary.

In prison, Chase agreed to be interviewed by FBI profiler Robert Ressler, who further noted significant oddities about Chase and his beliefs, which certainly point towards symptoms of paranoid schizophrenia. Chase insisted that he had killed to replenish his blood for his own survival and that anyone else would have done the same. At one point, he suggested that the Nazis should stand trial for the murders he had committed, as they had communicated telepathically with UFOs to command him to kill. He claimed to be Jewish, although he was not, and to have a Star of David on his forehead – it was for these reasons, he said, that the Nazis were after him. He believed they were also trying to poison him through his food and turn his blood to powder. Ressler discovered that Chase had been storing a large quantity of macaroni and cheese in his pockets so that he would not have to eat the prison food, which he believed was poisoned by the prison guards who were in league with the Nazis.

Chase was less than popular with his fellow prisoners.

While he was waiting on death row, the other inmates, who knew of his crimes and feared him, would try to incite him to kill himself. He was moved to a psychiatric hospital for a short time, but was soon returned to prison. On Boxing Day, 1980, the inmates of San Quentin Penitentiary got what they had asked for. When a passing guard checked in on Chase, he noticed that the prisoner was lying on his front, unresponsive. The guard called to Chase, but received no reply. The Vampire of Sacramento was dead.

The coroner was called and Chase's prison cell was searched. A suicide note was soon found, which indicated that he had been stashing away the Sinequan pills that had been prescribed for his depression and hallucinations. He had taken an overdose and committed suicide.

Discussion

Chase was guilty of horrifying crimes and the psychology behind them is complicated. Though Chase's plea of insanity was rejected, it is extremely likely that he suffered from schizophrenia, and that his murders were at least in part motivated by the delusions he experienced as a result. The medical criteria for a diagnosis of schizophrenia contains five groups of symptoms, namely: delusions (firmly held ideas that a person maintains even in the face of evidence or logic against them); hallucinations (sounds or other sensory input experienced as real although they occur only in the person's mind – auditory hallucinations are the most common in schizophrenia, though visual hallucinations are also relatively common); disorganized speech; grossly disorganized or catatonic behaviour (such as a decline in overall daily functioning or self-care or a lack of inhibition and impulse control); and a group of symptoms known as negative symptoms (such as diminished emotional expression and a reduced ability to function normally). A person must exhibit at least two of these symptoms most of the time during at least a one-month period.

Some – or most – of these are already evident in the history and crimes detailed earlier in this chapter. His beliefs about his blood evaporating and his fear of the Nazis and UFOs, for example, clearly stand out as abnormal. These beliefs, if truly held by Chase and not fabricated to reinforce his plea of insanity, are clearly consistent with delusions, which are the commonest symptom of schizophrenia, occurring in over 90 per cent of people who suffer from the illness.

It was most likely that his schizophrenia and the delusions that accompanied it prompted his murderous rampages, but a good proportion of people suggest that Chase suffered from Renfield's syndrome, or clinical vampirism, an obsession with blood-drinking behaviour associated with sexual gratification (as discussed in the earlier chapter on Peter Kürten, the Vampire of Düsseldorf). It has been pointed out that as clinical vampirism has not gained official recognition as a diagnosable psychiatric condition, people suffering from it are often diagnosed with other psychiatric conditions, most commonly schizophrenia – as in the case of Chase – or paraphilia.

When Chase was being interviewed pre-trial, one psychiatrist suggested that he was not schizophrenic but in fact psychopathic. There is some evidence to corroborate this theory; after all, people with psychopathy are aware of the difference between right and wrong, as opposed to people with psychosis, who lack this insight. This awareness, however, does not necessarily show in their behaviour. Their personal needs or desires can – and often do – override social rules. This psychiatrist claimed that Chase's thought processes were not disrupted. He was well aware of what he had done and that it was wrong – he simply chose to commit the crimes anyway. Two other psychiatrists who interviewed Chase claimed that he had expressed no signs of guilt for his crimes, which is consistent with the mindset of a psychopath unable to feel empathy or remorse for their actions. Chase described his murders to the psychiatrists in a simple, matter-of-fact way that suggested precisely this lack.

He did, however, demonstrate a certain fascination with his victims and their anatomy. In an interview, criminology professor David Wilson discussed the difference between act-focused and process-focused serial killers:

'Some serial killers will be act-focused. Other serial killers will be process-focused. By act-focused I mean that the psychological need for the killer to kill is achieved simply by the death of the victim. The killer will do nothing to the victim's body, because he's achieved whatever it is that he wants to have achieved. On the other hand, a process-focused serial killer will want to spend time with the body of his victim, and that's very common in relation to what Chase did with [his victims] . . . . He wants to explore the body. He wants to drink her blood. He wants to engage with the body in a sexual way, and the longer he's able to stay with the victim, the longer he's able to sustain some feeling of sexual satisfaction.'

It is difficult to assign Chase to a particular typology based on the Holmes and DeBurger method. Though it might be tempting to categorize him as the Hedonistic type of killer, elements of his story do not fit: he did not really kill for the pleasure it brought him. He saw it as a necessity, although the fact that he sexually gratified himself at the crime scenes might indicate otherwise. He might arguably belong to the Visionary type of killer: he certainly suffered from delusions and experienced severe episodes of paranoia. It was because of these delusions that he allegedly committed the murders. There is no direct account of his having heard voices or seen visions instructing him to kill, as Visionary killers do. His belief that the Nazis had communicated telepathically with UFOs to command him to kill, however, could be interpreted as such an instruction.

Considering the information relayed here, it is incredible that Chase was not identified as a threat and detained earlier so that these violent and horrific acts of murder could have been prevented. This is even more astonishing when we consider that, even before his crimes, this man was identified as a 'danger to others' and a neurologist who assessed him concluded that he possessed 'a psychiatric disturbance of major proportions'. Had Chase received the help he had asked for when he visited hospitals for his various perceived ailments, he might have had the treatment he required and his victims might have survived.

CHAPTER TEN

Jeffrey Dahmer – The Milwaukee Cannibal/ The Milwaukee Monster

'Skulls in lockers, cannibalism, sexual urges, drilling, making zombies, necrophilia, drinking alcohol all the time, trying to create a shrine, lobotomies, defleshing, calling taxidermists, going to graveyards, masturbating . . . this is Jeffrey Dahmer, a runaway train on a track of madness.'

Gerald Boyle

Introduction

'The Milwaukee Monster' is arguably one of the highest-profile serial killers of modern times. The name Dahmer is notorious even outside of the true crime genre, with his story featuring in numerous films, documentaries and books. Casual references to him are peppered throughout popular culture, usually as an efficient way of describing a worst-case scenario of someone gone wildly off the rails, such as 'he's gone Dahmer'. His very name has entered into modern slang: the Urban Dictionary defines 'Dahmer' in four ways:

1. 'To go crazy and insane. Inspired from the serial killer who killed and ate his victems [sic]'
2. 'To eat something with voracious enthusiasm, usually after prolonged hunger'
3. 'To roofie and rape'
4. 'The inability to pick up girls at a bar alone . . . without a wingman. Stems from serial killer, Jeff Dahmer, who stalked, killed, and eventually ate his victims.'

This infamous murderer, who rocked America with his barbaric and twisted acts of violence, strongly identified with the devil and began a macabre project of building an occult altar with his victims' body parts, believing this granted him supernatural powers to subdue and control his prey. He attempted to create living zombies out of the people he killed, drilling holes into their heads and pouring acid into their brains. He also indulged in cannibalism: he believed that by ingesting his lovers, he would never again be alone. He was ultimately responsible for taking the lives of 17 men and boys between the years of 1978 and 1991.

The bloody story began on 21 May 1961, when Jeffrey Lionel Dahmer was born in West Allis, Wisconsin, to parents Joyce Annette and Lionel Herbert Dahmer. Until the age of six, Dahmer appeared to be an average, happy child, outgoing and untroubled.

One incident from these carefree early years that is worth mentioning, however, occurred when Dahmer was four, when he witnessed his father removing dead animal bones from beneath their home. This is where Dahmer's fascination with dead animals was born; it would later mutate into something much darker. In a later interview, Lionel Dahmer stated that his son appeared to be 'oddly

Jeffrey Dahmer at his trial

thrilled' by the incident. This interest began relatively innocently, with Dahmer collecting dragonflies and butterflies inside jars. This progressed to collecting road kill and dissecting them to see what their insides looked like. Jim Klippel, a neighbour of Dahmer's, said years later that when he was 16 he found a mutilated dog carcass in the woods behind Dahmer's house, with the head mounted on a stick beside a wooden cross. The body had been gutted and skinned, and was nailed to a nearby tree.

In his early childhood, Dahmer experienced a series of unfortunate events in quick succession. He was forced to endure abdominal surgery to correct a double hernia, which reportedly left a significant emotional scar, as he was left exposed and vulnerable, not fully understanding what was happening to him as strangers clinically examined his body. His mother began to spend a lot of her time in bed due to various illnesses, becoming highly anxious over minor things. She even tried to kill herself with an Equanil overdose, a drug to which she had become addicted. According to reports, it was around this time that a noticeable shift in Dahmer's demeanour developed, and he became more introverted and withdrawn, noticeably lacking in self-confidence.

In October 1966, the family moved to Doylestown, Ohio where, in a new and strange environment, Dahmer's introversion continued to worsen. His mother was pregnant with Dahmer's younger brother at the time of the move. On 18 December 1966, when Joyce gave birth, his parents decided to allow Jeffrey to name the child so that he would feel more included. He named the baby David, but remained largely uninterested in his little brother's existence.

By the time Dahmer reached his teenage years, he was

mostly friendless and disengaged from his surroundings. Dahmer claimed that, at the tender age of 14, during his freshman year at Revere High School, he was already harbouring pervasive and disturbing urges that he was having a difficult time suppressing, including thoughts of both murder and necrophilia. His strange behaviour alienated him from his classmates, and he developed a reputation of being an outcast. He would regularly sneak alcohol into school and drink throughout the day. Despite his troubles, he was regarded as being highly intelligent, though his general apathy meant that he regularly only managed average grades.

The breakdown of his parents' marriage, which occurred during his teenage years, certainly did nothing to help his emotional well-being. Their relationship was growing increasingly hostile and the blatant animosity he regularly witnessed between his mother and father would doubtlessly have impacted on him, adding psychological stresses to his existing issues, perhaps acting as a catalyst for his later deadly actions.

It was around this time that Dahmer realized that he was attracted only to men, though he kept this aspect of himself secret from his parents for some time. He longed to be close to another boy. His sexual fantasies more often than not involved elements of dominance and control: he was preoccupied with the idea of a relationship with a subservient partner, where his own wants and needs took precedence over those of his lover. At the same time, thoughts of dissection – which had always preoccupied him – began to enter into his sexual fantasies.

When Dahmer was 16 his sexual needs became too strong to deny and he decided to take action: he took his baseball bat to a wooded area that he knew was regularly frequented by a jogger. The plan was to hide behind the bushes and then jump out at the jogger, knocking him unconscious, then sexually gratifying himself with the unconscious body. On that particular day, however, the jogger did not appear. Dahmer later admitted that this was his first attempted attack on another human being. He did not attempt the same plan again.

Although he was certainly far from popular at his high school, perceived by most as quiet and odd, he did become known around his school as a bit of a prankster. He would regularly pull tricks on others or do ridiculous things in order to amuse or get attention, including feigning cerebral palsy, allergies or seizures. At his school, pulling a prank became known as 'doing a Dahmer'.

By 1977, Dahmer's performance at school had not improved, hindered considerably by his increasing alcohol use and the fact that he was clearly uninterested in studying. His parent's relationship was not faring any better, though they were attending marital counselling in an attempt to save their failing marriage. It did not take long, however, before both realized that they were fighting a losing battle and decided to divorce. The divorce was not a civil one and their sons often witnessed their many arguments. A vicious custody battle for his younger brother, David, occurred, but as the older child Dahmer was largely disregarded. His father, Lionel, finally left the family home in early 1978, to stay in a nearby motel. Joyce was awarded custody of David, and the two also moved out later the same year, relocating to Chippewa Falls, Wisconsin, leaving 18-year-old Dahmer alone to indulge his increasingly overwhelming sexual and violent urges.

Crimes

Dahmer's extensive criminal career began early, at the age of 18. On 18 June 1978, three weeks after his high school graduation, he took the plunge from internal fantasies to murder. He picked up 18-year-old Steven Mark Hicks, who was trying to hitchhike his way to Lockwood Corners for a rock concert. Dahmer tempted him back to his parents' deserted house with the prospect of free alcohol and a good time. Together, they passed the time drinking beer, relaxing and having sex, but when Hicks decided he had to leave, Dahmer found he could not face the prospect of being left alone. In order to keep Hicks from going, Dahmer picked up a ten-pound barbell and, with two swift blows to the boy's head, killed his first victim.

His ensuing behaviour did not reflect that of someone suffering from any panic or stress, as might reasonably be expected, but rather that of someone with an almost clinical detachment. After killing Hicks, Dahmer stripped him of his clothes and stood over the body, pleasuring himself. He then took his time to dismember the corpse, and packed the body parts into separate plastic bags. He buried these in the woodland behind the house and left them there for weeks before finally digging them up and, with fascination, separating flesh from bone. He dissolved the flesh in acid and flushed the remnants down the toilet. Dahmer decided to crush the bones with a sledgehammer before taking them back outside and scattering them to the wind. Such was his first murder; it would be nine years before he struck again.

Dahmer's life following this murder was fragmented

and confused. Six weeks after the incident, Lionel visited the house and was surprised to find that his ex-wife had moved out, leaving his oldest son alone. Dahmer did not appear to be doing well on his own and, without any schooling, had no structure to his days. Lionel insisted that he enrol at Ohio State University, where he would major in business. Dahmer's attitude towards his tertiary education, however, mirrored that of his high school years: he was academically apathetic and his drinking problem had not abated; he spent most of his time too drunk to function. Dahmer dropped out after only three months, but Lionel did not give up trying to help his son. In January 1979, he got Dahmer to enlist in the US Army, where he was ultimately trained as a medical specialist. Though it is generally believed that Dahmer did not murder anyone during his time in the army, one soldier came forward in 2010 to state that when they were stationed at Baumholder together, Dahmer raped him repeatedly over a 17-month period.

Dahmer's alcohol dependency led to an honourable discharge from the army two years later, as he was unable to perform his duties adequately. Following his debriefing on 24 March 1981, Dahmer went to Miami Beach, Florida, to enjoy the sunshine and try to pull his life together. Although he found employment at a sandwich shop, he spent most of his earnings on alcohol and was kicked out of the motel room he was renting. In September 1981, he finally returned to his father in Ohio.

Following an arrest for drunk and disorderly conduct and at his father's insistence, Dahmer moved in with his grandmother. She was someone that Dahmer appeared to respect and love and it was hoped that her positive influence would prompt a change in his attitude and life. This appeared to work for a time, with Dahmer accompanying his grandmother to church and helping her out around her home. Although, in 1982, he managed to find a job as a phlebotomist at the Milwaukee Blood Plasma Center, for the majority of his time with his grandmother, he was unemployed and surviving on whatever money she gave him. As expected, his drinking problem persisted, leading to a further arrest in August 1982 for indecent exposure at the Wisconsin State Fair Park.

According to Dahmer, an incident in January 1985 reawakened fantasies of sexual dominance and control. A man approached Dahmer in a public library and passed him a note offering him oral sex. Dahmer ignored the invitation, but began to frequent gay bars and bathhouses. He also stole a mannequin from a clothing store, which he used to gratify himself before it was discovered by his grandmother. He began to visit the bathhouses regularly, but claimed that, far from satisfying his libido, he found the sexual encounters frustrating, as it annoyed him when his partners moved during intercourse. From June 1986 he took to slipping his partners drinks laced with sleeping pills: satisfying himself with their unconscious bodies was much more fulfilling to Dahmer than engaging in normal intercourse, despite the fact that, by all accounts, he was highly desirable within the communities he frequented.

The staff at the bathhouses eventually discovered Dahmer's use of sleeping pills and his membership was revoked. As he was living with his grandmother, at first Dahmer took his lovers to a motel. Around this time, he read a story in a newspaper about an 18-year-old boy who had recently passed away. He decided to find the grave, dig up the body and take it home to use as his own ideal sexual partner. He went as far as going to the graveyard, but found the soil too hard to dig through effectively and was unable to carry out his plan.

Dahmer claimed the life of his second victim on 15 September 1987, at Club 219, a popular gay bar in Milwaukee at the time. The man in question was 25-year-old Steven Tuomi, who returned with Dahmer to his room at the Ambassador Hotel. It is the one murder that Dahmer claims not to recall with any clarity whatsoever (this meant that, during his trial, Dahmer was not formally charged with Toumi's death, as his memory of the crime was insufficient to satisfy reasonable doubt). He simply remembered that they drank a substantial amount of alcohol. When he woke up the following morning, Tuomi was lying dead beneath him and Dahmer concluded that he must have beaten and strangled him to death. His chest appeared to have been crushed, there was blood leaking from his mouth and Dahmer noted bruises across his own fists and forearms. Once again, Dahmer did not panic. He left the room in search of a suitcase. Once he had bought one, he packed Tuomi into it and returned to his grandmother's house in a taxi. Notably, the taxi driver mentioned the heaviness of the suitcase, even jokingly asking whether it had a body inside. Once at home, Dahmer went to his room in the basement and, after indulging in necrophilia with the body, he dissected it. He removed Tuomi's head, legs and arms and once again removed the flesh from the bones. He chopped the flesh into small pieces before placing them into individual bags. As with his first murder, he beat the bones into fine pieces with the aid of a sledgehammer. All in all, this grim process took him only two hours.

To dispose of the evidence, he simply placed it on the curb with the remainder of the household waste. He did keep one souvenir from his second kill: Tuomi's severed head. He kept it wrapped in a blanket for two weeks, before boiling it in a bleach and detergent mixture in a bid to preserve it for masturbation. Unfortunately for Dahmer, this preservation process caused the bones in the head to become brittle, so he was forced to dispose of it as he had the rest of the body.

Dahmer stated in a later interview that, following this second murder, 'the compulsion to do it again was too strong, and I didn't even try to stop it after that'. He became more proactive and organized in his search for further victims, typically finding them in gay bars and bringing them back to his grandmother's house, where he routinely slipped them drugs and strangled them before indulging his dark sexual desires with their bodies.

Two months after Tuomi's murder, on 16 January 1988, Dahmer struck again when he met a 14-year-old male prostitute by the name of James Doxator. Dahmer tempted the young Native American back to his home with the promise of $50 in exchange for naked photographs of the boy. Once home, the two had sex before Dahmer drugged and strangled the adolescent boy. Doxator's body was left on the floor of Dahmer's basement room for a whole week before he began the process of dissecting the body. Once again, all body parts but the head were dissected and placed in plastic bags. As with Tuomi's head, Doxator's was kept for a time before being crushed and disposed of.

Dahmer now had a routine and no intention of giving

up. On 24 March, he met 22-year-old Richard Guerrero near The Phoenix, another gay bar in the area. Once again, Dahmer offered Guerrero $50 to spend the night with him. Like the others, Guerrero was drugged and strangled, this time with a leather strap, and Dahmer performed fellatio on the corpse. His method of dissecting and disposing of the evidence remained the same for this murder.

In September 1988, Dahmer's grandmother finally asked him to move out. She was a deeply religious woman and was displeased with her grandson's tendency to bring home young men. She had also noticed unpleasant smells in both the garage and Dahmer's basement bedroom. He moved out on 25 September to the Oxford Apartments on North 25th Street and the very next day was arrested for molesting and drugging a young 13-year-old Laotian boy by the name of Keison Sinthasomphone. However, this time the boy was able to escape and report the incident to the police. This resulted in a charge, in January 1989, of second-degree sexual assault. After Dahmer made a plea for leniency, saying that he had sexual and alcohol problems, Judge William Gardner issued a sentence of five years' probation and one year in the House of Correction with work release permitted. Two months before Dahmer received his sentence for this crime, completely undeterred, he was able to kill his fifth victim.

Victim number five was a 24-year-old man named Anthony Sears, whom Dahmer met at La Cage, the premiere gay bar in Milwaukee at the time. According to Dahmer, this murder was different from the preceding ones, in that he was not looking for a victim. In this case, Sears was the one who initiated conversation and Dahmer was taken aback by how 'exceptionally attractive' Sears was. Despite how it began, the kill proceeded as his others had, with Dahmer drugging and strangling his victim. The murder took place at his grandmother's house, as he was convinced that the police were keeping an eye on his apartment. He retained Sears' genitalia, scalp and skull, preserving them in acetone and storing them in a locker at his workplace.

One week after moving into a new apartment, on 14 May 1990, Dahmer claimed his sixth victim, male prostitute Raymond Smith. The 32-year-old was killed and, the following day, Dahmer bought a Polaroid camera so that he could pose Smith's body suggestively and capture the images. He then dismembered the body in the bathroom and boiled his limbs and pelvis in a steel kettle using Soilex[1]. He decapitated the body and retained the skull, dissolving the remainder of the skeleton in containers filled with acid. He then painted the skull with enamel spray-paint[2] and displayed it alongside Sears'.

Later that month there was another failed attempt at taking a life – Dahmer accidentally drank the drugged drink intended for his victim, who stole Dahmer's watch and $300 of his money. This failed attempt was followed swiftly by the murder of a seventh victim: 27-year-old Edward (Eddie) Smith. This time, Dahmer didn't follow his usual post-murder routine, opting instead to keep Smith's skeleton in his freezer for several months. When

---

1   An alkaline detergent meant to break down and emulsify the toughest grease and oil stains. 'The Soilex removes all the flesh,' he later explained, 'turns it into a jelly-like substance and it just rinses off.'

2   According to Detective Patrick Kennedy's later report, 'When asked why he used this spray paint on the skulls, he stated he sprayed them in order to give them an artificial look, in case someone would see them, they would feel they were not real.'

he finally got around to disposing of it, Smith's skull was accidentally destroyed. Dahmer put the head in his oven to dry it out, but, much to his dismay, the process caused the skull to explode. Being unable to keep any body parts from this victim was something Dahmer deeply regretted.

The next victim was 22-year-old Ernest Miller, whom Dahmer met on 3 September. This time, as Dahmer had an insufficient amount of sleeping pills, he had to kill Miller by cutting his carotid artery, causing him to bleed out in minutes. Once again, the victim's naked body was suggestively posed and photographs were taken of it and the body was dismembered. The head was preserved and Dahmer took to kissing and talking to it as he cut up the remainder of the body. He kept the head in his fridge for some time before stripping the flesh from the skull and coating it with enamel. During this murder Dahmer crossed the line into cannibalism, setting aside parts of Miller's flesh to eat, including his biceps and heart, keeping them in the fridge. Dahmer wanted to keep this victim's entire skeleton as a reminder and so bleached some of the bones in an attempt to dry them out.

On 24 September, 22-year-old David Thomas met his fate at Dahmer's hands. Once Dahmer had drugged him, he realized that he was not sexually attracted to him but was afraid of backing out, so he felt he had no other option but to go ahead with the murder. He intentionally did not retain any body parts this time, perhaps due to the fact that he did not feel any emotional or sexual ties to this victim as he had to the others, but he did take photographs of the body as he was dissecting it, which helped to identify Thomas at a later date.

Dahmer's tenth murder did not take place until 18

February 1991, when he killed 19-year-old aspiring model Curtis Straughter, whom he met at a bus stop near Marquette University. Dahmer drugged Straughter and strangled him with a leather strap while giving him oral sex. He retained the boy's skull, hands and penis.

This murder was quickly followed on April 1991 by 19-year-old Errol Lindsey's. This time, Dahmer began experimenting and wanted to see if he could create a living, submissive zombie that he could keep around and use for his own sexual pleasures. He drilled a hole into Lindsey's skull and poured muriatic (hydrochloric) acid into the cavity. Dahmer claimed that Lindsey awoke after this ordeal and complained of a headache. Dahmer decided that the experiment had been a failure and so once again strangled his victim. The decapitated skull was retained as usual and Dahmer tried to preserve the body in a cold water and salt solution. The body remained in this state for weeks, until Dahmer felt he had to get rid of the body as it had become too brittle. Unsurprisingly, it was about this time that Dahmer's neighbours began to take note of the foul smell that was coming from his apartment, as well as peculiar and suspicious noises, such as crashing and the sound of a chainsaw. When Sopa Princewell, the apartment manager, spoke to Dahmer about the issue, he had a number of excuses at the ready. He claimed at one point that the smell was due to his freezer breaking, and at another time he blamed the odour on the recent death of his tropical fish.

Dahmer's twelfth victim was a deaf mute named Tony Hughes, whom he met on 24 May 1991 at Club 219. He kept the 31-year-old man's body lying on his bedroom floor for a number of days before finally dismembering it. But before he could do so, he met 14-year old Konerak Sinthasomphone on 26 May: the younger brother of the Laotian boy he had been charged with molesting in 1988. Sinthasomphone was reluctant to accompany Dahmer back to his apartment, but did so with the promise of money. Once there, the boy posed for photographs in his underwear and was drugged. Once the boy was unconscious, Dahmer performed oral sex on him. He lay next to the boy's body for some time, drinking a number of beers. He then left his apartment to go out to a bar and buy more alcohol, returning in the early hours the next morning.

When he came home, he found the teenager naked and sitting outside his apartment, talking to three women. Dahmer tried to talk his way out of the situation by explaining that the boy was actually 19 years old and his lover and then tried to take the boy back to his apartment. The women were unconvinced by his story and told him that they had already called the police. Two officers, by the names of John Balcerzak and Joseph Gabrish, arrived not long after. Dahmer told them the same story, claiming that the boy had simply become drunk after an argument. The three women attempted to draw the officers' attention to the fact that Sinthasomphone was bleeding and struggling against Dahmer's attempts to get him back in the apartment, seemingly terrified. Their protests fell upon deaf ears, however, as the police informed them this was a domestic incident and they could do nothing about it. Sinthasomphone was, astonishingly, escorted back into the apartment by the officers.

As proof of their relationship, Dahmer showed the officers the photographs he had taken earlier that evening,

Tony Hughes, one of Dahmer's victims

of the boy posing in an openly sexual manner. At a later date, the officers claimed that they had smelled a peculiar odour inside the apartment, which was no doubt coming from Hughes' decomposing body. Extraordinarily, the officer who cast a glance inside Dahmer's bedroom failed to notice the dead body lying inside. They simply left with instructions for Dahmer to take care of his partner.

Following the departure of the police, Dahmer got to work killing his next victim. He drilled a hole into the boy's head, once again pouring muriatic acid inside the cavity, killing him almost immediately. He took the following day off work in order to properly dismember the two bodies in his house. He retained both of their skulls and added them to his growing collection. The murder of Sinthasomphone was completely preventable had the police at the scene run a simple background check and discovered that Dahmer was on probation for child molestation. There had, in addition, been more than sufficient evidence within the apartment to convict Dahmer of multiple counts of murder, had they taken the time to have a closer look around. As it was, Dahmer was left free to kill again, a little more than a month later.

On 30 June 1991, Dahmer met 20-year-old Matt Turner and brought him home under the pretence of offering him a professional photo shoot. Once he was drugged and killed, Dahmer once again placed his flesh in the fridge for later consumption. After five days, Dahmer met 23-year-old Jeremiah Weinberger and, before killing him, poured boiling water into his skull. This caused Weinberger to go into a coma, from which he never recovered. He died two days later. Oliver Lacy, also 23 years of age, followed not long after Weinberger, on 15 July. After the murder, Dahmer had sex with the body, and the victim's head found its place in Dahmer's freezer, next to Weinberber's skull and an open box of baking soda to lessen the smell. His heart was also preserved, as was his skeleton, which was placed in the freezer. After taking yet another day off from his job at a chocolate factory to dispose of his victims' bodies, Dahmer was finally fired on 19 July.

Dahmer did not take the loss of his job well. He went off in search of another victim and found 25-year-old Joseph Bradehoft, whom he tempted back to his apartment. After strangling him to death, Dahmer left Bradehoft's body on his bed for two days. On 21 July, Dahmer removed the sheet that had been covering the body only to discover that the head was infested with maggots. Undeterred, Dahmer simply decapitated the body, cleaned the head and, once again, set it inside the fridge. The torso he placed inside a barrel filled to the brim with acid.

Most serial killers get to a point in their criminal careers where they become less and less careful, leading to their eventual capture. Dahmer was no exception and, following Bradehoft's murder, his terrible, and successful, murderous streak had finally come to an end. His next attempt at murder would lead to his discovery and arrest.

Dahmer met 32-year-old Tracy Edwards on 22 July 1991. According to Edwards' own account, he noted the stench the moment he entered Dahmer's apartment, as well as the boxes of muriatic acid. Dahmer's behaviour shifted from congenial to threatening almost instantly – he attempted to place Edwards in handcuffs and then produced a knife, pointing it at his intended victim.

Edwards decided the safest course of action was to play along, so he unbuttoned his own shirt and agreed to naked photos. Dahmer pressed his head against Edwards' chest, listened to the beating of his heart and expressed his intention to cut it out. During later questioning, Edwards revealed that Dahmer appeared to be obsessed with the film *The Exorcist III*, which was playing on his television. He also began rocking back and forth, and chanting in a trance-like manner.

Edwards was only able to escape after he managed to convince Dahmer that they were friends, that he had no intention of running away and wanted, in fact, to remain in the apartment. He seized the opportunity to escape the instant he saw a break in Dahmer's concentration: he punched Dahmer in the face, ran out of the front door and soon flagged down two police officers, Robert Rauth and Rolf Meuller. With the two officers in tow, Edwards returned to Dahmer's apartment.

It did not take long for the two police officers to find the collection of Polaroid pictures in Dahmer's apartment, some of which depicted Dahmer's dismemberment process. It was clear to the officers that the photos had been taken in that same apartment. When confronted with the photographic evidence, Dahmer tried to resist arrest, but the officers overpowered him. One of the officers opened his fridge and was confronted with the sight of a severed head. A further search uncovered more severed heads in the freezer and various containers in his closet filled with different substances, such as chloroform, formaldehyde and ethyl alcohol, together with glass jars in which body parts had been preserved, including male genitalia.

Trial and Sentence

After Dahmer was escorted to the police station, the Criminal Investigation Bureau performed a more extensive search of 924 North 25th Street. There were so many body parts to be found in Dahmer's home that the Chief Medical Examiner is quoted as saying that 'it was more like dismantling someone's museum than an actual crime scene'. In the kitchen, four severed heads were found. In Dahmer's bedroom detectives found seven skulls, some of which were bleached or painted. Human hearts and arm muscles were found in the fridge, carefully wrapped in plastic bags. In the freezer, the team found a torso along with other organs, some of which were stuck to the ice lining the bottom of the appliance. Three other torsos were found in the apartment, still in the process of dissolving in acid, as well as entire skeletons and other body parts. Investigators removed from the address severed hands and penises and a preserved scalp. Victim identification was made easy for the detectives, as they discovered 74 photographs that Dahmer had taken of his lovers over the years, all of which amounted to damning evidence against him.

Dahmer's intense questioning began on 23 July 1991 and was carried out by Detective Patrick Kennedy. Kennedy claimed that during the early stages of the interview, Dahmer 'moved around kind of in a rage', ranting and raving and unwilling to co-operate. Kennedy handled the situation carefully and treated the suspect 'as almost fragile'. His approach paid off three hours later, when Dahmer finally began to talk. He said to Kennedy, 'Pat, when I tell you what I'm going to tell you, you probably will hate me.' He then added, 'When I tell you this, Pat, you'll be famous.' Kennedy and Detective Patrick Murphy interviewed Dahmer numerous times, resulting in over 60 hours of questioning. Dahmer decided to waive his right to have his lawyer present at this stage and was honest and open during the entire interrogation, giving the exact number of victims killed over the years and demonstrating a frighteningly accurate recall of all his crimes. One of the forensic psychiatrists who assessed him, Dr Park Dietz, would later reflect on Dahmer's incredible memory of his murders, saying that he could recall every detail, including how the blood of his victims tasted and what movies he watched with his victims in their final hours.

When asked why he appeared to have increased the number of murders recently Dahmer stated that his compulsion to be with someone else, whatever the cost, had been overwhelming and all-consuming. The only criterion for his victims seemed to be that they were good-looking. This need to be with someone else and create what he thought to be a 'bond' was with him every hour of the day.

When Dahmer was questioned about the bones and skulls that were found in his apartment, he told the detectives that he had been creating an altar to place on his black living-room table. Dahmer explained that he had planned to buy a blue lamp for the altar and use incense sticks to further add to the atmosphere. Once the altar of his victims was completed, he had intended to sit in front of it in a black leather chair. During an interview conducted on 18 November 1991, Dahmer stated that the altar had been intended as a place where he could feel at home and for meditation, a place from which he might be able to draw a sense of 'power'.

Dahmer was formally charged on 25 July 1991 with four counts of murder. This was increased on 22 August, with the murder count rising to 11. Once Ohio had conducted their own investigation in the woodland behind Dahmer's childhood home and discovered hundreds of bone fragments, he was also charged on 17 September with the murder of Steven Mark Hicks. Following Dahmer's arrest, the judge set his bail to $1 million. This was soon raised to $5 million, when evidence came to light to suggest that there might have been as many as eight more murders than initially thought, and the victim count continued to rise. Dahmer was subdued and quiet during the preliminary hearings, barely saying a word.

Initially, Dahmer was planning to enter a plea of not guilty, but, contrary to the advice of his lawyer, Gerald Boyle, he changed his plea to guilty on 13 January 1992 on the premise that he had been legally insane during the commission of his crimes. This meant that, rather than trying to convince a jury that his client was innocent of all charges, his lawyer had to do his best to demonstrate the true horror of Dahmer's crimes, shocking and disgusting the jury in an effort to convince them that a sane man could not have been capable of the acts that Dahmer had performed.

The trial itself was eventful and provoked a great deal of media coverage and tension, especially in the African-American community, to which most of Dahmer's victims belonged. Controversially, given Dahmer's victim profile, there was only one African-American on the jury, which caused a significant amount of discontent. Beginning on

30 January 1992, the trial was heard by Judge Laurence Gram. Throughout, Dahmer had the quiet support of his father, Lionel, and Lionel's second wife.

The trial opened with Boyle explaining the twisted mentality of his client and his preoccupation with subjects of a dark or evil nature. He explained how Dahmer identified with the most evil characters in his favourite horror films, believing that he was the 'personification of evil' and perhaps even the devil himself.

The courtroom heard from two detectives who read aloud from Dahmer's 160-page confession. The things that Dahmer testified to would have been nearly impossible for the average, well-adjusted citizen to understand. The jury got a real insight into Dahmer's mind, his disgust at his own actions and the innate excitement he felt when committing his crimes. Notably, he knew what he had done was wrong and this is reflected in his fear of being caught. He was simply unable to stop himself. Detective Dennis Murphy quoted Dahmer during the trial as saying, 'It's hard for me to believe that a human being could have done what I've done, but I know that I did it.'

Due to the fact that Dahmer entered a guilty plea, the only pressing issue during the trial was his state of mind and whether or not he was legally insane. Experts had to determine whether he suffered from a personality disorder or some other mental problem. The prosecution argued that, whatever disorder Dahmer may or may not have been suffering from, his ability to understand the nature of his actions remained unimpaired. He knew right from wrong and he also had the capability to resist his desires if he had chosen to; he simply decided to commit his crimes anyway. By contrast, the defence argued that Dahmer was incapable of controlling himself, as he was compelled by his obsessions and desires, notably his necrophilic drive. Dr Fred Berlin testified that Dahmer's need to sexually gratify himself with dead bodies was an urge he simply could not control. Another expert for the defence, forensic psychiatrist Dr Carl Wahlstrom, argued that Dahmer had borderline personality disorder.

The assertion that Dahmer suffered from necrophilia was something that the prosecution rejected entirely. Testimonies were given to refute this, including that of Dr Phillip Resnick, a forensic scientist, who argued that Dahmer actually preferred live partners, as he had had sex with most of his partners while they were still living. He did, however, agree with the assertion that Dahmer suffered from borderline personality disorder. This diagnosis was agreed upon by all: fellow prosecution experts Dr Fred Rosdel, psychiatrist, and Dr. Park Dietz, forensic psychiatrist and criminologist, also diagnosed him with borderline personality disorder.

On 12 February, Dietz suggested that Dahmer's behaviour was reflective of a cunning individual who had carefully crafted and planned out his crimes, stating that, 'Dahmer went to great lengths to be alone with his victim and to have no witnesses.' It was clear that Dahmer's crimes were calculated and that each act had been premeditated and deliberately prepared. Interestingly, Dietz touched on the fact that Dahmer had been habitually drunk while committing his crimes. The psychiatrist stated that if Dahmer had indeed had a compulsion to kill and cause pain, he would not have had to numb himself in some way to get through the experience.

As well as the defence and prosecuting experts, independent mental health professionals were called in to ensure objectivity and fairness. Two of these experts were clinical psychologist Dr Samuel Friedman and forensic psychiatrist Dr George Palermo. Palermo was of the opinion that the crimes were the result of Dahmer hating his own sexual orientation and the murders a manifestation of him trying to 'kill the source' of these urges. He, together with the other experts, diagnosed Dahmer with borderline personality disorder, as did Friedman, who asserted that Dahmer possessed an extreme longing for friendship and companionship, which paradoxically prompted him to kill. Interestingly, most of the experts reported feeling a sort of sympathy for Dahmer, or liking him to some degree. Friedman himself described him as 'amiable, pleasant to be with, courteous, with a sense of humour, conventionally handsome and charming in manner . . . a bright young man'.

In a final attempt to convince the jury that Dahmer's actions were not those of a sane, rational human being, Boyle stated:

'Skulls in lockers, cannibalism, sexual urges, drilling, making zombies, necrophilia, drinking alcohol all the time, trying to create a shrine, lobotomies, defleshing, calling taxidermists, going to grave yards, masturbating . . . this is Jeffrey Dahmer, a runaway train on a track of madness.'

To this the prosecuting lawyer, E. Michael McCann, responded: 'He wasn't a runaway train, he was the engineer . . . ladies and gentlemen, he's fooled a lot of people. Please don't let this murderous killer fool you.'

The trial lasted two weeks and closing arguments were delivered on 14 February. The court reconvened the following day to hear the verdict. The jury decided that Dahmer was in fact sane: that he was aware of the nature of his evil acts and that he did not deserve to spend his life in a hospital. The jury only took five hours to find him legally sane and, therefore, guilty on all counts. The death penalty was not an option in the Wisconsin courtroom, having been abolished in the 19th century, but Dahmer was sentenced to 15 consecutive life terms, equating to 957 years in prison.

Three months later, Dahmer was extradited to Ohio and found guilty of a sixteenth murder on 1 May 1992. Of his crimes, Dahmer said this:

> 'I know how much harm I have caused . . . .Thank God there will be no more harm that I can do. I believe that only the Lord Jesus Christ can save me from my sins . . . . I ask for no consideration.'

Dahmer adapted well to life in prison and was, by all accounts, a model prisoner. He served his time at the Columbia Correctional Institute and was initially separated from the other inmates over fears that his safety would be compromised. Eventually, he managed to convince the authorities to grant him contact with other prisoners, meaning that he was able to eat with fellow inmates and make use of the communal areas. Along with janitorial work, his time was spent finding religion and, in May 1994, he was baptized by Roy Ratcliff, who visited Dahmer on a weekly basis afterwards. Dahmer regularly asked Ratcliff whether it was a sin for him to remain alive after all that he had done. According to his mother, Joyce, Dahmer had repeatedly stated in their weekly phone calls that he was unafraid of dying and that he was prepared for his own death.

Life among the other prisoners was, however, not without its dangers. Dahmer was attacked on 3 July 1994 by a fellow inmate, Osvaldo Durruthy, while attending a chapel service. Durruthy attempted to slash Dahmer's throat with a toothbrush that had a razor blade embedded inside it, but Dahmer escaped with only superficial wounds.

Dahmer was far less fortunate on 28 November 1994, when he was working on an unsupervised bathroom detail with two other inmates, Jesse Anderson and Christopher Scarver, a delusional schizophrenic. Twenty minutes after they had begun their shift, a prison guard checked in on them and discovered Dahmer lying face down in a pool of his own blood. His head had been beaten in. Anderson was, likewise, lying in a shower surrounded by his own blood. Dahmer had reportedly been beaten with a large blunt object (which some allege was a weight bar from the prison gym). His head had also been repeatedly hit against the bathroom walls and floor. He was still alive when discovered and was rushed to a nearby hospital. He died of his injuries en route, however, and was pronounced dead at 9.11 am.

Many have wondered why these three men were left to their own devices and stated that it was an extremely poorly thought-out situation, given that Scarver was African American, highly unstable and bore strong grudges against Anderson and Dahmer: Anderson had blamed a murder on an African American and Dahmer had killed many African American men. During a 2015 interview with *The New York Post*, Scarver stated his belief that the prison officials knew how much he had hated Dahmer and were likely aware of what would happen if they were left alone, as they had been.

Joyce reacted angrily to Dahmer's death, asking the media, 'Now is everybody happy? Now that he's bludgeoned to death, is that good enough for everyone?' In accordance with Dahmer's will, no services were held and he was cremated in September 1995, with his ashes (following a court battle) being divided between his two parents.

During his time in prison, Dahmer had been sued many times for damages, but he had had no money to offer. Following his death, his estate was awarded to his victims. A civic group entitled Milwaukee Civic Pride purchased Dahmer's estate for $407,225, promptly destroyed all of his belongings and buried them in a landfill. This was done as there was concern that items such as Dahmer's fridge might one day be memorialized in a museum, something that the recovering city of Milwaukee was not prepared to accept. The apartment block that had once been home to Dahmer was demolished in November 1992 and the land remains derelict as an eerie reminder of the murderer who once lived there.

Discussion

Dahmer's mental state was a complicated mix of fears, desires and obsessions. Books upon books have been written on this topic and the public's fascination with Dahmer and his pathology is seemingly insatiable. In this chapter we have touched on his pathologies and para-philia, to provide a brief insight into his tumultuous mind. There was undoubtedly a dark psychological driving force within Dahmer. He felt he was possessed, somehow, by sinister compulsions that he claimed he could not begin to control. Eventually he gave up the fight entirely, and simply succumbed to his murderous instincts. During his talks with Dietz, Dahmer discussed his favourite films, including *Hellraiser III*, *The Exorcist III* and the *Star Wars* series. Although it seems a childlike topic for discussion, it is psychologically significant in that Dahmer always identified with the villain, whom he believed was possessed by the same internal demons that he himself wrestled with. He respected them, particularly for the power they exercised over others. Dietz is quoted as saying, 'He really loved the power that Darth Vader had to intimidate and influence those around him.' Power in general was deeply important to Dahmer, and is a pervasive theme in his murders.

An interesting aspect of Dahmer's murders is that, from time to time, he would experiment with changing his killing and dismemberment routine. Rituals developed, he became more efficient with dissolving body parts and he took to keeping mementos of his victims. He developed a relatively effective means of disposing of the bodies, which must have involved a great deal of trial and error with various acids and substances. He even took to lobotomizing his lovers in an attempt to keep them alive but subdued, a clear example of his desire for power and control.

When discussing his motives during an on-air inter-view, Dahmer explained that killing, for him, was actually the least satisfying part of the process and that it was merely a means to an end. He had great difficulty forming normal relationships and appeared to perceive his crimes as an extreme attempt to surround himself with people he loved and who would never leave him. On the topic of his cannibalism, for example, Dahmer admitted, 'I suppose in an odd way it [cannibalism] made me feel as if they were even more a part of me.' This explains his cannibalistic habits and his tendency to keep body parts around his home, but the root problem was that he was simply unable or unwilling to attempt a traditional relationship. Dahmer, by all accounts, was emotionally unstable and dysfunctional, and could not cope with the give and take of a traditional relationship. He did not want a lover, with desires and needs that he would then have to take into consideration. From an early period of his life he knew he wanted his lovers to do as they were told and to be quiet and subservient to his needs.

Dahmer's victim selection has often been discussed and analysed. Most of his victims were of an ethnic minority and many argue that this was due to the fact that Dahmer believed it more likely their absence would go by unnoticed. Others argue that his victim selection may well have been a matter of chance. He lived in a neighbourhood that had a high proportion of African American residents. His victims were also largely homosexual men: although Dahmer would have naturally selected these particular men because of his own sexual orientation, many psychologists argue that his series of murders were actually due to the hatred he felt toward his homosexuality. However, one theory why Dahmer surrounded himself with body parts is that he was trying to prevent abandonment, as discussed earlier, while other forensics experts attest that it was the result of an unconscious desire to punish and demonstrate his disgust at himself because he was extremely uncomfortable with his own homosexuality. This was a side of his life that he never dealt with healthily; he did not even come out to his family until long after the death of his first victim.

The issue of control once again presents itself when we consider his tendency towards necrophilia. Experts generally agree that necrophilia is heavily associated with the desire to exercise control over other people. This, however, is the least of his psychological issues: the preparation for his 1992 trial included a number of psychiatric examinations and the general consensus was that Dahmer had multiple co-morbid pathologies. The examining experts stated that Dahmer suffered feelings of extremely low self-esteem, as well as suicidal thoughts and an ever-present fear of abandonment. Many have suggested that the last stemmed from the fact that the devotion and attention he received from his parents in his very early years stopped by around the age of five, when his mother had less time for him and his father was busy finishing his PhD in chemistry. He was uprooted a number of times, which may have affected his feelings of stability and his ability to make friends, and when his younger brother was born, he received even less attention from his parents. He was then effectively abandoned at the age of 18, compounding his sense of rejection and neglect.

In addition to these issues, and despite the fact that he was deemed sane at his trial, he suffered from borderline personality disorder (BPD), signs of which were picked up by his psychologists following his 1988 arrest for molestation. BPD is one of the ten types of personality disorders in psychiatry and a serious mental illness that significantly affects how an individual interacts with and behaves around other people. It is associated more frequently with women, although it is believed that this may be because fewer men come forward for treatment. It manifests in problems with emotional regulation, impulsive and reckless behaviour and unstable relationships with those around the sufferer. *The Diagnostic and Statistical Manual for Mental Disorders* (5th edition), has the following criteria, among others, for its diagnosis:

1. Impairments in self-functioning, either in terms of self-direction or self-identity, with an unstable self-image 'often associated with excessive self-criticism; chronic feelings of emptiness; dissociative states under stress'.
2. Impairments in interpersonal functioning, marked by either a lack of empathy ('compromised ability to recognize the feelings and needs of others') or problems with intimacy ('intense, unstable, and conflicted close relationships, marked by mistrust, neediness, and anxious preoccupation with real or imagined abandonment; close relationships often viewed in extremes of idealization and devaluation and alternating between over involvement and withdrawal').
3. Emotional liability ('unstable emotional experiences and frequent mood changes; emotions that are easily aroused, intense, and/or out of proportion to events and circumstances'), anxiousness and separation insecurity ('fears of rejection by – and/or separation from – significant others, associated with fears of excessive

dependency and complete loss of autonomy').

4. Depressivity: 'frequent feelings of being down, miserable, and/or hopeless; difficulty recovering from such moods; pessimism about the future; pervasive shame; feeling of inferior self-worth; thoughts of suicide and suicidal behavior'.

5. Disinhibition, characterized by: a) impulsivity ('acting on the spur of the moment in response to immediate stimuli; acting on a momentary basis without a plan or consideration of outcomes; difficulty establishing or following plans; a sense of urgency and self-harming behavior under emotional distress') and b) risk-taking.

6. Antagonism, characterized by hostility.

In short, individuals with BPD generally have a real dread of being alone yet experience great difficulties with intimacy and close relationships, have a poor sense of self or self-image, indulge in impulsive, hostile or damaging behaviours and struggle with long-term feelings of rejection and loneliness. All of these sound extremely familiar in the case of Jeffrey Dahmer. They can also – notably in this case – experience strong feelings of aggression and antagonism, which they find hard to control.

Dahmer's interest in the occult is also something that should be mentioned in this chapter. He went through what some term a 'satanic phase', where he researched satanic verses and intended to use them to control his victims. He also claimed to have performed certain occult rituals over the dead bodies of his victims. Though this part of his life was short, it tells us a great deal about his tendency towards superstition and desire for power, not just of a physical and emotional nature, but also a spiritual one. In his book *I Have Lived in the Monster*, FBI Special Agent Robert Ressler reveals that an interview with Dahmer uncovered the fact that Dahmer attempted to use the occult to tap into more power. He admitted to visiting occult bookshops and looking for certain materials to use in rituals. He claimed not to have used them yet, but had he been at large for longer, it is likely that he would have become more involved in occult practices, particularly in relation to his murders.

Firmly placing Dahmer in a particular type using the Holmes and DeBurger typology is problematic, as he appears to fit in a number of them. The overall opinion is that Dahmer suits the third variety of serial killer: the Hedonistic type. This is the most common category of serial killer, and those who fall within it generally kill for the thrill it gives them, or for their own enjoyment. They also kill for their own sexual pleasure, as was the case with Dahmer. He has often been placed in the subtype of Hedonistic Lust Killer, given the extent of sexual involvement in his murders, as well as his practices of cannibalism and dismemberment.

The argument could be made that Dahmer also fits within the Power/Control type, due to the amount of control he needed to exercise over his victims. This began with sleeping pills to subdue them and quickly evolved into murder. He also attempted to turn some of his victims into zombie-like slaves for his own sexual use by pouring acid and boiling water into their skulls. In Dahmer's own words: 'Lust played a big part of it. Control and lust. Once it happened the first time, it just seemed like it had control of my life from there on in.'

Dahmer's crimes devastated Milwaukee, and rocked both the African-American and gay community. His murders were unforgivable, terrifying and tragic. Years after his death, his mental state and motives are still of considerable interest to experts and the general public alike, all attempting to understand the mind behind the man who wrought such destruction, and how a boy who had once been so innocent and quiet grew into the merciless killer known as 'The Milwaukee Monster'.

CHAPTER ELEVEN

Adrian Lim: The Toa Payoh Ritual Murderer

'To say that Lim was less than a coward who preyed on little children because they could not fight back; killed them in the hope that he would gain power or wealth and therefore did not commit murder, is to make no sense of the law of murder.'   Deputy Public Prosecutor Glenn Knight

Introduction

Adrian Lim is something of a deliberate anomaly in this book. He did not hold a supernatural moniker, such as 'werewolf', 'witch' or 'vampire' and, with an official victim count of only two, he was not technically a serial killer[1]. Lim is included, however, because of his clear supernatural leanings, especially in his work as a medium, the ruthless murder of the two innocent children who were his victims and the element of the supernatural in their deaths as ritual blood sacrifices. The Toa Payoh ritual

---

1   Although if we count Benson Loh Ngak Hua's death, which is discussed later in the chapter and clearly attributable to Lim, then Lim could quite objectively be termed a serial killer.

murders, as they came to be known, stunned the citizens of Singapore, many of whom could hardly have imagined vicious acts such as these taking place in a country known for being orderly and safe.

Lim was born on 6 January 1942 in Singapore, the eldest of three children in a middle-class family of Chinese origin. Not a great deal is known about his early years, though during his trial his sister attested to the fact that he had always been a 'hot-tempered' boy. Lim left the world of academia at an early age, dropping out during his first year of secondary school at an Anglo-Chinese School.

Lim began work as an informer for the Internal Security Department before moving on in 1962 to join Rediffusion Singapore, a cable radio company. For the first three years, he installed and serviced radio sets, and then was given a promotion and became a bill collector. In April 1967, he married his childhood sweetheart, Lillian, converting to Catholicism for the union. The two went on to have two children and lived in a rented apartment until 1970, when they were able to buy a public housing flat: unit 467F on the seventh floor of Block 12, Lorong 7, Toa Payoh – an address that was to gain infamy in the small city-state in which Lim lived.

It was not long after the married couple moved that Lim met a bomoh (a Malay shaman), known as Uncle Willie. Uncle Willie gave Lim lessons in spells and curses and Lim soon found himself fascinated with the craft. He fell further and further into the world of dark magic and witchcraft and, from 1973, officially began part-time work as a medium, whose services included communicating with the deceased and acting as a bridge between the physical and spiritual worlds. Ever the showman, Lim would seemingly go into trances in front of his clients, affecting different accents and speaking different languages. He would also make proclamations that he could cure illnesses and, despite his newfound Catholic faith, he began to pray to gods from different religions, including Phra Ngan, a powerful underworld deity associated with the Thai occult, and the Hindu Goddess Khali. Lim described Phra Ngan as a 'Siamese sex god' and would pray to him in order to gain sexual favours, offering up soiled sanitary pads or female undergarments to the deity.

In order to conduct his medium business, Lim rented a room, where he primarily preyed upon women and elderly clients, tricking them into believing he truly had supernatural powers and frequently cheating them out of large sums of money. He was also sought out by bargirls and prostitutes who were brought to him by his landlord. His targets were desperate and gullible girls and women, who were usually more superstitious and with deep-seated issues for which they were seeking an otherworldly cure. Lim made promises that he would be able to erase their earthly problems, increase their beauty and make their businesses and lives more successful and, in exchange, they would pay him in money or sexual services. Frequently, he made use of ritual massage, where he would order the girls to strip naked and then knead every part of their body, including their genital area. On occasion, he would also have sex with his clients in view of a Phra Ngan statue.

Apart from massage, a popular treatment Lim employed was electro-shock therapy. He would place his client's feet in a tub of water, attach wires to his or her temples and send electric currents through the wires, assuring the client that it would cure headaches and repel evil spirits.

In 1974, a bargirl named Catherine Tan was referred to Lim by one of her colleagues. She was seeking help for depression, as she was in mourning for her grandmother and unable to cope with her overwhelming grief. She had been sent away by her parents at the age of 13 and was, furthermore, struggling with issues relating to estrangement from her family. Over time, the frequency of Tan's visits increased, the two became close and, eventually, began an affair. Tan moved in with Lim in 1975, despite the fact that his wife and two children were still living with him. Lim reassured his wife that he was being faithful to her, but when she discovered that this was a lie, she moved out of their home and took their children with her. The divorce became official in 1976 and he chose to take Tan as his 'holy wife'. In June 1977, they registered their marriage.

Married life for Lim and Tan was far from idyllic. Lim was abusive and domineering, frequently beating his wife and manipulating her through threats and lies. In order to help support her husband, Tan worked as a stripper and, at his request, a prostitute. Tan was apparently extremely trusting of Lim, revering him and his opinions. He told his new wife that having sexual relations with other young women would help her stay healthy and that sex with young men would keep her young. According to one source, this led to her having intercourse with a Malaysian teenager and even her own brother. In time, Lim was able to leave his day job and become a full-time medium. His business had become extremely profitable and was continuing to grow.

In 1979, Lim met the woman who would become integral in the murders of his two young victims. Her name was Hoe Kah Hong and she was brought to Lim by her own mother, who hoped that Lim would be able to cure Hoe of her foul temper and an ever-present headache. During her visit, Lim performed one of his favourite tricks, known as the 'needle and egg' trick. He would blacken needles using a burning candle, then insert these needles into an egg and seal the small, delicate hole with powder. Someone looking at the egg would not be able to tell that it had been tampered with. The ritual he performed would then require his client to chant while he passed the egg over her body. Finally, he would give the egg to his client and ask her to crack it open, revealing the darkened needles inside. These needles, he would tell his client, were symbolic of the evil spirits that consumed her.

Although Hoe was already married, Lim set his sights on her and decided to put a plan into motion to isolate her from her family and friends. He convinced her that she was not a legitimate child of her parents but the result of one of her father's affairs and that her family had been lying to her about her parentage her entire life. Over time Hoe began to believe Lim's lies and, eventually, severed ties with her family.

Lim also told Hoe that her husband, Benson Loh Ngak Hua, had been the one to corrupt her with evil spirits, by casting dark spells and curses on her. On 7 January 1980, when Loh came to Lim's flat to see his wife undertake her treatments, he was talked into taking part in an electro-shock treatment. Lim was more liberal with the electric current than usual and Loh died instantly. Hoe claimed, during the subsequent police investigation, that Loh had died after being electrocuted by a faulty electric fan. No further investigations were carried out. Shortly afterwards, Hoe moved in with Tan and Lim, only three months after they were introduced, becoming yet another 'holy wife'. Like Tan, Hoe had an unfaltering devotion to her new husband and did exactly as he requested at all times.

Before long, Lim and his two 'wives' would be involved in one of the most notable criminal cases in Singapore's history.

Crimes

Lim was lucky to get away with his reckless criminal behaviour for as long as he did. Events that took place in late 1980, however, saw his luck come to an end. At this time, a door-to-door salesperson by the name of Lucy Lau met Lim when she was attempting to promote her cosmetic products to Tan. On 19 October, Lim convinced Lau that her grandmother's evil spirit had taken up residence in her body and that he needed to perform certain rituals to rid her of it. These rituals involved Lau having sex with Lim, but the girl was reluctant and declined. The persistent Lim was determined, however, and emptied two capsules of the sedative Dalmadorm (a benzodiazepine derivative) into a glass of milk, which he gave her to drink, telling her that it had holy qualities. After drinking it, Lau became disorientated and dazed and Lim was able to take advantage and rape her.

In November, Lau reported the incident to the police. Lim was arrested on rape charges, and Tan on charges of aiding and abetting rape. The two were subsequently released on bail. Lim persuaded Hoe to tell the police –

untruthfully – that she had been present at the time of the alleged rape but had seen no crime committed. This did nothing to stop the investigation. Every fortnight, Lim and Tan had to go to the police station in person to extend their bail. This situation greatly angered and shook the trio. In his frustration, Lim concocted a diabolical plan: he and his wives would divert the police's attention from the rape case with murder. The murder would also act as a form of sacrifice to his deity, the goddess Kali, whom he believed would then help them by drawing the rape investigation away from him. Affecting spiritual possession by Kali, Lim told Tan and Hoe that the goddess wanted them to kill children in order to take revenge on Lau. He also told them Phra Ngan had decreed that he must have sex with their female victims.

Their first victim was nine-year-old Agnes Ng Siew Heok, whom Hoe met on 24 January 1981. Agnes was a schoolgirl from the Holy Innocents Chinese Girls' School. She met Hoe at the Church of Risen Christ in Toa Payoh, where she was last seen alive. Hoe asked the young Catholic girl for help, and then convinced her to follow her home by taxi. At a later point, during their trial, the trio confessed to drugging the girl with Dalmadorm before sexually abusing her and smothering her with a pillow. Lim then pierced the girl's fingers and the three drank her blood straight from her hands before smearing the blood over a painting of Kali. She was then drowned in a bucket of water. To ensure that she was dead, live wires were put into the water and a current was passed through it.

To dispose of the body, the girl was simply placed inside a brown bag and dumped outside an elevator near the neighbouring block of flats, Block 11. Her body was found the following day, 25 January. The post-mortem revealed her cause of death as asphyxia, and the report also indicated that her body had been sodomized.

The trio's second and final victim was abducted on 6 February 1981. Ten-year-old Ghazali bin Marzuki was approached by Hoe as he was playing with his cousins in a playground in Clementi, an area in the west of Singapore. Once again, Hoe pretended that she needed help and the little boy obliged. Like Agnes, he was dosed with sleeping pills, but proved more resistant to the drugs than the killers expected. He took some time to fall asleep, so Lim tied him up. While they waited for the child to fall asleep, the trio went out for a seafood dinner. When they returned and noticed Ghazali struggling against his ropes, they stunned him with strikes to the neck. When he was out cold, they once again drew blood from their victim and drowned him. The post-mortem report later revealed burn marks across his back, as well as a puncture wound on his arm. The death and the disposal of the evidence in the young boy's case were not as straightforward as they had been in that of Agnes. Ghazali's nose kept bleeding after he was killed, leaving behind a substantial trail of blood. Tan attempted to clean the house while Lim and Hoe took the body outside, leaving it under a tree in a grassy area near Blocks 10 and 11. The three were far from careful and took no measures to prevent the blood leaking from the boy's nose, and failed to clean up the blood that had leaked. As a result, there was an incriminating trail of bloody evidence leading from the tree straight to Lim's apartment in Block 12. The body was found the following day, on 7 February, and all the police had to do was to follow the trail of blood.

Inspector Pereira, who led the investigation, knocked on the door of 467F to be greeted by Lim himself. Lim appeared agreeable, allowing the inspector into his home and explaining his living situation. Pereira noted the strange amalgamation of religious relics both at the entrance and inside his home, including Hindu and Chinese idols (which were smeared with blood), crosses and altars. He also found traces of blood, which Lim tried to explain away, first as dried candle wax, and then as chicken blood. He then changed his story again, stating that Ghazali had come to him recently, asking for his help as he had been suffering from a bleeding nose. The evidence against Lim, however, piled up steadily as the investigating team found slips of paper within the flat, with both Agnes and Ghazali's names written on them, along with other personal details. During the police search, Lim noticed a few strands of hair in the flat. Believing them to belong to one of the children, he tried to excuse himself to flush them down the toilet, but the police intervened and took them into evidence. They later determined that the hair had belonged to Agnes.

The investigating team put in a request for a background check on the medium. It did not take long for Pereira to be informed that Lim was on bail pending rape charges. Overhearing this, Lim became visibly distressed, as did Tan and Hoe. They began arguing and shouting at the officers, managing only to compound the suspicions that all three were involved in the two recent murders. Sealing the apartment as a crime scene, Pereira and his team took Lim, Tan and Hoe back to the station for questioning. By this time, Lim and his influence had grown to such an extent that he had 40 'holy wives', although the only ones that were involved in the murders of the two innocent children were Tan and Hoe.

Trial and Sentence

Two days following their arrest, Lim, Hoe and Tan were formally charged in the Subordinate Court on two murder counts. This came about after substantial questioning and forensic and medical examinations. From the moment of his arrest, Lim did nothing to refute the allegations levelled at him, but was far from co-operative with the police. He refused legal representation and insisted on defending himself during the Subordinate Court hearings. While Hoe and Tan declared their innocence, Lim asserted that he had sole responsibility for the murders.

Their case was brought to the courts for a committal procedure on 16 September to ensure that there was sufficient evidence to formulate a substantial case against the accused. During this procedure, Deputy Public Prosecutor Glenn Knight was extremely thorough and brought forward 58 witnesses before the magistrate, as well as 183 pieces of implicating evidence. It was duly decided by the magistrate that there was indeed a strong enough case to be heard at the High Court. Until this time, the trio remained in custody and investigations into their histories and their crimes continued.

The 1983 trial, which lasted 41 days, was the second longest murder trial to be heard in Singapore. There was a fierce amount of media and public attention paid to the trio, and people gathered in large crowds at the High Court, wanting to hear for themselves the details of the crimes and the rampant sexual perversion inherent in

Lim's business as a medium. Details had emerged in the media regarding the drinking of human blood, spiritual possession and the blatant cruelty of the murderers. Word spread that Lim had a deep interest in black magic: the media focused on this aspect of the case, and the public, unused to crimes of such violence occurring in their relatively peaceful society, was rapt with horrified fascination.

Interest in the case increased further when the trial commenced, with regional newspapers describing in minute detail its gory nature. Unsurprisingly, given how extreme the crimes were, the reported stories seriously offended a number of people. One concerned vicar, Canon Frank Lomax of Saint Andrew's Anglican Church, even contacted *The Straits Times*, the largest national newspaper, to complain about the material published about the case, insisting that the disturbing reading might have a lasting and corrupting impact on the youth of Singapore, a viewpoint which was heavily supported by a number of readers. Despite this, the open reporting persisted. It was generally acknowledged that, although the crimes were without doubt terrible, relaying details of the case helped to raise awareness of possible dangers to a public that enjoyed, on the whole, very low crime rates. As the case and media coverage continued unabated, Lim became further established in the minds of Singaporeans as 'evil incarnate'.

The High Court case was held in Courtroom No. 4 of the old Supreme Court Building. It began on 25 March 1983 and was presided over by Judge Thirugnana Sampanthar Sinnathuray and Justice Frederick Arthur Chua. The detectives involved had gathered such a substantial amount of damning evidence that denial was impossible. All three defendants pleaded guilty. During the trial, Knight put forward the evidence that the police had gathered, including photographs of the crime scenes, drugs, religious artefacts and, of course, the papers with the children's names written on them. The fact that Knight had no eyewitnesses to the murders did little to hinder his case.

The three defendants each had a lawyer standing for them. Tan was represented by J. B. Jeyaretnam, Hoe by Nathan Isaac and Lim by Howard Cashin. Although Lim had previously defended himself, Singapore law requires citizens to have legal representation in capital offence cases, though Cashin was not helped much by his reluctant client. Throughout the trial, Lim's almost constant refrain was 'no comment'. Although Cashin, as a court-appointed lawyer, had no choice but to represent Lim, he became a very unpopular man in Singapore at the time. Many people simply could not understand his willingness to defend Lim, given his crimes, and were unreserved with expressing their disapproval. He received a number of angry phone calls, as well as a few death threats[1].

The three lawyers were united in their decision not to argue their clients' innocence. Instead, they attempted a defence of diminished responsibility and argued that their clients had not been in their right minds at the time of the murders and, therefore, could not be held responsible for their actions. Various psychiatrists were brought in for their professional opinions. After interviews with the

---

1   Knight, on the other hand, was regarded as a hero. The fact that he would ultimately bring Lim to justice significantly boosted his career as a criminal lawyer. His stellar reputation lasted for seven years, before he was convicted for corruption.

defendants, expert witnesses for the defence claimed that they showed symptoms of manic disorder, as well as schizophrenia, psychosis and depression. In response, the prosecution argued that, whatever illnesses they might or might not have been suffering from, they had been well aware of their actions and had known the difference between right and wrong while committing their crimes. They had made sufficient preparations beforehand, furthermore, to indicate that the murders had been premeditated.

The court heard testimonials from acquaintances and family members of the accused, including a number of the other 'holy wives' Lim had acquired. Details of their personal lives together were given, along with accounts of disturbing character traits. Doctors Yeo Peng Ngee and Ang Yiau Hua, both general practitioners in Toa Payoh, were questioned and admitted to providing Lim with sleeping pills and sedatives, with little or no questions being asked about their intended purpose. One important witness stated that he had been outside Block 12 shortly after midnight on 7 February 1981 and had witnessed Lim and a lady walking, carrying a 'dark-skinned boy'. The defendants' confessions were read out in court by an Inspector Suppiah, including a statement given by Lim in which he admitted to killing the children for revenge, as well as to sodomizing Agnes. It was clear from the three confessions that all three defendants had played a part in the crimes.

Lim took to the stand on 13 April, insisting that he was the sole perpetrator of the murders, but that he was not guilty of raping Agnes or Lucy Lau. When confronted with his own confession in which he admitted to these crimes, Lim stated that the confession was false, as he had only admitted to the crimes to stop the interrogators asking further questions.

Throughout the criminal proceedings, Lim was far from helpful. His behaviour did not improve in the High Court. He answered only those questions that he believed supported his case. When he did not like a question, he would resolutely remain silent. Hoe and Tan were much more accommodating, answering all the court's questions. Together, they painted a vivid portrait of a manipulative and evil man, who kept them both in a near perpetual state of fear for their lives. They both stated that they believed him to have supernatural abilities and so felt compelled to obey his orders, rendering their own freewill virtually non-existent. This story, however, failed to hold up under Knight's questioning. The prosecutor got Tan to admit that she had helped Lim deceive clients in the past and that she had known exactly what she had been doing on the night of the murders.

As there was no dispute over the fact that the trio had murdered the two children, the majority of the case came down to psychiatric evaluation. Psychiatrist Dr Wong Yip Chong asserted that, judging by his sexual promiscuity and delusional belief in the goddess Kali, Lim probably suffered from a mild manic depression, adding that it was clear that Lim was not mentally well, as no sane person would dump his victims' bodies so close to his own house for fear of attracting suspicion, especially considering that the initial aim had been to distract the police from their rape investigation. To refute this diagnosis, the prosecution put forward psychiatrist Dr Chee Kuan Tsee, of Woodbridge Hospital (now the Institute of Mental Health). Chee asserted that Lim was, in fact, 'purposeful in his pursuits, patient in his planning and persuasive in his performance for personal power and pleasure'. He added that Lim's belief in Kali was a religious belief, not a delusional one, and that his use of religion for his own sexual and financial gain suggested that he possessed full self-control, and was not suffering from mental illness.

As to Tan's state of mind, a psychiatrist named Dr R. Nagulendran asserted that Tan had been suffering from a reactive psychotic depression at the time of the crimes, which meant that she could not be held legally responsible for her crimes. Nagulendran stated that this was a disorder that predated her acquaintance with Lim, with roots in her family environment, but that the condition worsened after her relationship with Lim deepened. Her depression had been exacerbated by the threats and physical abuse that she had received from Lim throughout their time together. Added to the fact that she had begun taking drugs, Tan began to hallucinate and had had no real defence against the devious medium and his lies. Chee's rebuttal was that Tan had lived a contented and happy life, enjoying the luxuries provided to her by Lim's profitable business. She had been the recipient of slimming courses, expensive clothes and salon treatments – none of which would have been very attractive to a woman in the grips of reactive psychotic depression.

Interestingly, both Chee and Nagulendran agreed that Hoe had suffered from schizophrenia before she met Lim. Following a brief stay at Woodbridge Hospital after the death of her husband, she had appeared to show significant recovery. The two doctors disagreed, however, on the likelihood of a relapse. Nagulendran stated his belief that, during the time of the murders, Hoe was flung back into the grip of schizophrenia, while Chee disagreed, stating that in the six months of follow-up checks conducted by Woodbridge Hospital following her discharge, not one of the highly trained doctors had expressed concern over signs of a relapse. Rather than demonstrating traditional warning signs of a psychotic episode, in fact, Hoe had been helpful and integral to the murders, abducting the children and then assisting in the killings. Chee summarized by expressing disbelief that three separate individuals, with varying mental illnesses, would share an identical delusion that a god would want them to kidnap and kill two innocent children.

In the defence's summation, Lim was portrayed as a once normal, traditional family man who had become insane after mingling with the occult, believing that by killing these children he was doing as the goddess Kali instructed. Tan was depicted as an automaton – 'a robot' – without free will, under the twin influences of depression and Lim's abuse, who had done as she had been instructed and who had barely been mentally present enough during the crimes to be convicted as a murderer. Hoe, on the other hand, was painted as a delusional schizophrenic under the belief that if she killed the children, they would go straight to heaven rather than growing up evil like their parents. The defence even went as far as criticizing Chee, the prosecution's expert witness, for not noticing the signs of real mental illnesses.

The prosecution, on the other hand, used its closing statement to reiterate Lim's cold, calculating character and the premeditated nature of his killings. Warning of the grave consequences of failing to find the defendants guilty of their crimes, Knight said:

'My Lords, to say that Lim was less than a coward who preyed on little children because they could not fight back; killed them in the hope that he would gain power or wealth and therefore did not commit murder, is to make no sense of the law of murder. It would lend credence to the shroud of mystery and magic he has conjured up in his practices and by which he managed to frighten, intimidate and persuade the superstitious, the weak and the gullible into participating in the most lewd and obscene acts.'

Outside the Supreme Court Building, Singaporeans gathered in their masses to hear the verdict on 25 May 1983. It took Justice Sinnathuray only 15 minutes to return with a guilty verdict, deciding that all three of the accused had been legally sane while committing their crimes. Had the judges accepted the defences of diminished responsibility the three would have faced life in prison. As it was, they were all sentenced to be hanged. The two women had no visible reaction to the announcement, while Lim smiled widely and said, 'Thank you, my Lords!' as he was led out of the courtroom.

Lim made no move to appeal against his death sentence and, in fact, signed an affidavit confirming that he would not do so. He remained cheerful while awaiting execution. He was visited by Catholic priests in prison and Father Brian Doro even described him as being a 'rather friendly person'[1]. In an uncharacteristic move, Lim, who had shown no remorse for his misdeeds, also signed a consent form

---

1   This, of course, is not uncommon. Many serial killers are known to be able to 'flip on' a charismatic personality, which serves to draw in victims. This trait is most common in psychopathic personalities.

to donate his eyes, kidneys and other organs upon his death, in order to 'give life to others'. He also offered a 'gesture of atonement' to the families of Agnes Ng and Ghazali bin Marzuki in the form of $104,000 (all that remained of his savings), which was rejected.

His 'holy wives', however, did their best to save their own lives, with a number of appeals based on the fact that their lawyers believed their medical histories had not been adequately considered. In August 1986, the Court of Appeal, presided over by Chief Justice Wee Chong Jin, Justice L.P. Thean and Justice Lai Kew Chai, rejected their appeals. The women also approached London's Privy Council and Wee Kim Wee, then the president of Singapore, but both of these appeals were also turned down.

As the day of the executions drew near, Lim begged Father Doro for absolution and received Holy Communion, while Hoe and Tan converted to Catholicism and received Holy Communion and forgiveness for their sins. Their date of execution was 25 November 1988, and *The Straits Times* reported that Lim smiled on his walk to the hangman's noose in Changi prison. The three were cremated at Mount Vernon Crematorium on the same day, after a church service at the Church of the Holy Family in Katong.

Discussion

Lim, Tan and Hoe's court case was interesting to legal experts not because of any contention over whether the crimes had been committed, but because of the strategy adopted by the defence. The case became a noteworthy example used by local law and psychology academics in the study of diminished responsibility. It captured the interest and imagination of the public and the intense attention of the media. However, although Singapore is one of the most developed countries in South-east Asia, it is also one of the youngest and many members of its multiracial migrant population, only second- or third-generation settlers, retain superstitious or supernatural beliefs from their cultures of origin. This was even more so in the 1980s and the people of Singapore, alarmed by the nature of the murders and their supernatural element and unaccustomed to such vicious and violent crimes occurring in a country with a relatively low crime rate, followed the significant media coverage surrounding the case closely. In the years following the crime, the case stayed uppermost in the Singaporean consciousness. It was deemed the most sensational case of the 1980s, with journalist Ben Davidson in a 1990 newspaper article branding it 'the talk of a horrified city as gruesome accounts of sexual perversion, the drinking of human blood, spirit possession, exorcism and indiscriminate cruelty unfolded during the 41-day hearing'.

Two Singaporean films, *Medium Rare* and *God or Dog*, and an episode of a true crime programme, *True Files*, were released in the 1990s based on the case, together with a number of books and references scattered throughout local legal and psychiatric articles.

Although Adrian Lim was only convicted of two murders, the case could be made for labelling him a serial killer if the murder of Hoe's husband is taken into account, as, arguably, it should be. He might also be thought of as a religious cult leader, if one considers the scores of women he managed to trick into believing he had supernatural powers. There is ample evidence to suggest that

Lim was a persuasive and charismatic character, one who could attract and then manipulate new followers. He used religious icons and ideology to keep his followers in place, but also to ensure that they believed his word to be law. Tan and Hoe, according to their testimonies, did not even consider defying or arguing with him and his instructions; dissent was not allowed.

There are other attributes that resemble cultism, including the fact that Lim and his wives were living communally, with neither of the wives having connections with the outside world. Lim deliberately and carefully severed their ties with their families and, in Hoe's case, her husband. Both women were extremely vulnerable, with troubling family backgrounds and emotional or psychological issues that Lim used to his advantage, forming an effective 'us against them' mentality, allowing him even greater power and control over the women. As in many other cults, Lim utilized mind-altering techniques such as chanting, meditation, suggestion and even speaking in tongues to give an aura of authenticity. He was also certainly preoccupied with bringing in more members and money, as is evident from the number of 'holy wives' he had by the end of his life and the lucrative business he had built.

Lim was a particularly interesting and complicated character and showed signs of psychopathy, as indicated on Robert Hare's PCL-R Checklist, a psychological assessment tool used to assess the presence of psychopathic traits. These traits include a grandiose sense of self-worth, which Lim certainly possessed and frequently demonstrated; a lack of remorse, which was evident during his trial and incarceration; a failure to accept responsibility for his actions, which can be seen from his constant denial that he had ever committed rape; promiscuous sexual behaviour, as can be observed in the sexual manipulation of his clients and the fact that he had many 'wives' and was unwilling or unable to remain faithful to one person; impulsivity; irresponsibility; criminal versatility; manipulation and pathological lying.

Difficulty arises in categorizing Lim according to the Holmes and DeBurger typology, as he seems to fit in a number of categories, yet none completely satisfactorily. The Visionary killer seems the first obvious choice to consider: a killer who kills because voices or visions demand lethal action against a defined and identified cohort of people. Though Lim was, from his own perspective, acting in the service of the goddess Kali, he neither heard voices nor saw visions demanding that he kill his two child victims: they were selected quite randomly by Hoe. Furthermore, as argued by Chee, his belief in Kali was a religious belief and not a delusion and, therefore, was not indicative of psychosis – a sentiment that was, ultimately, supported by the court.

Given Lim's history of exploiting religion and other people for his own sexual and financial gain, it might also be apt to consider if he fits within the Hedonistic type of serial killer, who kills because it is pleasurable (or because it enhances the murderer's social or personal status). The element of sexual abuse in the murder of Agnes Ng suggests that Lim might be further categorized into the Lust killer subtype of the Hedonistic category and further supports the underlying assumption here that Lim may simply have enjoyed the act of killing.

Finally, Lim may belong to the Power/Control type of

serial killer, who kills because he or she enjoys the feeling of being in complete control of another person. It is clear from his history – and from the testimonies of Hoe and Tan – that Lim had a great need for power and control over those around him. It is possible that this need might have grown homicidal in nature, extending to the need for power and control not only over the lives of those around him, but also their deaths.

The answer to the question of the real motivation behind these murders, however, may well have been taken to the grave with the Toa Payoh Ritual Murderer. Whether Adrian Lim truly held deep religious beliefs or was a confidence trickster, and whether he was truly mentally ill or – as the court decided – mentally sound and legally responsible for his crimes, are questions that still stir debate.

CHAPTER TWELVE

Ricardo 'Richard' Leyva Muñoz Ramírez –
The Night Stalker

'I love to kill people. I love watching them die. I would shoot them in the head and they would wiggle and squirm all over the place, and then just stop. Or I would cut them with a knife and watch their faces turn real white. I love all that blood. I told one lady to give me all her money. She said no. So I cut her and pulled her eyes out.'   Richard Ramirez

Introduction

Ricardo 'Richard' Leyva Muñoz Ramírez, known affectionately as 'Richie' to his immediate family, was an American serial killer, burglar and rapist who terrorized the citizens of San Francisco and the greater Los Angeles area. Before the media knew his identity, he was nicknamed the 'Night Stalker'. He would eventually become notorious for his ruthless nature, his marked lack of human compassion and his dedication to Satanism. Using a range of weapons, including knives, machetes, guns and hammers, Ramirez tortured and raped more than 25

Ricardo Ramírez in custody

people and murdered at least 13. His dark fascination with the supernatural transformed this already remarkably terrifying figure into someone whom the American public would forever remember as a merciless monster.

Ramirez was born in El Paso, Texas, on 29 February 1960.

His parents were Julian Tapia Ramirez and Mercedes Ramirez and together the couple had five children, with Richard being the youngest. His father was at one time a policeman in Mexico, later becoming a labourer for the Santa Fe railroad. He was a man with a temper, which often resulted in acts of physical violence towards his children.

As is typical for many serial killers, Ramirez's childhood was troubled and eventful. He suffered several head injuries in his early years, providing yet another common denominator between him and a number of other killers featured in this book. When he was only two years old, Ramirez suffered a forehead laceration after a cupboard fell on top of him, an injury which required 30 stitches to repair. Three years later, at the age of five, Ramirez was knocked unconscious when a swing struck his head in a local park. Following this event, he was prone to epileptic seizures, which continued to occur throughout his childhood and teenage years. To complicate his neurological issues further, he began taking drugs at a very young age, which may have had an effect on his brain and psychology. By the age of ten, he was a frequent marijuana smoker, a habit that continued throughout his life.

When Ramirez turned 12, he became close to his older cousin, Miguel, whom he knew as 'Mike'. His cousin was a decorated US Green Beret and frequently discussed his less-than-noble exploits with his young cousin. He had recently returned from Vietnam and regaled Ramirez with tales of rape, torture and mutilation that he had experienced during his time in the army. He made these stories even more real for Ramirez by showing him photographs of the women he had tortured. In one particular photograph, Mike stood posing with the severed head of one of his female victims. This worrying influence notably took hold at a very impressionable time in Ramirez's life, when his own sexuality was beginning to develop and, no doubt, contributed to the devastating behaviour he would later exhibit.

Together, Mike and Ramirez would smoke marijuana and discuss their mutual interest in the practice of Satanism, which would have been a significant shift for Ramirez, who came from a staunchly Catholic family. His spiral into deviance continued as he began to steal and commit other petty crimes in order to procure the money to support his drug habit. These criminal acts and worrying behaviour drove a wedge between Ramirez and his parents, with the result that Mike was able to play an even bigger role in his life. Mike took to teaching Ramirez life skills, such as those he learned in the military, including stealth killing. In his early teens, Ramirez started to seek relief from his father's frequently alarming temper by sleeping in a local cemetery.

On 4 May 1973, Ramirez experienced a life-altering event when he witnessed his cousin Mike shoot his wife, Jessie, in the face with a .38 calibre revolver during an argument. Jessie died from her injuries, but Mike was ultimately found not guilty of murder by reason of insanity, with his military history and subsequent troubles factoring into the decision. He was committed to the Texas State Mental Hospital, where he stayed for only four years.

Ramirez was irrevocably changed by this murder and became much more insular and sullen, withdrawing from friends and family. The boy who had once been described as 'nice', 'friendly' and 'funny' effectively retreated from society. He made the decision to move in with his sister

Ruth and her husband Roberto. However, his problems worsened: his interest in Satanism increased, he began taking LSD and by the ninth grade he had dropped out of Jefferson High School.

Ramirez's criminal career began with petty crime in 1977, for which he was tried and placed in a juvenile detention facility. His lesser crimes soon escalated into more serious ones. While working at a local Holiday Inn, Ramirez would habitually use his pass key to enter the rooms of sleeping guests and steal their possessions. He was eventually fired when one hotel guest returned to his room to find Ramirez trying to rape his wife. The guest in question seriously injured Ramirez in a fight, but charges against the youngster were ultimately dropped when the couple left the state and decided against returning to testify in court.

In 1982, at the age of 22, Ramirez received a probationary sentence for possession of marijuana. Shortly after this time, he made the decision to move to San Francisco, California, and then to Los Angeles. His addiction to drugs now extended to the use of cocaine, and his criminal tendencies also increased in severity when he began using weapons during his burglaries. Experts and academics studying Ramirez have said that although the mind-altering effects of the drugs he abused may well have gone some way towards affecting and escalating his behaviour, the drug use in itself was in no way causative. They did not create the need or urge to kill – this need was already present within him.

Following a car theft in 1983, Ramirez received a one-year prison sentence. Upon his release, he was far removed from the young schoolboy who had once appeared so sweet and innocent. He had left his childhood behind and was fully transformed into a remorseless criminal with a keen interest in Satanism and no plans to change.

Crimes

Ramirez began his series of killings in 1984, at the age of 24[1]. On 10 April 1984, nine-year-old Mei 'Linda' Leung was discovered hanging from a pipe in the basement of a hotel in the Tenderloin district of San Francisco. Leung had gone to the basement with her eight-year-old brother, in search of a dollar bill that he had lost. Somehow, the two became separated and Leung was attacked. She was beaten, raped and then stabbed to death. Her brother discovered her body soon after.

An investigation was carried out into Leung's death, but no convincing suspects were ever arrested. However, this murder remained in the memory of a young police officer by the name of Holly Pera. It was thanks to her that, years later, when she became a cold case detective, Leung's case was reopened. On 22 October 2009, DNA technician Matthew Gabriel was able to conclusively match Ramirez's DNA to trace evidence obtained from the crime scene. It was later discovered that at the time of the murder, Ramirez had lived roughly six blocks from Leung. His first victim was also, tragically, his youngest.

Ramirez went on to kill again on 28 June 1984, when he entered the Eagle Rock apartment of 79-year-old Jennie

---

1 His first official murder, however, was not tied to him until 2009, 25 years after the perpetration of the crime, when advances in DNA technology finally allowed a cold case detective to solve the murder.

Vincow. It was a hot summer's day and the elderly woman had decided to leave her window ajar – something Ramirez took full advantage of, by prying it open further and allowing himself access. Later, when her body was discovered by her son, Jack, she was found nearly decapitated from a deep slash in her throat. She had also been repeatedly stabbed and sexually assaulted. The only clues left behind by Ramirez were four fingerprints, but as forensic science was not as advanced in the 1980s as it is today, this was not much for Mike Wynn and Jesse Castillo, the two LAPD homicide detectives involved, to go on.

Nearly nine months later, on 17 March 1985, Ramirez struck again. As 22-year-old Maria Hernandez was pulling into the garage of her apartment block, Ramirez took aim with a .22 calibre handgun, intending to shoot the young woman in the face. In a miraculous stroke of good fortune, the bullet intended for her ricocheted off the keys she was holding, which she had lifted to protect herself. Hearing the gunshot, Hernandez's housemate, Dayle Okazaki, hid behind a kitchen counter. She heard Ramirez enter the kitchen and stole a glance above the counter, at which point Ramirez shot her in the forehead. This murder was followed an hour later on the very same day by that of 30-year-old Tsai-Lian 'Veronica' Yu, whom Ramirez dragged out of her car in Monterey and shot twice with his handgun. The fact that these two murders and one attempted murder had taken place in such quick succession caused a flurry of public concern about a murderer the media had taken to calling 'The Valley Intruder' and 'The Walk-in Killer'.

On 27 March 1985, Ramirez struck again when he let himself into a house in Whittier that he had burgled the year before. At roughly 2am, Ramirez shot and killed 64-year-old Vincent Zazzara with his usual .22 calibre handgun. He went on to attack Zazzara's wife, Maxine, who had been awakened by the noise. He tied her up and demanded that she tell him where the valuables were kept in the house. When he went off in search of them, Maxine was somehow able to free herself and run for an unloaded shotgun that her husband kept hidden under the bed. When Ramirez returned, he was furious at her escape and shot her three times with his gun before grabbing a carving knife from the kitchen and stabbing her a number of times. Ramirez then cut out Maxine's eyes and placed them inside a jewellery box, which he took away with him as a grim souvenir of the crime.

The Zazzaras' son, Peter, discovered the horrific murder scene and the bodies of his parents two days later. This time, Ramirez had left footprints in the flowerbeds, which the police determined as having been left by a pair of Avia trainers. They photographed and cast the footprints for future reference. The bullets found at the crime scene were also tested and found to have come from the same gun that had been used in the previous two murders. With this evidence, the police now knew that they were dealing with a serial killer.

Ramirez continued on his random killing spree, unde-terred by media coverage or the possibility of being detected. On 15 April 1985, he went in search of another victim in Monterey Park, where he happened upon the home of 66-year-old William Doi. Entering his home, Ramirez shot Doi in the face as the man was reaching for his own gun, and went on to hit him as he lay dying. Ramirez then encountered 63-year-old Lillian, Doi's invalid wife, whom he bound with thumb cuffs and raped, after searching the house for items he could sell. Strangely, Ramirez let Lillian live, which is extremely uncharacteristic behaviour for a serial killer.

After Doi's murder, Ramirez began to incorporate elements of Satanism and the occult into his murders. On 29 May 1985, he attacked two women: 84-year-old Mabel 'Ma' Bell and her sister, 81-year-old Florence 'Nettie' Lang. Ramirez drove a Mercedes-Benz, which he had stolen, to Monrovia and stopped at their house. After rummaging through their kitchen and finding a hammer, he tied Lang up in her bedroom and beat her nearly to the point of death. He then attacked Bell with the hammer and shocked her with an electrical cord. He went on to rape Lang and used a lipstick belonging to Bell to paint a pentagram on her thigh. He also drew a large pentagram on the walls of both sisters' bedrooms. The women were not found until 2 June, when their gardener came upon their bodies. Remarkably, though near death, both women survived the initial attack. Bell later died of her injuries on 15 July, while Lang lived on.

It was approximately around this time that Ramirez became known to the press as 'The Night Stalker' and his unpredictable crimes, to all appearances in the name of Satan, began to arouse real fear in the local community. Despite the June heat, people began sleeping with their windows closed at night, in an effort to keep themselves and their families safe from any possible intruders. Gun sales in southern California skyrocketed as residents of the area felt the need to have some form of self-defence against any possible attack from the killer.

On 28 June, the police were called to another crime

scene, this time for the murder of 31-year-old Arcadia teacher Patty Elaine Higgins. She had been sodomized, beaten and stabbed multiple times. Her throat had been slashed so deeply and profoundly that she was almost decapitated. This style of killing was repeated shortly afterwards, on 2 July, when the body of 75-year-old Mary Louise Cannon was found in her home. Ramirez had once again stolen a car, broken into his victim's house and ransacked it for valuables after beating her to death, this time with a bedside lamp. Cannon had been sleeping in her bed at the time of the break-in. Once she was unconscious from the repeated battering to her head, Ramirez went into her kitchen and found a knife. He then went on to stab her numerous times in the throat; the police tied this murder to that of Higgins a few days earlier due to the similar manner in which the killer had fixated on and attacked the throat of the two victims.

Although this similarity was picked up on by the police, the majority of Ramirez's behaviour was otherwise remarkably inconsistent for a serial killer. He rarely acted in the same way more than once and used a wide variety of weapons. The prevailing opinion was that the murders thus far were committed by a number of different attackers, but a small number of people believed that one man was responsible for all the deaths, despite the differences between them.

Three days later, on 5 July, Ramirez attempted to kill yet again when he broke into a Sierra Madre home belonging to the family of 16-year-old Whitney Bennett. While she lay sleeping in her room, Ramirez struck her with a tyre lever, ensuring that she would remain unconscious while he went to the kitchen to get a knife. Not finding one sufficient for his purposes, he returned to the girl and tried to strangle her with a telephone cord. When, simultaneously, sparks flew from the cord and Bennett began to breathe, Ramirez took this as a sign that Jesus was interfering to save the girl. He ran from the building and Bennett survived, but required over 120 centimetres of sutures to her head in order to close the wound inflicted by the tyre lever.

On 7 July, Ramirez entered the home of 61-year-old Joyce Lucille Nelson. Ramirez saw that she was sleeping on her sofa and, this time, rather than utilizing a weapon, used his own fists to beat her to death, kicking her in the head afterwards to ensure that she was dead. This kick left the imprint of his shoe, which the police were able to match to the Avia imprint found previously. On the same night, Ramirez went to Monterey Park and claimed another victim, 63-year-old Sophie Dickman. Ramirez handcuffed the woman, assaulted her and tried to rape her before stealing her jewellery. He asked her if he had taken everything of value from her and refused to take her word for it until she agreed, at gunpoint, to 'swear on Satan'.

Ramirez's next bout of murderous violence occurred on 20 July, in Glendale, when he killed 68-year-old Maxon and 66-year old Lela Kneiding, attacking them with a machete and then shooting them in the head with his handgun, once again stealing any valuables he could find in their home. He then drove to Sun Valley and, at roughly 4 am, he entered the home of the Chovananths. Immediately, Ramirez shot 32-year-old Chainarong to death, and then proceeded to repeatedly beat, sodomize and rape his wife, Somkid. He tied up the couple's eight-year-old son and forced Somkid to escort him around the

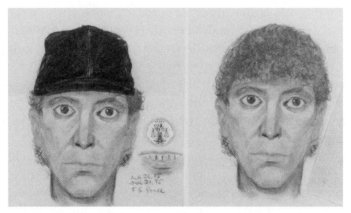

Identikit pictures of the Night Stalker that were circulated by police.

house, pointing out the most valuable items for him to take, once again forcing his victim to swear to Satan that she was not holding back on him.

Shortly after this incident, on 8 August, he broke into the home of Elyas Abowath and his wife, Sakina. He shot the sleeping Elyas in the head and handcuffed Sakina, demanding that she reveal where her valuables were kept. He raped and sodomized her, commanding her to swear to Satan that she would not scream as he attacked her. Horrifyingly, the couple's three-year-old son entered the room while Sakina was being attacked. Ramirez tied the boy up and continued to rape Sakina. Once Ramirez had made his escape, Sakina was able to release her son and order him to go to the neighbour's house to get help.

Ramirez was keeping track of the coverage of his murders in the press and knew that he needed to move away from his current area in order to evade suspicion. So he left southern California and headed to San Francisco where, on 17 August, he claimed his next victims. Once inside the house of 66-year-old Peter and 62-year-old Barbara Pan, he shot Peter in the head and sexually violated Barbara. Ramirez then used Barbara's lipstick to paint a pentagram on the bedroom wall, together with the phrase 'Jack the Knife'. The police were able to link these attacks to 'The Night Stalker', thanks to the now infamous Avia trainer marks that were also left at the Pan's house. This was leaked through the media – unfortunately tipping Ramirez off and giving him the opportunity to dispose of his trainers by throwing them from the Golden Gate Bridge before returning to the Los Angeles area.

The fact that he had not yet been captured or killed after so many violent attacks over such a long period was having an effect on Ramirez, who was likely beginning to think himself untouchable. This was evidenced by his behaviour during the next attack, on 24 August. Ramirez shot 30-year-old Bill Carns several times after letting himself in through the back door of Carns' house. He went on to tell Carns' 29-year-old fiancée, Inez Erickson, that he was 'The Night Stalker'. He attacked the terrified woman, bound her with neckties and forced her to swear her love for Satan as he sodomized and raped her. Before he took his leave, he instructed Erickson to 'tell them that the Night Stalker was here'. Erickson ran to her neighbours to get help for her fiancé, who defied the odds and survived the attack after two bullets were removed from his head.

As Ramirez ran from Erickson and Carns' home, he was seen by 13-year-old James Romero III. The police now had enough eye-witness statements to put together a fairly definitive portrait of the killer. Romero was also able to supply the police with the information that the attacker had driven a 1976 orange Toyota, even managing to provide them with a partial licence plate number. The police found the car on 28 August, but it was almost completely devoid of fingerprints. Thankfully, one remained and so, at long last, the detectives had a breakthrough and were able to match the print to ex-convict Ramirez.

Initially, the investigating officers struggled with the decision to make his identity and photograph public: if they released the information, it would tip him off and give him the chance to lie low. If, however, they kept it quiet, it would leave him free to wander unrestricted in public and continue his attacks. Ultimately, it was agreed that the safety of the public was the topmost priority and identikit pictures of the real Night Stalker were circulated, so at last everyone now knew what the notorious killer looked like.

Ramirez's photograph was plastered over nearly every newspaper and was shown regularly on television news reports. The police arranged a press conference, in which Ramirez was taunted with the following words from Los Angeles Country Sheriff Block: 'We know who you are now, and soon everyone else will. There will be no place you can hide.'

On 29 August, after paying a visit to his brother in Tucson, Arizona, Ramirez returned to Los Angeles. Upon entering a local shop, Ramirez noticed that he was attracting a lot of attention and that some people were actively avoiding his gaze. One or two Mexican women whispered the words '*el matador*' ('the killer') behind his back. All of which made sense to Ramirez when he reached the check-out counter and saw the newspapers with his own face staring back at him. Wasting no time, Ramirez ran.

Ramirez scaled garden fences, bolting from garden to garden. As he did so, residents noticed and began to make calls to the police about the peculiar intruder in their gardens. This allowed the police to stay hot on his trail. Finally, he ran across the Santa Ana Freeway – at this point, Ramirez had run over three kilometres in 12 minutes. Exhausted, he tried to steal a woman's car, but was seen off by witnesses, who recognized him and gave chase. Eventually, they had him cornered and one of them, in an effort to keep him restrained, hit him over the head with a large metal bar. They were able to keep Ramirez captive until the police arrived and, finally and much to the relief of the whole of California, took him into custody.

Trial and Sentence

Initially, when questioned, Ramirez claimed his innocence, stating that he had been wrongly identified. However, once it became clear to him that the police possessed enough forensic evidence to arrest him, he relented and admitted to the numerous murders he had committed. He is quoted as saying to Deputy Sheriff Jim Ellis, on 10 October 1985:

'I love to kill people. I love watching them die. I would shoot them in the head and they would wiggle and squirm all over the place, and then just stop. Or I would cut them with a knife and watch their faces turn real white. I love all that blood. I told one lady to give me all her money. She said no. So I cut her and pulled her eyes out.' He also expressed frustration at his capture: 'I killed 20 people in California. I was a super-criminal. No one could catch me. Then I fucked up and left one goddamn fingerprint and they caught me.'

Jury selection began nearly three years after Ramirez's arrest, on 22 July 1988. His first court appearance was dramatic and he started as he meant to go on: he entered the courtroom shouting 'Hail Satan!', showing off a pentagram on the palm of his hand to all who were present. The dramatics continued, with his antics and eerie stares frequently disturbing the courtroom. On 3 August 1988, Ramirez made the headlines once again. This time, the *Los Angeles Times* reported that a few employees at the jail had heard Ramirez making plans to shoot his prosecutor with a gun that he was planning to sneak into the courtroom. A metal detector was afterwards situated outside the courtroom and intensive body searches conducted on everyone entering in order to prevent this from happening.

Ramirez and the details of his case had become so notorious and widespread that over 1,600 jurors had to be called in for selection. Ramirez changed his legal counsel a number of times, delaying the trial. In addition, certain aspects of the case were causing legal issues that led to further delays. One such issue was the geographic spread of his murders, which created some uncertainties relating to legal jurisdiction and resulted in some charges having to be dropped.

Ramirez's trial ended up costing a staggering $1.8 million in total. At the time, it was the most expensive court case in Californian legal history[1]. Throughout the trial, Ramirez enjoyed a degree of notoriety and, bizarrely, admiration from fans, with both men and women alike pledging their devotion to him. He received a large number of letters from these fans, who also took the time to pay him regular visits in prison.

The trial itself was dramatic, exacerbated by Ramirez's overt and seemingly 'Satanic' behaviour. Some observers at the court cried when accounts of the attacks were relayed. Peter Zazzara, the son of two of Ramirez's victims, found it impossible to sit through the trial. In 2006, during a CNN interview, Peter said, 'It's just evil. It's just pure evil. I don't know why somebody would want to do something like that. To take joy in the way it happened.'

Once closing arguments were made, the jury was sent away to consider the fate of the 'Night Stalker'. Thirteen days into their deliberations, on 14 August 1989, discussions were halted when one of the jurors, Phyllis Singletary, failed to arrive in the courtroom. She was found later that same day, beaten and shot to death in her flat. Rumours abounded that Ramirez had been in some way responsible for the murder, with some claiming that he had arranged the death from inside prison and others suggesting that his demonic minions had carried it out. These rumours were, of course, discovered to be unfounded: the murderer in Singletary's case had been her boyfriend, who had gone on to use the same gun to kill himself in a hotel room. Regardless, the jurors were understandably shaken by the event and frightened for their own safety.

---

1   This remained true until the notorious O.J. Simpson murder case shook the nation in 1994.

Superior Court Judge Michael Tynan had a difficult decision to make regarding the trial proceedings that were to follow. The defence claimed that it would be unreasonable to proceed at this point, as the jurors were evidently too affected by the incident to resume their duties, especially given the fact that the murder was so very similar in nature to the murders committed by Ramirez himself. With no legal precedent to guide him, Tynan decided that the jury should continue with their deliberations, declaring, 'We must get on with the task life has given us.' Singletary was replaced with an alternative juror, who was reportedly so nervous in her role that she was afraid to return home. Later, the jury insisted that, although it was tragic, Singletary's death had not affected their decision-making process.

The jury returned their verdict on 20 September 1989, delivering a unanimous guilty verdict on 33 charges, including 13 counts of murder, five counts of attempted murder, 11 of sexual assault and 14 of burglary. On 7 November 1989, the court reconvened for sentencing. Before receiving his sentence, Ramirez was given the chance to speak:

'It's nothing you'd understand, but I do have something to say. In fact, I have a lot to say, but now is not the time or place. I don't know why I'm wasting my time or breath. But what the hell? As for what is said of my life, there have been lies in the past and there will be lies in the future. I don't believe in the hypocritical, moralistic dogma of this so-called civilized society. I need not look beyond this room to see all the liars, haters, the killers, the crooks, the paranoid cowards – truly trematodes of the Earth, each one in his own legal profession. You maggots make me sick – hypocrites one and all. And no one knows that better than those who kill for policy, clandestinely or openly, as do the governments of the world, which kill in the name of God and country or for whatever reason they deem appropriate. I don't need to hear all of society's rationalizations, I've heard them all before and the fact remains that what is, is.'

Judge Michael Tynan sentenced Ramirez to death, which was to be carried out in California's gas chamber. The judge commented that Ramirez had demonstrated 'cruelty, callousness and viciousness beyond any human understanding'. In an interview in the press at a later date, Tynan added that, 'The Richard Ramirez case was the most difficult trial I ever handled. It was an experience I will never forget and I'm glad the ordeal is over.'

After hearing his conviction and upon being escorted from the building, Ramirez gave the media a two-fingered sign of the devil and remarked, 'Big deal. Death always went with the territory. See you in Disneyland.'

Ramirez lived out the rest of his life on death row in San Quentin State Prison, where he continued to attract followers and Satan worshippers. He received a number of love letters from interested women, many of whom had attended his trial. One of these women was Cindy Hadan, a juror who had actually convicted him. Another was freelance magazine editor Doreen Lioy, who had been in contact with Ramirez since 1985. Convinced of his innocence, Lioy had fallen in love with the killer. Her family were, understandably, unimpressed with her decision to pursue Ramirez, describing her as someone who lived in a fantasy world. Of Ramirez, Lioy told CNN, 'He's kind, he's funny, he's charming. I think he's a really great person. He's my best friend; he's my buddy.'

By 1988, in fact, Ramirez had proposed to Lioy and the two were married on 3 October 1996. Lioy was initially so dedicated to her husband that she insisted for years that she would commit suicide when he was executed. Some time during the period of his incarceration on death row, however, the two separated.

On 7 August 2006, Ramirez appealed his sentence, with his lawyers insisting that his case should never have been tried in Los Angeles and that he had been incompetent to stand trial. On 7 September, however, the California Supreme Court upheld his sentence. Undeterred, Ramirez continued to file appeals until the time of his death.

At the age of 53 and after 23 years on death row, Ramirez died at Marin General Hospital in Greenbrae, California at 9.10am on 7 June 2013. The cause of death was determined to be liver failure as a result of B-cell lymphoma. He had also been suffering from a chronic hepatitis C viral infection and the effects of long-term substance abuse.

Discussion

Ramirez wreaked so much havoc in California during his life that it is natural to focus more on his terrible acts and the impact he had on countless lives than the psychology behind why he committed his crimes. Indeed, many documentaries focusing on Ramirez and his murders tend to disregard events from his childhood that may have moulded his psyche, instead claiming that he was a normal boy from a normal family. Given what we know about his childhood, however, the reality is certainly more complicated.

Albert Bandura's Social Learning Theory suggests that children learn aggressive behaviour from their environment, the family members around them and their role models. Children are also far more likely to imitate and reflect the behaviour of those whom they think are similar to themselves. This is, more often than not, someone of their own gender. As already mentioned, although he was a hardworking and lawful man, Ramirez's father had a bad temper and occasionally beat his own children. It is not hard to imagine that the effect of this abuse from a respected father figure might have been damaging to a young child. Ramirez grew afraid of his father, his most significant role model, who used his own children as an outlet for his anger – to the extent that, as a child, Ramirez ran away from home to avoid his father's beatings and slept in a local cemetery[1]. As a young child struggling with such an intense amount of frustration and fear, Ramirez would doubtlessly have been attempting to find a way to deal with his situation. As pointed out by forensic psychologist Dr N.G. Berrill, 'one way to do that is to become a frightening person yourself'. Instead of simply avoiding his father, Ramirez may have decided to take the necessary steps to become a scarier and even more dangerous monster than the person he feared.

---

1   Here, among the dead, the young Ramirez found the solitude and calm he desired. This may have been where his interest in the grim and macabre originated. He would later confide in author Philip Carlo that he felt a connection with the dead, bordering on the mystical.

A substitute father and role model for Ramirez came in the form of his older cousin, Mike, who had a long-standing history of violence, one that he could demonstrate to Ramirez with photographic evidence. Discussion relating to Ramirez would be woefully incomplete without making mention of this incredibly strong and damaging influence. The young Ramirez spent a great deal of time with this man, who was himself dealing with some profound psychological issues and problems in controlling his violent and sexual urges. Ramirez was introduced to this violence at a very vulnerable period, when his personality and sexual identity were developing, which no doubt gave rise to an association between sex and violence for Ramirez, as well as deviant sexual fantasies. Mike normalized the violence for Ramirez, with casual pictures of severed heads and tales of rape and torture. With every story, Ramirez's respect for his mentally unstable cousin grew and his reaction to accounts of violence became, in all likelihood, less overwhelming and less negative.

The final straw came when Mike decided to shoot his wife: Ramirez had been taught to capture and kill animals by his cousin and had, to some degree, become accustomed to killing and death. The murder of another human being, however, was above and beyond anything he had ever seen first-hand. Even though Mike was arrested and tried for this crime, he got off incredibly lightly, only serving a short amount of time in a mental institution. Witnessing his first murder, Ramirez saw how easily it could be done and how insignificant the consequences could be.

Other possible contributory factors to Ramirez's violent urges were his early head injuries and resulting episodes of epilepsy. As described in the discussion of

Fritz Haarmann in Chapter 5, a number of studies have examined – and found evidence of – the link between brain injuries and violent tendencies. Furthermore, there is evidence to suggest that marijuana smokers, especially early onset marijuana smokers (a group to which Ramirez belonged, beginning the habit at a very young age), exhibit performance and behavioural differences from the general population, such as, among others, higher levels of impulsivity.

Interestingly, the detectives involved in Ramirez's case noted that he did not act like a traditional sexual serial killer. He frequently opted to make use of 'impersonal' and long-range weapons, such as guns, while most serial killers relish contact with their victims, so that they can see their destruction at work and fully experience the power they have over their victim's lives. These killers traditionally use methods such as blunt force trauma and manual strangulation. Although he did utilize these methods on occasions, Ramirez was varied in his approach, which is another way in which he differed from the norm. He killed with a machete, with knives, with a hammer, with a tyre lever and with other random objects. He had no specific and reliable modus operandi. He had, further-more, no specific or preferred victim type. His victims varied heavily in both age and race. He killed both genders. It is typical for serial killers to target those who habitually put themselves in the way of danger or who are less likely to be missed, such as prostitutes or the homeless. The way in which Ramirez selected his victims was frighteningly random: nobody was safe; everyone was in danger of being the next target of the 'Night Stalker'.

Ramirez fits rather comfortably in two categories in the

Holmes and DeBurger's typology: the Hedonistic type and the Power/Control type. He was a hedonistic killer in that killing itself gave him pleasure and it was a thrill-seeking exercise for him. There is no doubt that he revelled in what he did, as his murders were not quick. They were often drawn out, involving rape and mental and physical torture. He humiliated his victims, asking them to pray to Satan to save themselves or to declare their love for Satan. He loved the sight of blood, as he admitted during his time in prison, and killing was simply something he enjoyed. He also, however, fits in the Power/Control type, as killing certainly gave him the upper hand that he had sought in his childhood. Part of the thrill of killing for him would have been the fact that his victims were defenceless, completely at his mercy and under his control.

Ramirez is a very recent serial killer and, as such, his crimes are still fresh in the minds of the citizens of California. It is hard to imagine not only the evil carried out on the innocent victims themselves, but also the sheer mental torture Ramirez's presence had on the entire area. Stifling in the heat of a sweltering summer, people penned themselves in, frightened within their own homes to even open a window to let in a breeze. Not knowing who to look out for or how to avoid capture, the people of California lived in fear of a faceless, satanic 'Night Stalker', who died unrepentant of his catalogue of unthinkable crimes.

CHAPTER THIRTEEN

Tsutomu Miyazaki – The Little Girl Murderer/ Dracula/The Otaku Killer

'Please tell the world that I'm a gentle man.'

Tsutomu Miyazaki

Introduction

The record of serial killers with violent, unloved or abusive childhoods is one that recurs again and again throughout this book and, indeed, in the annals of murderous crime. These individuals who go on to commit terrible, unforgivable acts of violence leave an indelible mark on criminal history. Analysing their stories and developing an understanding of how their monstrous impulses are created is of great forensic importance, as it aids the early identification of the risk factors in certain individuals and may even prevent future atrocities. This understanding is not merely an attempt to make sense of their barbaric acts, it serves a wider function in criminology and forensic psychology: to protect us as a society.

The story of one such serial killer began in Tokyo on

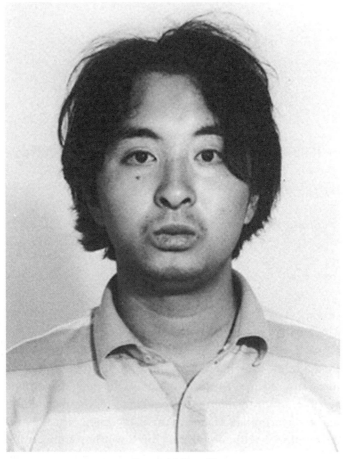

Tsutomu Miyazaki

21 August 1962 and resulted ultimately in four terrible murders in Tokyo and Saitama Prefecture, part of the Greater Tokyo Area. This was to become the story of one of the highest-profile serial killers in Japanese history,

with crimes spanning the range of abnormal criminal psychology: paedophilia, necrophilia, sadism, cannibalism and vampirism. The murders, the victims of which were innocent young girls, shocked Saitama Prefecture, which had not before seen many crimes against children, much less crimes of such a violent, sexual and disturbing nature.

At the centre of these crimes was an outwardly gentle, unassuming young man named Tsutomu Miyazaki. Miyazaki was born to a well-to-do family, but he had a childhood that was far from easy. He was born prematurely, weighing less than five pounds and with a permanent, debilitating deformity. His hands were visibly gnarled and the bones of his hands were fused directly to those of his forearm, meaning that he had no wrist joints. In order to move or rotate his hand, Miyazaki had to move his entire forearm from the elbow down. This greatly affected his self-image, self-esteem and social development. At Itsukaichi Elementary School, which he attended as a boy, he was either viciously bullied or shunned and wholly unaccepted among his peers. He was mocked for having 'funny hands', a wound that remained with him and left a psychological scar that would, arguably, later emerge as part of his modus operandi.

At home, he was regarded with undisguised disgust by his own sisters, who found his hands repulsive. Furthermore, his relationship with both of his hardworking parents was distant. At a young age, Miyazaki was forced to become a solitary figure and a reluctant loner. From the age of five, he exhibited behaviour that related to his self-esteem issues, being a quiet child who tended to prefer solitude. An interesting early behavioural oddity was that from the age of five, he never opened his eyes during family photos.

Miyazaki attended Meidai Nakano High School, initially achieving excellent grades, and dreamt of going to Meiji University to read English and become a teacher. Unfortunately, this dream went unrealized after his grades plummeted towards the end of high school, leaving him with a class ranking of 40 out of 56. Instead of becoming an English teacher, he attended a local junior college and enrolled in a course to become a photo technician. The loneliness of his childhood continued into his adolescence and teenage years. He turned inwards, becoming increasingly isolated, and developed an unhealthy obsession with Japanese comic and fantasy books, which he spent a great deal of time reading. Among his main interests were horror films and anime and graphic pornography and he amassed a significant collection of videos from these genres. He would later blame this habit as being a defining influence on him and his criminal tendencies. Miyazaki's obsession with horror developed to such a degree that he carried the nickname of '*otaku*', a Japanese term used to describe fanatical followers of manga, anime, video games or computers, whose obsession can become so advanced that they become isolated from society, or even divorced from reality.

Miyazaki claimed that all that he really desired was 'being listened to about his problems', but believed that his family would not have been willing to do so. His sisters had always expressed disgust over his deformity and he was not close to them. Miyazaki's father owned a newspaper in Itsukaichi and the family was a prosperous and influential one within the town; Miyazaki believed that they prioritized wealth and material concerns over feelings and sentiment. After his arrest, he said of his parents that if he had attempted to open up to them, they 'would not have heard me; I would have been ignored'. He had begun to contemplate suicide, even at this early, pre-criminal period in his life.

Miyazaki had no history of any healthy, functional romantic or sexual relationships. He was apparently highly sexualized, as evidenced by his interests and, later on, his crimes, but was completely unable to explore this aspect of his life in a normal way. According to one of his classmates from high school, Miyazaki developed an inferiority complex about the size of his genitals, and was unwilling to interact with adult or older women. He attended college sports events in order to take photographs of the participants, which he would later masturbate over. At the age of 21, Miyazaki developed a keen interest in child pornography.

Rejected by his sisters and emotionally unsupported by his parents, the one family member Miyazaki felt he could relate to was his grandfather. Three months prior to Miyazaki's first murder, however, his grandfather passed away, further adding to his sense of isolation. In a desperate attempt to 'retain something from him', Miyazaki took a portion of his grandfather's ashes and consumed them.

This, shocking in itself, was merely the beginning of a long streak of strange behaviour. A few weeks after this incident, one of his sisters was showering and was shocked to find Miyazaki watching her. She shouted at him to leave, but instead he physically attacked her. Miyazaki's mother soon learned about the incident. When she reprimanded her son, demanding that he spend more time away from his videos and more time working, he attacked her as well.

Crimes

Between August 1988 and June 1989, Miyazaki murdered four young girls in Tokyo and the Saitama Prefecture, none of whom was older than seven.

Serial killers often commit their first murders in their mid-twenties and Miyazaki was no exception. His first attack took place one day after his twenty-sixth birthday, and the victim was four-year-old Mari Konno, who vanished while playing at a friend's house. The crime took place on 22 August 1988. On this day, Miyazaki convinced the little girl to get into his black Nissan Langley. He then took Konno to a bridge near a wooded area, where he parked the car. He apparently sat next to the girl and spoke to her for about half an hour convincing her to let him take photographs of her, before he strangled her to death. After she was dead, Miyazaki undressed her body and sexually abused it. He then dumped the naked four-year-old body in the hills near his home, leaving the corpse to decompose. He took Konno's clothes home with him, and returned to the corpse five months later to chop off his victim's hands and feet, which he took home and kept in his wardrobe: trophies of his first kill.

Later, he further dismembered Konno's body and burned the remaining bones in his furnace, which he then ground and sent to the victim's family, along with some of her teeth and photos of her clothes. Included among these items was a postcard, which chillingly read: 'Mari.

Cremated. Bones. Investigate. Prove.' In the future, he would also send letters to the media, under an assumed female name, Yuko Imada, claiming responsibility for the crimes. The name, in Japanese, has the double meanings of 'now I have courage' and 'now I will tell you'.

On 3 October of the same year, Miyazaki saw seven-year-old Masami Yoshizawa taking a walk by herself. Miyazaki persuaded the girl to get into his car and drove to the second murder site. Again Miyazaki strangled the little girl to death. After Yoshizawa had died, he stripped and sexually abused her body, taking her clothes with him as he had Konno's. He left Yoshizawa's body at the murder scene, where it remained undiscovered.

Miyazaki's third murder heavily reflected his first two. Roughly two months after Yoshizawa's murder, on 12 December, Miyazaki went on to kill four-year-old Erika Nanba, when he found her walking home from a friend's house. As with Konno and Yoshizawa, Miyazaki talked the little girl into his car and drove to a car park in Naguri, Saitama before he forced her to take her clothes off in the back seat, photographed her and strangled her to death. After she died, Miyazaki tied the girl's hands and feet behind her back and covered her with a bed sheet. He then stored her in the boot of his car until he was able to get rid of her body in a nearby car park. He discarded her clothes in a nearby wooded area.

This time, Miyazaki thought he might have been seen at the scene of the crime, which shook his confidence and caused him to refrain from murder for the following months. He did, however, send another postcard, this time to Nanba's family that read, 'Erika. Cold. Cough. Throat. Rest. Death.'

Tsutomu Miyazaki (with his head covered), accompanied by police at an inspection of the site of one of his murders.

Following Nanba's murder, the police began to tie together Miyazaki's killings. They investigated and questioned witnesses, some of who claimed to have seen a suspicious car in the area, which they described for the authorities. The police also interviewed the victims' families, who all said that they had received silent and unsettling phone calls. If the families ignored these calls, their phones would ring for as long as 20 minutes. In addition to describing these calls, the families also gave the police the grim, eerie postcards they had received about their children, which comprised words, seemingly describing their murders, cut out of magazines. With this information and the consistent patterns reported by the victims' families, it was clear that the Japanese police force had a serial killer on their hands.

Miyazaki's next murder took place on 6 June 1989, when he abducted five-year-old Ayoko Nomoto from a park, after taking photos of her. This time, after strangling the young girl in his car, he took the body home, where he could videotape the corpse and take photos of it in different positions. He spent the next two days engaging in sexual acts with the body. When the body began to decompose, he proceeded to dismember it. He drank Nomoto's blood and ate parts of her flesh, including her hands. After this, he took her head to bury in the nearby hills and deposited the rest of her body in a cemetery. Two weeks later, anxious that the hidden parts of the corpse would be found, he returned to his hiding places and retrieved the decomposing remains, carrying them back to his apartment to keep. It was not long after this that Miyazaki made his first mistake that would result in his capture.

Trial and Sentence

Ultimately, Miyazaki was caught because he was neither a very organized nor a very careful criminal: the random manner in which he picked his victims meant that little or no planning was involved. He acted more or less on instinct, leaving a lot of room for error. On 23 July 1989, two young sisters caught Miyazaki's eye in the Hachiko neighbourhood. He approached both of them and tempted one away. The other girl, sensing that something was wrong, escaped and ran home for help. She returned to the scene with her father in tow, while at home her grandfather called the police. When the girls' father got to the dry riverbed in the park that Miyazaki had planned to use as his fifth murder scene, he caught Miyazaki photographing his six-year-old daughter's genitals and attempting to insert a zoom lens into her vagina. Miyazaki fled the scene, completely naked and on foot, but later returned to the park to get his car. The police were waiting for him and arrested him immediately.

During questioning at the police station, Miyazaki admitted to killing four female children and eating some of the remains of two of them. It was also discovered that in addition to mutilating the bodies of his victims, he also slept next to some of the corpses and drank their blood. A search of Miyazaki's home revealed a collection of 5,763 videotapes, reportedly depicting graphic torture pornography and violent live-action films and anime. Police also found photographs and video footage of his atrocities, as well as the remains of Mari Konno, his first victim.

Miyazaki's video collection is a contentious issue. The

official police report stated that among his extensive library were a substantial number of horror films, including some of the Guinea Pig films, a series of seven Japanese 'slasher' horror films from the 1980–90s[1]. He claimed to have used the second film, *Flower of Flesh and Blood*, as an outline for one of his murders. He also had the fourth Guinea Pig film, *Mermaid in a Manhole*, which is generally believed to be one of the goriest films ever made (its connection with Miyazaki subsequently led to it being taken out of production in Japan).

Some people dispute the fact that Miyazaki even possessed the disturbing video collection at all. One writer by the name of Elji Otsuka proposes that the collection was in fact a forgery by a photographer, done in order to exaggerate Miyazaki's depravity to the public. Others suggest that the majority of the videotapes contained regular anime programmes, which were neither sexually depraved nor violent in nature. Japanese social critic Fumiya Ichihashi has suggested that the released information regarding the videos was playing to the public's existing distaste for *otaku*, in order to aid in securing a conviction.

Whatever the case, what followed was an extensive legal process that dragged on for two decades. Miyazaki's initial trial lasted from 30 March 1990 until 1997. Throughout the course of the trial, Miyazaki never once uttered a word of remorse for his crimes or expressed regret for the torture he had caused the victims and their families. He maintained a calm and composed demeanour,

---

1   The series contains scenes of extreme violence and gore, and gained notoriety when an investigation was made into its first two films to prove that none of the cast was actually injured or killed.

seldom appearing concerned about his fate or the consequences of his dreadful crimes.

Four years into Miyazaki's trial, his father was unable to deal with the shame his son had brought to his family. He committed suicide by jumping from a bridge into a river in 1994. When Miyazaki was given this news, far from being affected, he is known to have sent a letter to a publisher, declaring that the news left him feeling 'refreshed'. In his spare time, Miyazaki continued as he had always done outside prison. His mother brought him comic books on her weekly visits, which he would read day after day, and he would watch anime on a small television in his prison cell.

Miyazaki's psychological condition was also something that proved contentious. He would often speak in a strange, nonsensical way in court. He would also occasionally and bizarrely insist that, rather than being culpable himself for what had transpired, an alter ego, named 'Rat Man', was to blame. Miyazaki told Hirokazu Hasegawa, the prison clinical psychologist, that Rat Man had made him commit the murders of the four girls in order to bring his dead grandfather back to life. He even went on to draw cartoon images of this persona. He would, from time to time, declare, 'A rat man has appeared', and then remain silent and incommunicative for a significant period of time. At one point, Miyazaki demanded that the authorities return his car and his videotape collection.

On 17 January 2006, the court decided that Miyazaki had an 'extreme character disorder'. Both the defence and the court-appointed psychiatrists agreed that Miyazaki was mentally ill. Opinion, however, is divided: some insist that Miyazaki had schizophrenia, while other specialists assert that he had multiple personality disorder. Despite the unanimous belief that Miyazaki suffered from some form of mental illness, although it was not clear which, it was decided that he was technically legally sane, as he seemed entirely able to tell right from wrong at the time of his crimes. The court claimed that his motive for murder was 'to satisfy his own sexual desire and appetite to own videotapes with footage of corpses'.

Miyazaki was finally sentenced to death by hanging on 14 April 1997. He fought his fate and appealed the ruling, but his capital sentence was upheld by the Tokyo High Court on 28 June 2001 and the Japanese Supreme Court on 17 January 2006. After the Supreme Court finalized his death sentence, Miyazaki is known to have said, 'This has to be wrong. I'll be proved innocent someday.'

Miyazaki was to be executed by hanging, for which he had a deep objection and he petitioned to be executed by lethal injection. In a 2007 letter to Hiroyuki Shinoda, the editor of *The Tsukuru*, a monthly Japanese magazine, he wrote:

'Under the current execution method, death row inmates have to suffer great fear at the time of their execution, and therefore won't have a chance to feel regret for what they've done. For this reason, we should switch to lethal injections of the kind used in the United States.'

Miyazaki wrote more than 300 letters to Shinoda, who published the correspondence in February 2006. In the course of this correspondence, Miyazaki discussed the

Supreme Court's decision, making such statements as: 'This is silly. That judge will be sorry. He must be an idiot.' He also demonstrated his severe lack of remorse in one letter, where he discussed his murder victims: 'There's nothing much to say about them. I'm happy to think I did a good deed.' In fact, right up to the date he was executed, Miyazaki maintained his claim of moral innocence and described his terrible crimes as an 'act of benevolence'. Shinoda stated that, 'he never wrote anything that indicated he was scared of the execution. He behaved as if it was something that was going to happen to someone else.'

At the age of 45, Miyazaki was finally put to death on a Tuesday, 17 June 2008, two years and four months after the Supreme Court had finalized his death sentence. Politician Kunio Hatoyama signed his death warrant and stated, 'I ordered the execution because the cases were of indescribable cruelty . . . We are carrying out executions in order to achieve justice and to firmly protect the rule of law.'

Miyazaki's last words to Hasegawa, his clinical psychologist, were: 'Please tell the world that I'm a gentle man.'

Discussion

Serial killers would be infinitely easier to understand and identify if they appeared every inch the criminals they are on the inside. Most of the time, however, when a killer is exposed it comes as a surprise to those who know them. Often they are described as having been 'unassuming' or even 'charming'. Miyazaki himself was described as 'mild-mannered' and 'quiet', as well as being an 'obedient employee' by his colleagues.

Although Miyazaki certainly had a particular type of victim that he preyed upon, his style was relatively random. He was not an organized killer; he did not set out with a plan. Miyazaki is difficult to categorize using the Holmes and DeBurger typology, due to the contradictory information we have regarding his mental state and his motivations. However, using what we know about his upbringing, his insecurities and character, it is most likely that Miyazaki fits into the Power/Control serial killer category. He had precious little control over his life. From the moment he was born, he was burdened with a deformity that markedly separated him from the majority of his peers. His familial relationships were tenuous. He was not close to his mother or his father, who had to spend most of their time working and who reportedly favoured his sisters. His sisters in turn did not hide their disgust for him. He was unable to develop normal, acceptable relationships with friends or girlfriends. When he was very young his grandfather, the only person with whom he had a good relationship, died – arguably the catalyst for his killing spree. This 'mild-mannered', quiet human being was no one of note and possessed no degree of authority or control over any other person. The young girls he eventually chose as his victims would have been easy to control and exert power over. Miyazaki did not look at, or lust over, women of his own age, perhaps because he felt inferior to them. Children would most likely have been less intimidating to him.

Another interesting aspect of Miyazaki's case are the notes that he sent to his victims' families and the media.

For a serial killer to send a note might seem strange; it might even seem like the behaviour of a man looking to be caught. There have, in fact, been a number of serial killers who have left notes or even contacted the police regarding their crimes, notably the BTK killer in Kansas[1]. Retrospective analysis has revealed that a characteristic common to many serial killers, particularly of the psycho-pathic variety, is an incredibly inflated ego. They believe that they are cleverer and more able than the average person. The notes demonstrate that their authors believe in their abilities to such an extent that they feel safe in taunting investigators with hints and clues, believing that these suggestions will do little or nothing to hinder their murderous careers. Unfortunately, in this case, Miyazaki was to a certain extent correct. After sending his first note to Konno's family, he remained undetected and was able to go on and kill again.

Miyazaki remains something of a mystery to forensic psychology, largely due to the fact that he himself never fully explained the motivation behind his murders, other than to blame them on a nebulous alter ego, 'Rat Man'. Mental health expert witnesses, furthermore, were divided regarding what mental illness he suffered from – and the courts did not recognize his disturbed mind as legal insanity at all. What sense we make of his motivations

---

1   Dennis Rader was the BTK killer, who murdered ten people in a killing spree spanning almost two decades from 1974 to 1991 in Wichita, Kansas. Throughout this time he sent taunting letters to newspapers and the police containing details of his crimes and even poems, together with a drawn symbol intended to be his BTK calling card. His moniker, 'the BTK killer', originated from a letter he wrote to a newspaper of his first kill-ings, in which he wrote, 'the code words for me will be Blind them, toture [sic] them, kill them: B.T.K.'.

and his psychology are retrospective analyses of the available information.

The two provisional diagnoses suggested for Miyazaki were schizophrenia and multiple personality disorder. Schizophrenia, as discussed in the earlier chapter on Richard Chase ('The Vampire of Sacramento'), consists of five groups of symptoms, namely: delusions, hallucinations, disorganized speech, grossly disorganized or catatonic behaviour and negative symptoms. It is possible to argue that Miyazaki suffered from all of these. He demonstrated evidence that he was able to sense the physical presence of Rat Man, whether by sight or hearing, which might be indicative of auditory or visual hallucinations. He claimed to believe that the murders were committed at Rat Man's behest in order to resurrect his dead grandfather, which could certainly be considered a delusion. His strange, nonsensical speech during his trial could certainly have been a type of disorganized speech. A lack of inhibition or impulse control is a common example of grossly disorganized behaviour, which Miyazaki certainly showed signs of in the course of his murderous attacks – especially considering that his victims were selected randomly and his murders committed on impulse. Even his oddly calm demeanour while on trial might, arguably, be evidence for this diagnosis: diminished emotional expression is a common presentation of the negative symptoms of schizophrenia.

Multiple personality disorder, known now as Dissociative Identity Disorder (DID), on the other hand, has a reputation as one of the more controversial disorders in the field of psychiatry, with no clear consensus in the field regarding its diagnosis or management. The word 'dissociation' itself, in medical terms, can mean a number of different things, ranging from a daydream or fantasy, lapses in attention, memory lapses caused by medication, to pathological dissociative disorders.

According to the *Diagnostic and Statistical Manual of Mental Disorders* (5th edition) (DSM-5), DID is one of these dissociative disorders. It is a mental disorder characterized by a disruption of identity, with two or more relatively enduring and distinct personality states that alternately control a person's behaviour. Alternating between these personality states brings associated changes in mood, behaviour, perception, cognition, sensory-motor functioning and memory. A caveat is that these symptoms must not be accounted for by substance abuse or other medical conditions, nor by fantasy or imaginative play (especially in children). It is possible to argue that 'Rat Man' was Miyazaki's alternate personality state and that he suffered from DID. It is easy to see why the diagnosis might have been suggested for him.

Another caveat that is commonly associated with DID, however, is that malingering – i.e., feigning or exaggerating illness – should be considered if there is potential financial or forensic gain. In Miyazaki's case, the forensic gain was clear and enormous: to aid in a plea of not guilty by reason of insanity, mitigate his sentence and potentially avoid his execution.

It is impossible to now know for certain whether Miyazaki truly suffered from either – or perhaps both – of these mental illnesses, if he suffered from others in addition, or none at all. What we do know, however, is that in the course of his criminal career he certainly tapped into a deep well of sexual depravity and dark psychological scars.

An interesting recurring theme in his life and criminal career was that of cannibalism. It began with the ingestion of his grandfather's ashes – a shocking act, yet one that stemmed from trying to 'retain something' of his grandfather, perhaps the only human being he ever felt close to, or affection for. This was to extend later in his life to something even more horrifying: the cannibalism of body parts from the corpses of the young girls he had murdered.

Criminal cannibalism refers to the consumption of human flesh or organs. Laws governing criminal cannibalism, however, vary considerably between cultures and countries. In many countries cannibalism is not a crime and is only recognized legally when it occurs together with another crime. In the UK and the US cannibalism is not illegal, but is, for obvious reasons, socially unacceptable. Those who have been found to engage in cannibalism have usually violated other laws related to it, such as with the Miyazaki murders, desecration of corpses or necrophilia.

There are four main forms of criminal cannibalism: sexual cannibalism (performed to amplify or satisfy sexual gratification), aggression cannibalism (performed for a sense of power or control), spiritual and ritual cannibalism (performed for religious or ritualistic purposes, or to attain some sort of spiritual connection to the person eaten) and epicurean (or nutritional) cannibalism (primarily motivated by a liking for the taste of the flesh or nutritional value).

These different forms often overlap with one another and it can be hard to extricate one from another. For example, in Miyazaki's case, taking into account the paedophilic and necrophilic aspects of his crimes and his history of sexual depravity, the most obvious form is likely to be sexual cannibalism. Sexual cannibalism is a psycho-sexual disorder in which the consumption of another person's flesh gives an individual a sexual thrill, or allows the individual to release sexual frustration or repressed anger. It is thought to be a kind of sexual sadism and frequently occurs together with the act of necrophilia, as in Miyazaki's case. He may have consumed human flesh for other purposes, however, such as to achieve a sense of power and control, either over his victims themselves, or perhaps over a society that his victims represented – a society which had always shunned him and denied him that sense of power and control. This would be consistent with aggression cannibalism.

Miyazaki may also have combined these factors in a more subtle way. For example, we know that he ate his grandfather's ashes in order to 'retain something of him', suggesting that, on that particular occasion at least, he indulged in cannibalism in order to reach a spiritual affinity with the person he ingested. Taking this into account, it is fascinating that he should choose to canni-balize the hands of one of his victims, considering that his own deformity, which caused him so much trauma as a child, was a deformity of the hands. From a psycholog-ical perspective, it is possible that he chose the hands to cannibalize in order to in some way 'retain' them, to compensate for his own deficit in this respect, thereby also attaining a kind of affinity – albeit of a more physical nature – with his victims, while simultaneously achieving an intense sexual gratification in the process.

Additionally, Dr Clancy McKenzie, a psychology professor at Capital University in Washington, DC, suggests that cannibalistic urges may result from psychological trauma, especially trauma experienced in childhood. McKenzie believes that a baby experiences separation anxiety when weaned from its mother's breast. The baby's oral fixation around its mother can develop into fantasies about devouring her. Once an adult, the individual may regress back to this stage after suffering stress or trauma, leading him to seek the gratification he has been denied by resorting to cannibalism. Considering the extreme lack of fulfilment in Miyazaki's childhood, this theory may fit as a psychological aetiology for his cannibalistic urges.

Whatever inner demons he possessed, Miyazaki's actions ensured that his name and reputation will live on, a sinister example of the horrifying potential of human nature. If Miyazaki had only enjoyed a more encouraging childhood, without the scorn of his sisters and peers and the resulting isolation and torment, he might perhaps have gone on to live a happier existence. He might have been able to receive support or professional help and treatment for his mental health issues. As it was, instead of learning to experience acceptance and love and to sustain meaningful, functional relationships, Miyazaki grew up to be every inch the monster that he believed others perceived him to be.

CHAPTER FOURTEEN

Andrei Chikatilo – The Rostov Ripper/The Forest Strip Vampire/The Butcher of Rostov

'I am a mistake of nature. A mad beast.'

Andrei Chikatilo

Introduction

Andrei Romanovich Chikatilo has earned his place in the history books as one of the most prolific serial killers to emerge from the former Soviet Union. Targeting the most vulnerable in society, including vagrants, prostitutes and children, Chikatilo sexually assaulted, mutilated and murdered over 50 people between the years of 1978 and 1990, often eating intimate body parts from his victims. These crimes and his astonishing number of victims earned him a number of nicknames, including the 'Butcher of Rostov', the 'Rostov Ripper' and the 'Forest Strip Vampire', due to the fact that he would habitually drag his victims into a nearby forest or into woodlands to carry out his terrible offences.

Chikatilo was born on 16 October 1936, in Yabluchne,

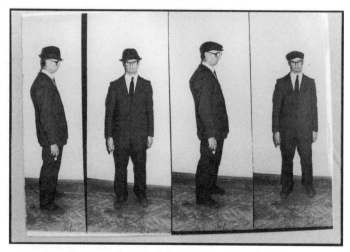

Andrei Chikatilo

a village in the heart of rural Ukraine. His childhood was an amalgamation of various misfortunes and traumatic events, beginning with the fact that even as he was born, Ukraine was gripped by a debilitating mass famine. This was caused by the forced collectivization of agriculture, imposed by Joseph Stalin from 1928 to 1940. The farmers of Ukraine were compelled, in the name of communism, to hand over their crops for state-wide distribution. Ukraine soon became known as the 'breadbasket' of the Soviet Union and the collectivization measures led to nationwide hardships, famine and death. In a bid to survive, people took cats and dogs from the streets for food, while reports of cannibalism soared.

Chikatilo himself was born into and raised in a household that never had enough food. He claimed that he was 12 years old before he tasted bread and survived sometimes on grass and leaves. From the young age of five, his mother told him repeatedly that before he was born, he had had an older brother, Stepan, who, at the age of four, had been captured and eaten by their neighbours. This has never been substantiated in any way and no birth or death records for Stepan Chikatilo have come to light, but it is not difficult to imagine the impact that this information may have had on the young Chikatilo and the environment of scarcity and fear in which he grew up.

Chikatilo's parents, Anna and Roman, were both farm labourers. Their family was poor and lived in a one-room hut, with Chikatilo and his parents all sleeping in a single bed. At birth, Chikatilo reportedly suffered from hydrocephalus – an abnormal accumulation of cerebrospinal fluid in the brain leading to increased intracranial pressure within the skull, a condition that can be fatal if left untreated and often results in headaches, visual problems, seizures and mental disabilities. One particular symptom that Chikalito suffered from was urinary incontinence, which persisted throughout his childhood. This is something that infuriated and frustrated his mother, who beat and mocked her son for his bedwetting[1].

Chikatilo did not have a loving or supportive relationship with his mother, who showed no genuine affection for her son, preferring instead to tease or torment him. His father was the more affectionate and caring parent, but he was drafted into the Red Army in 1941 to fight in the Second World War. Roman was subsequently captured

---

1   Interestingly, persistent bed wetting over the age of five, or enuresis, is one of the three behavioural characteristics constituting the MacDonald, or Homicidal, Triad).

and taken prisoner by the Germans. He would later be ostracized for this by his fellow countrymen – he had, in the eyes of his peers, brought shame upon himself and his family for allowing himself to be captured. This was something that Chikatilo, too, felt the impact of, as he was teased and bullied at school for the actions of his father, the 'coward'.

While Roman was away at war, Anna gave birth to a girl, Tatyana, in 1943. The paternity of the child is unknown, although some sources claim that Anna was likely raped by a German soldier. Considering the fact that the family had a one-bedroom hut, it is reasonable to assume that Chikatilo may have witnessed his mother being raped. Chikatilo and his family continued to suffer throughout the war, witnessing shootings, bombings and fires. They even watched as their own home was burned.

In September 1944, Chikatilo began his first days at school, where he was generally regarded as shy and withdrawn. He was significantly myopic, which meant that he was unable to see the blackboard properly. Years of starvation also meant that he was weak and lacking in energy, and he would often succumb to the effects of hunger and faint on his trips to and from school, all the while being teased by his stronger and more resilient classmates.

As Chikatilo entered puberty, he noticed that his body did not function in the way that he had expected. He was excruciatingly shy and found that he was unable to sustain an erection. His only romantic interest in school came in the form of Lilya Barysheva, whom he admired from afar at the age of 17. He did not have the confidence to approach her, suffering as he did from debilitating nerves. Not long afterwards, however, he experienced his first sexual encounter, when he attacked a friend's 11-year-old sister. Chikatilo tackled the girl to the ground and ejaculated as she writhed and attempted to escape, inviting yet more scorn and derision from his friends. This may well have marked the origin of his association between sex and violence, which certainly escalated in his later years.

Despite the torment he suffered at school, his enthusiasm for studying and learning remained undiminished. He had a flair for memorizing data and a love for reading. He showed sincere devotion to his education and pursuit of knowledge. By the age of 14, Chikatilo was the editor of his school newspaper and a committed communist, eventually becoming the chairman of the school's communist committee at age 16. He graduated from school in 1954 with very respectable grades but although he passed the entrance exam to his desired university, Moscow State, his scholarship application was ultimately rejected. The reason for the rejection was, in all likelihood, simply an abundance of intelligent and capable students vying for limited places, but Chikatilo was convinced that it was in fact due to his father's reputation.

Disillusioned with the prospect of higher education[1], Chikatilo moved to Kursk and began work as a labourer, enrolling in a two-year course in a vocational school three months later, in order to become a communications technician. In 1955, Chikatilo began a relationship with a woman, but his impotence put a strain on the relationship and it ended after 18 months.

---

1   Chikatilo would eventually obtain a correspondence course degree in Russian Literature from Rostov University, but not until 1970.

After two years of working on a construction project in Nizhny Tagil, Chikatilo was conscripted to the Soviet Army in 1957, where he served in a KGB communications unit in Berlin until 1960. By all accounts, he served well in his post and when he returned from service he was reunited with his parents and lived with them once again. His return marked a rocky period in his life: not long after moving back home, Chikatilo began a three-month relationship with a divorcée that failed due to his impotence issues. After seeking advice from friends, word got out that Chikatilo was unable to maintain an erection, something that caused him to feel great shame. Chikatilo eventually revealed in a 1993 interview that his shame caused him to attempt suicide:

'Girls were going behind my back, whispering that I was impotent. I was so ashamed. I tried to hang myself. My mother and some young neighbours pulled me out of the noose . . . I had to run away from there, away from my homeland.'

In 1961, Chikatilo moved to Rodionovo-Nesvetayevsky, Russia, and worked as a telephone engineer. He was joined soon after by his younger sister, Tatyana, who lived with him for six months before marrying. She grew concerned about her brother's inability to sustain a romantic relationship and decided he needed her help. In 1963, Tatyana introduced Chikatilo to Feodosia 'Fayina' Odnacheva. The two married two short weeks after their initial meeting. Feodosia was understanding when it came to his impotence and the couple had a very limited sex life. They both wanted children, so they came up with their own solution to procreation: Chikatilo would use his fingers to insert his semen into her vagina. Incredibly, the couple conceived two children in this manner: Lyudmila, who was born in 1965 and Yuri, born 1969.

Chikatilo began his teaching career in 1972, after completing a correspondence course degree in Russian Literature. He taught Russian literature and language in Novoshakhtinsk, but was an unremarkable teacher, once again the result of his mild and reserved character. He was largely unable to command respect from his students, who either refused to pay attention or chose to tease their teacher, sometimes smoking right in front of him. He was nicknamed 'goose' by the children, a derogatory name for someone one has no respect for. He began to notice the teenagers around him falling in love and forming functioning, traditional relationships. This was something that angered Chikatilo, who was still wholly incapable of a traditional sexual relationship.

Not long into his teaching career, Chikatilo began sexually molesting and harassing his students. In May 1973, he groped a 15-year-old girl's genitals and breasts. This incident was discovered, but no action was taken against him. When this was followed by another similar sexual assault, however, the school director informed Chikatilo that he would either have to leave voluntarily or be sacked. Although he found other positions, Chikatilo's teaching career finally came to an end in March 1981, after numerous molestation charges were levelled at him from both girls and boys that he had taught.

By this point, Chikatilo had been killing and evading capture for nearly three years.

Crimes

Most serial killers commit their first murder in their mid to late twenties, so it is unusual that Chikatilo did not take his first life until he was almost 42 years old, in December 1978. Chikatilo had recently moved to the coal-mining town of Shakhty in September. The victim in question was nine-year-old Yelena 'Lena' Zakotnova. On 22 December, Chikatilo convinced the young girl to return with him to a dilapidated three-room house in a run-down area, which he had bought specifically for the purpose of murdering his intended victims. He had promised Zakotnova bubble gum: a rare and enticing treat for the children in the area.

Once in the shed, Chikatilo tried to rape Zakotnova, but his usual sexual problems prevented him from achieving an erection. He then stabbed Zakotnova three times in the stomach before strangling her to death. In the process, as the girl struggled and fought for her life, Chikatilo found that he was able to achieve orgasm. Afterwards, he threw the girl's body into a river nearby, where it was found two days later.

This was far from the perfect, organized murder and, as such, there were several clues leading back to Chikatilo. Once the locals learned of the poor girl's death, a witness came forward to say that he had seen Zakotnova talking to a man at a bus stop, even giving a detailed description that closely resembled Chikatilo. An investigation revealed traces of blood in the snow, close to Chikatilo's dilapidated house, and witnesses asserted that he had in fact been in the house on 22 December. Zakotnova's backpack was found not far from the house, near the bank of the river.

Things were not looking good for Chikatilo, but he had some elements working in his favour: he was a dedicated communist party member, he was married and had a family and he had no previous criminal record. He was not, in the eyes of the locals and the investigating police, a likely suspect.

In a lucky (for Chikatilo) turn of events, a 25-year-old man named Aleksandr Kravenko was arrested for the murder. Kravenko had a history of vandalism dating from his teenage years and had been previously convicted on one count of rape. Despite fairly flimsy evidence and the fact that his wife was able to provide him with an airtight alibi, backed up by friends and neighbours, Kravenko was eventually convicted of the murder in 1979. Some sources suggest that the conviction was the result of a confession procured from a violent and extensive interrogation. He was eventually executed by firing squad on 23 March 1983, aged 29. Years later, the judge who imposed the sentence was quoted as saying, 'At the time I had no doubts whatsoever concerning Kravenko's guilt.'

After this extreme near-miss, Chikatilo lay low for the next few years, and did not take another life until 1981. A realization had dawned and a desire awakened in Chikatilo, who had discovered through Zakotnova's murder that the only way he could reach sexual gratification was through enacting violence on another human being. Later, Chikatilo claimed that he had tried to resist this compulsion initially, but that the urges eventually became overwhelming and all-consuming.

His second victim, Larisa Tkachenko, was killed on 3 September 1981. Chikatilo came upon the 17-year-old student at a bus stop as he was leaving a library in Rostov city centre. With promises of alcohol, Chikatilo convinced the girl to accompany him to a forest by the Don River, but almost as soon as they reached their destination, Chikatilo attacked Tkachenko. He threw the teenager to the ground and ripped her clothes away, once more attempting, and failing, to rape his victim. Frustrated, he stuffed her mouth with mud, so she could not alert anyone nearby, and strangled her to death. He then ripped off one of Tkachenko's nipples and disfigured her corpse using a stick and his own teeth. This murder set a precedent for Chikatilo: from then on he made a habit of targeting people at both bus and train stations before coaxing them away to more secluded areas where he would mutilate and kill them.

Chikatilo's third murder took place on 12 June 1982, when he met 13-year-old Lyubov Biryuk in the village of Donskoi. Biryuk was walking home and taking the same path as Chikatilo, who took advantage of the lack of onlookers and dragged the girl to some nearby bushes, once again ripping off her dress and stabbing her to death. Her body was not found until 27 June. The medical examiner reported 22 wounds to her body, including her pelvis, head, chest and neck. On this occasion, Chikatilo also focused on mutilating the girl's eyes, an area he would later regularly fixate on during his attacks. Chikatilo would later explain the reason behind this: he believed in the old Russian superstition that the last thing an individual saw before he or she died would be imprinted on the eyes. By destroying the eyes, he reasoned that his identity would remain safe and unknown.

After this murder, Chikatilo's rate of killing increased considerably and he made no attempt to curb his

Four of Chikatilo's victims

disturbing addiction to violence and his reliance on it for sexual release. His method of killing remained the same: death by either strangulation or stabbing. He rarely made a significant effort to hide the bodies of his victims. He went on to kill five victims between July and September 1982, whose ages ranged from nine to 19. At this point, the authorities began to take note of the murders and the mutilations. In the Soviet Union, serial killings were extremely rare and almost unheard of, while cases of murder or child abuse were frequently suppressed by the media in order to protect the public, maintain order and prevent panic. However, due to the very specific eye mutilations in these attacks, it was becoming evident that a serial killer was on the loose. The public began speculating about the murders – the more superstitious among them even talked of werewolf attacks.

Far from abating, Chikatilo's violence only seemed to escalate as time went on. On 11 December 1982, Chikatilo met ten-year-old Olga Stalmachenok, on a bus ride home from her piano lessons in Novoshkhtinsk. He convinced the girl to get off the bus with him and a number of witnesses later reported that they had seen her walking hand-in-hand with a middle-aged man. In a cornfield, Chikatilo stabbed the girl 50 times in her head and body, paying particular attention to the eyes, before eviscerating her by ripping open her chest and cutting out her uterus and lower bowel.

By January 1983, with public fears reaching new heights and a victim count on the rise, Moscow detective Major Mikhail Fetisov was brought in to take control of the investigation. He hired forensic analyst Viktor Burakov to head the investigating team. In April, Stalmachenok's body was found and Burakov took note of the damage to her eyes, which convinced him that the murder was committed by their serial killer. By September 1983, Chikatilo had killed a further six people, whose deaths were connected by the authorities by the distinctive manner in which they were killed.

The investigation pressed on, with the detectives focusing primarily on known sex offenders and the mentally ill. Unfortunately, as a result of the method of interrogation, a number of false confessions were offered by susceptible and mentally ill individuals. All of the accused would eventually be released, because murders continued to take place even as they were in custody and being questioned.

The investigating team had several other theories, based primarily on the bloody and savage nature of the murders, as well as the often precise, ritualistic method of cutting involved. At one time, they considered the possibility that the murders were committed by a group that was harvesting organs for sale on the black market. It was also thought that they could have been human sacrifices, conducted by a cult of Satanists. Although the team was no closer to identifying the true killer, they were able to solve over 1,000 other, unrelated crimes, including 95 murders.

As the murders continued throughout January and February 1984, the police were given more detailed descriptions of Chikatilo by witnesses who had seen the victims during their final hours in the company of a strange man. A big break through came when the body of ten-year-old Dmitry Ptashnikov was found on 27 March, three days after his death. From the scene, the police were able to extract a footprint as well as hair, saliva and semen samples from Ptashnikov's clothing, from which they were able to determine the killer's blood type to be AB.

The year 1984 was a bloody one for Chikatilo, who deviated from his usual method of killing on a number of occasions. On 25 May, instead of killing strangers, Chikatillo killed Tatyana Petrosyan and Svetlana, her ten-year-old daughter, people that he had known for several years. On 7 August, Chikatilo took deliberate steps to prolong the suffering of his victim, 17-year-old Lyudmila Alekseyeva, in a way he had not done before. On the banks of the Don River, Chikatilo wounded Alekseyeva in ways that he knew would be agonizing but not instantly fatal. He sliced off her upper lip and placed it inside her mouth once she had finally died. He stabbed her 39 times and carefully disembowelled her. By the time her body was found the following morning, he had left the area entirely on a business trip to Tashkent, where he killed two more people, beheading one and butchering another to such an extent that the police attributed the death to an accident with a harvesting machine. On 28 August, Chikatilo killed 11-year-old Aleksandr Chepel in the same location, strangling him before cutting out his eyes and castrating him. By the end of 1984, Chikatilo had killed a staggering total of 32 people and was no closer to being caught.

With 15 known victims having lost their lives in 1984, the police were under pressure to find the killer responsible. Knowing that he tended to target train stations and bus terminals, surveillance cameras were mounted so that, were another victim taken, the police would be able to identify the perpetrator.

On 13 September, one week after killing 24-year-old Irina Luchinskaya in Aviators' Park, Chikatilo was arrested and detained after he had tried to coax away another young woman from a bus station. He resembled past descriptions of the mysterious and prolific serial killer, so the police searched his belongings and found a knife and a rope. Chikatilo's murders might have come to an end on that day, but he was eventually released when a blood sample was taken from him and his blood, which was determined to be type A, did not match the blood type that they knew to belong to the killer, based on semen samples found on six victims: type AB.

His details were placed in the index file of suspects, which at this time numbered over 25,000, and the charges were dropped. He was, however, found guilty on a count of theft, levelled at him by a former employer, and was sentenced to one year in prison. He served only three months and was released on 12 December 1984.

Chikatilo then refrained from killing until 31 July 1985, perhaps worried about yet another close call with the police. On this occasion, the victim was 18-year-old Natalia Pokhlistova, whom he abducted near Domodedovo Airport while on a business trip to Moscow. Chikatilo dragged the girl into some woods, where he strangled and stabbed her 38 times. The police recognized the method of killing as belonging to the unknown serial killer from Rostov and assumed that the murderer had travelled by air to Moscow. They diligently checked all the flight records from July to August, not knowing that Chikatilo had actually made his way to Moscow by train.

Surveillance measures were renewed with vigour, and regular police patrols were established at the railway stations in Rostov. Issa Kostoyev, a special prosecutor brought in to guide the investigation, contacted psychiatrist Dr Alexandr Bukhanovsky, which was a significant step as it was the first time that a psychiatrist had been consulted in relation to a serial killer in the Soviet Union. Bukhanovsky provided a psychological profile 65 pages long, indicating that the murderer was likely to be between 45 and 50 years of age. This was vitally important information for the police, who had assumed that the killer was much younger. Bukhanovsky added that the killer was also likely to be married or divorced and of average intelligence. He would, most likely, be an antisocial character and, if he was in a relationship, it would most likely not be a sexual one. Bukhanovsky described the murderer as being a 'necro-sadist' – a person who achieves sexual satisfaction from witnessing the suffering or death of another human being. The psychiatrist was also able to deduce that, because the murders occurred near stations, and usually on weekdays, the murderer was likely someone who had to travel for work.

Chikatilo took a great interest in the investigation, which was detailed by the local media. Perhaps concerned that the police might be closing in on him, Chikatilo took a break from murder from 27 August 1985 to August 1986. This did not reflect his usual high rate of killings and the police took note, thinking perhaps the killer had died, or had perhaps already been imprisoned for some other unrelated offence. Another theory was that the killer was simply being more careful about his murders and taking steps to bury his victims' bodies or conceal them more effectively. This theory was backed up when 18-year-old Irina Pogoryelova was found on 18 August 1986 in Bataysk. Pogoryelova's body had been subjected to all of Chikatilo's usual mutilations, with her body slit open from her neck to her genitalia. One of her breasts had been sliced from her body and her eyes had been removed. Her killer, however, had obviously made a substantial effort to bury the body and hide it from view. Chikatilo would later confess to this murder during his trial.

In the following years, Chikatilo's victim count continued to mount. Evidence suggests that he became increasingly blasé, taking risks and varying his methods. In 1988, he killed one unnamed woman by clubbing her with a slab of concrete after restraining her with rope, filling her mouth with dirt and cutting off her nose. On 8 March 1989, Chikatilo killed 16-year-old runaway Tatyana Ryzhova in his own daughter's apartment, dismembering her body and disposing of the body parts in the sewers. This murder was not initially tied to the serial killer that the police were after, as he had never before been known to dismember his victims. In this way and many others, Chikatilo was able to confuse the police and prevent his later murders from being connected to those committed earlier, which had followed a more distinct and linking pattern.

The murders began again in earnest and, with the body count growing ever higher, the police were under even more pressure to find the murderer who had managed to evade capture for so long. Victor Burakov devised a scheme to flush out the killer, which took effect on 27 October 1990. He suggested having a large, conspicuous police presence at the larger Rostov stations, which the murderer would obviously notice and shy away from. He would opt instead to target the smaller stations in the area, which would also be under police surveillance. The police at these stations, however, would be undercover and thus be barely noticeable to the killer. Given the fact that these smaller stations (including Donleskhoz, Kirpichnaya and Lesostep) were far less busy, any suspicious individuals or unusual behaviour would be far more likely to be detected by the police. Any man seen talking or associating with a woman or a child would be approached and questioned. After this plan had been put in place, three more victims were claimed by the 'Rostov Ripper' and the final one – that of 22-year-old Svetlana Korostik on 6 November 1990 – finally drew attention to Chikatilo.

After murdering Korostik in the woods, Chikatilo was noticed by an undercover policeman as he left the crime scene with grass stains on his coat and soil marks on his elbows. Most incriminating of all, perhaps, was a bloody red smear on one of his cheeks. The officer knew that some people in the area liked to venture into the woods to collect wild mushrooms, but Chikatilo stood out to him because he was dressed in formal work clothes – hardly the usual sort of outfit people wore to forage for food. The officer promptly approached Chikatilo and demanded to see his papers. Other than a gut feeling that something was not quite right, however, the policeman had no real reason to detain Chikatilo, so he let him go and reported the incident when he returned to the station.

Once Korostik's body was found on 13 November, the police began to investigate Chikatilo more thoroughly, with some even recalling the man from 1984, when he had been formally questioned. He was also already on their official suspect list. In addition, the investigation uncovered the sexual assault complaints from his teaching days. This amounted to enough evidence to place Chikatilo under surveillance, beginning on 14 November. The police almost immediately noticed Chikatilo's tendency to approach women and children travelling alone. He was careful in the way that he carried out his crimes – if the woman or child appeared reluctant to talk to him, or were overly uncomfortable, he would step away and find another target after a short period of time. When his efforts to approach and lure children away from stations and parks continued, the police finally made their move. The 54-year-old, seemingly innocuous grandfather was arrested on 20 November.

Initially, Chikatilo claimed no involvement at all in any killings, pointing out that he had already been arrested in connection with these murders at an earlier date and released. The police officers were not dissuaded, however, especially when they noticed a wound on one of Chikatilo's fingers, which they later determined to be a human bite mark. Chikatilo's finger had been broken, the nail had been bitten clean off and yet he had not attempted to seek treatment for the injury, which struck the investigating officers as peculiar. Furthermore, at the crime scene of the killer's penultimate crime, the police had found numerous signs pointing to a violent struggle having taken place between victim and murderer. Once again, a search of Chikatilo's belongings was carried out and a knife and rope were found.

The police also repeated a blood typing test on Chikatilo, which once again showed his blood type to be A. This, again, was incompatible with the AB type previously found in the killer's semen samples at the crime scenes. Between 1984 and 1990, however, the police had gained new forensic knowledge about blood typing: the Ministry of Health had circulated information that stated ABO typing in bodily secretions was not necessarily always an accurate match to that in the blood. Unusual 'paradoxical' cases existed, in which the two did not match. With this knowledge, the police obtained a semen sample from Chikatilo, which was found to be AB: a match with the killer[1].

Questioning began in earnest on 21 November, carried out by Issa Kostoyev. The police knew that, at the time, they did not have a strong case against Chikatilo. It was composed mostly of circumstantial evidence and guess-work, but they were certain they had the right man. They had ten days in which to convince Chikatilo to confess. After that time, under the law, they would be forced to release him. Kostoyev decided to move carefully: he behaved sympathetically, suggesting to Chikatilo that he was mentally ill and in need of help. With this approach, the police hoped that Chikatilo would think that he had a chance of being found not guilty by reason of insanity and, therefore, would be encouraged to confess. Although he admitted to his history of sexual molestation, however, Chikatilo continued to assert his innocence of any murders.

By 29 November, Burakov and Fetisov were impatient to obtain a confession before time ran out. They contacted Alexandr Bukhanovsky, the psychiatrist who had originally written the serial killer's psychological profile in 1985, who was permitted to question Chikatilo. The officers told Chikatilo that the purpose of the questioning was to deepen their understanding of the mind of a serial killer, a concept that Chikatilo seemed to find flattering.

The doctor's approach was vastly different from the

---

1   Medical tests revealed that Chikatilo's blood type was A, but his semen had a weak B antibody. This meant that, from the semen samples, it appeared that his blood type was AB, even though it was not: his was the rare 'paradoxical' case.

one that the police utilized – it was completely free from blame or accusation and something about this worked to convince Chikatilo, finally, to talk. Within two hours, he confessed to the murders. The turnaround was incredible: Chikatilo admitted that his actual victim count was approximately 56, far greater than the 36 that he had initially been accused of, and even offered to lead the officers to several undiscovered bodies.

Chikatilo co-operated with the police in their subsequent investigations, recalling and even re-enacting his murders so as to best illustrate the final moments of his victims. 'I'm a mistake of nature. A mad beast,' he stated, during his confession, in which he admitted to killing an extraordinary number of people, drinking their blood and eating parts of their bodies. The extent of his recall for each and every murder was chilling. He was even able to give the detectives sketches of the crime scenes and illustrate the positions he had left the bodies lying in.

He recalled his attack on Tkachenko in 1981, for example, in which he had used his teeth to bite off one of the 17-year-old girl's nipples. 'At the moment of cutting her and seeing the body sliced open,' he said, 'I involuntarily ejaculated.' It was with such intimate and disturbing detail that he described each of the murders to the police. Sometimes he had behaved in the same way as a predator, studying his victims' routines and habits and learning how to lure them away or get them alone. At other times, his victims had simply been in the wrong place at the wrong time and his attack had been spontaneous and opportunistic.

Chikatilo described his usual method of killing, beginning with tying the hands of his victims with rope behind their backs. The subsequent stabbings were usually a frustrated, enraged response to his own impotence and failed attempts at raping his victims. He had quickly come to understand that he could not get aroused without violence: 'I had to see blood,' he said.

So he would proceed: with shallow, painful but not life-threatening stab wounds, then quickly moving on to inflicting 30 to 50 deeper cuts. Finally, he would gut his victims in a number of ways, learning in the course of his murderous career how to crouch next to his victims so as to avoid staining his clothing with their blood, which he demonstrated for the police with a mannequin. He claimed to have shaken with pleasure while drinking the blood of his victims, finding a raw and primal joy in the act. He also confessed that he would use his own teeth to rip off body parts, including tongues, lips and genitalia, which gave him an 'animal satisfaction'. Before discarding the bodies of his victims, he had, on occasion, chewed on the uteruses (which he described as 'pink and springy') and the testicles of some of the males. He never, however, entirely admitted to actually eating the body parts, though there were missing remains that the police were never able to find.

'The whole thing,' Chikatilo said, 'the cries, the blood, the agony – gave me relaxation and a certain pleasure.'

With this extensive confession, the police were well equipped to press ahead with the case against him. Chikatilo was formally charged on 30 November.

Trial and Sentence

On 20 August 1991, with the investigation and interrogations completed, Chikatilo was transferred from

Rostov-on-Don to the Serbsky Institute in Moscow. There, he underwent a psychiatric evaluation that lasted 60 days, carried out by a psychiatrist by the name of Dr Andrei Tkachenko. This evaluation was meant to ascertain whether Chikatilo was legally insane, or whether he was able to stand trial. Despite the fact that the psychiatrist found evidence of borderline personality disorder and sadistic features, Chikatilo appeared to know right from wrong. On 18 October, Tkachenko completed his evaluation and found the killer to be legally sane.

Details of Chikatilo's arrest and crimes were delivered in a press conference in December 1991. The media was both fascinated and disgusted by the killer and his crimes, with sensational headlines dominating the front pages of the local newspapers and a number of chilling names created for him. They often referred to Chikatilo as a 'maniac' and a 'cannibal', the latter a nickname that would have been particularly disturbing to the local people, who had grown up with tales of cannibalism in the famine of the earlier half of the century.

Chikatilo was brought to court for the beginning of his trial on 14 April 1992, which was when the media and the public were allowed their first glimpse of the killer. Chikatilo's hair had been shaved off, a standard procedure at the time to guard against the spread of lice, and this prompted the media to describe him as resembling a 'shaven-skulled demon'. People gathered in droves on the steps of the House of Justice to see the monster that had preyed upon the women and children for well over a decade.

Chikatilo's own wife was disgusted, confused and ashamed of the whole situation. She felt guilty for having had no idea what had been going on, which was reflective of Chikatilo's cold and calculating nature. He was able to commit his grisly murders, then return home and play the part of a loving husband and father, betraying no hints of his darker side and the terrible acts of violence he had indulged in. Feodosia said of Chikatilo, 'I could never imagine him being able to murder one person, let alone 53 . . . he could never hurt anyone.'

Feodosia visited her husband only once in prison, in order to get his authorization to access their savings. Chikatilo was unable to look his wife in the eye during her visit and said to her, 'If only I had listened to you . . . if only I had listened to your advice and got treatment.'

After receiving death threats, Feodosia was forced to change her name and move away from the area. She said afterwards to writer Peter Conradi, 'I crossed him out of my mind as if he never existed.'

Chikatilo's court case was presided over by Judge Leonid Akubzhanov. His defence lawyer was Marat Khabibulin and, for the majority of the hearing, the prosecutor was Nikolai Gerasimenko. Chikatilo was charged with 53 counts of murder and five charges of sexual assault, which he had committed during his teaching days. Throughout his trial, Chikatilo was kept in a large iron cage for his own protection, as the courtroom was filled with many family members of his alleged victims. The furious onlookers shouted at him as he entered and, to all appearances, were seeking any opportunity to exact their own revenge on the man who had killed and mutilated their children and loved ones. This meant that he was unable to sit near his lawyer and converse, as is traditional in most court cases.

It took the first two days of the trial for Judge

Akubzhanov to read out the charges against Chikatilo, describing each count individually and in detail, with victims ranging from the ages of nine to 45. Often, the family members of the deceased would be overcome with grief and begin to cry, or faint from hearing first-hand what their loved ones had been subjected to. Judge Akubzhanov explained the importance of the trial: 'Let this trial at least teach us something, so that this will never happen anytime or anywhere again.'

On 16 April, Chikatilo was given the opportunity to address the court. For two hours, he spoke about his life's misfortunes and how he was a victim of his own circumstances, blaming his upbringing, his parents and even his blood group at one point for what he had become. He stated that he was a man 'robbed' of his genitals and that he was ultimately driven to commit murder due to his lifelong struggle with his own sexual inadequacy and frustration. His murders were never planned, he explained. He was simply seized by an uncontrollable urge causing him to lose control. This speech did nothing to quell the hatred of those present in court and their anger toward him was almost palpable.

Throughout the trial, Chikatilo's behaviour was theatrical at worst and noncommittal at best. On occasion he would appear almost manic, talking nonsense and singing socialist anthems. At one point, he pulled down his trousers and exposed his penis to the court, shouting, 'Look at this useless thing. What do you think I could do with that?' He also requested that the trial be conducted in Ukrainian and stated that he was being targeted by the KGB, who were firing invisible rays at him. It was generally believed that this extreme, dramatic behaviour was a desperate bid to appear insane and therefore provoke a degree of sympathy[1]. At times, however, his cold-hearted nature shone through his manic displays. While discussing his search for victims, Chikatilo said, rather dispassionately, 'I did not need to look for them. Every step I took, they were there.'

The partiality of the judge was obvious and it was clear from a very early stage that Chikatilo would receive a guilty verdict. The judge would regularly overrule Chikatilo's lawyer, disparage Chikatilo and order him to shut his mouth. Khubibulin noticed that this hostility endured even when Chikatilo was attempting to be co-operative, which prompted him to protest against the judge's conduct, stating that he was unfit to preside. The assumption of innocence before being judged guilty was sorely lacking throughout the trial. The prosecutor, Gerasimenko, supported the defence, suggesting that the insults and lectures that had been directed at Chikatilo were inappropriate procedural violations. He supported the defence's move to have the judge replaced. Instead, Gerasimenko himself was replaced.

Closing arguments were delivered on 9 August, and the judge took two months to deliver his verdict, which was read on 15 October 1990. Unsurprisingly, Chikatilo was found guilty on 52 murder charges, and sentenced to death. When reading the sentence, the judge said: 'Taking into consideration the monstrous crimes [Chikatilo] committed, this court has no alternative but to impose the only sentence that he deserves. I therefore sentence him to death.'

---

1   If he had been found not guilty by reason of insanity, Chikatilo would have received a stay in a mental institution, rather than the death penalty.

People broke into applause upon hearing these words. Chikatilo, in fury, kicked a bench, causing it to fly to the other side of his cage. He shouted and protested but when he was allowed the opportunity to speak a few words, made no comment, no excuses for his behaviour and no apologies for the hundreds of lives he had devastated.

Although some people were content with the death sentence, others were dissatisfied with the legal execution, wishing to dole out the justice themselves. Some of the bereaved cried out, 'Give him to us. Let us deal with him,' as Chikatilo was led to his cell at Novocherkassk prison to await his execution. The judge responded: 'I understand your feelings and your inability to hold yourselves back. I understand. But we must have due process of law.'

Chikatilo and his lawyer attempted to appeal his sentence with the Russian Supreme Court on the grounds that his psychiatric evaluation had been biased, but his appeal was promptly rejected in 1993. His last appeal for clemency was rejected by President Boris Yeltsin on 4 January 1994. In some way, Chikatilo must have known the futility of his endeavours to appeal, stating, 'And now my brain should be taken apart piece by piece and examined, so there wouldn't be any others like me.' On 14 February, Chikatilo was taken to a soundproof room in Novocherkassk prison and, with a single shot to the head, put to death.

Discussion

Chikatilo was a uniquely terrifying serial killer. He carried out acts of murder so numerous and so barbarous that it is hard to imagine that he was also capable of leading a double life as a functional and normal member of society. He was, however, a husband, father, grandfather and friend to a great many people, none of whom suspected that the congenial man they knew had the capacity for such depravity. As a killer, he was able to emotionally compartmentalize and leave his murders behind when socializing with his family and friends. Once his crimes came to light, he was dramatically described by the press as a 'shaven-skulled demon' and had words like butcher, demon, monster and vampire used in association with him: there was a persistent effort to separate the vicious killer from the rest of humanity, to distance him as far as possible from the rest of us, using pseudonyms that suggested something foreign, inhuman or even supernatural. It is remarkable that for years before his capture, he had lived and walked among his fellow citizens and was utterly indistinguishable as somebody capable of such evil.

The fact that Andrei Chikatilo began his series of killings in his forties is worthy of note. Typically, serial killers take their first victim in their mid to late twenties. Chikatilo, however, was able to contain or manage his violent urges until later in life, only giving in to them aged 42. It is unclear what changed at this point to finally break him; the fact that he bought a house specifically in which to kill his victims certainly indicates a degree of premeditation, although he did not have a specific victim in mind. It is very likely that his lifelong struggle with his sexuality was a constant reminder of his very first satisfactory sexual experience, where he violently held down a struggling girl and achieved a long-desired sexual gratification. This cemented his association between sex and violence, and provided him with a specific fantasy that took hold of him over the years, becoming increasingly harder for him to resist enacting in real life.

Although Chikatilo was intelligent, he was not a commanding or authoritative man. His teaching career was a failure due to his inability to control his students and to command respect. His impotence also created a lack of control in his life. He went from one job to another and was frequently reprimanded for different infringements. The only time he ever felt powerful was when he had his victims at his mercy, with their hands tied behind their backs and unable to fight for their lives. When placing Chikatilo into a Holmes and DeBurger type, it is important to bear in mind that one of the driving forces behind his need to kill was the influence and power he held over his victims. With this in mind, Chikatilo seems to fit comfortably in the Power/Control type. With his knife, he elevated himself from an insignificant and powerless man into someone with a substantial degree of influence. As serial killer Ted Bundy once said, 'What greater power can one have than control over life and death?'

It was also only at this time, when witnessing his victims in pain or dying, that he was able to achieve sexual gratification. This was another primary motivation behind his murders and which characterizes him quite clearly as a Hedonistic Lust killer. Lust killers often stab and mutilate their victims, cutting them or removing their sexual organs. They also have a tendency to 'display' the bodies of their victims, placing corpses in certain positions that are generally derogatory or overtly sexual and humiliating. Although there is no recorded evidence of Chikatilo posing his victims, he certainly fits the other characteristics of a lust killer, such as removing his victim's sexual organs and chewing on them. He never openly admitted to consuming these body parts, although he did confess to drinking blood on occasion. Both of these acts are also associated with lust killing.

We can more specifically label him as an 'organized' killer, given the torture he carried out on his victims. Their lives were not brought to a quick and painless end: he admitted to inflicting shallow but painful cuts on his victims, to disembowelling several of them and ensuring that they suffered before they died. Organized killers are usually intelligent and educated, calculating and methodical. This is reflected in Chikatilo's behaviour: he kept track of the investigation against him and his murders were generally carefully executed, which is why he was able to get away with murder for so long. A period of killing as long as Chikatilo's is extremely uncommon. Organized killers also honour ritual, which is evident in the characteristic manner in which Chikatilo killed his victims, as well as in the fact that he nearly always found his victims in travel hubs. This was his 'comfort zone' and it was also convenient, given the fact that he so regularly used trains and buses for work. An organized killer will, as Chikatilo did, usually target strangers of a particular type that are easily controlled; in Chikatilo's case they were usually children, or other vulnerable members of society susceptible to his manipulation.

An organized killer is, furthermore, usually sociable, with friends and family, and will not stand out as being peculiar or off-putting. Finally, the organized killer will bring their own weapons with them, rather than utilizing whatever is at hand, as in Chikatilo's case with his knife and rope. Where Chikatilo does not fit the profile of a typical organized killer, however, is in the way he treated the bodies of his victims. He did not dispose of or hide them. If he did decide to bury them, they were typically not far from the surface, in a shallow and poorly dug grave. But usually, they were left out in the open in plain sight.

The fact that Chikatilo went on to kill so many people and that he took such delight in the murders makes him one of the most memorable and frightening serial killers to date. In the words of Jack Levin, professor of Criminology at Northeastern University in Boston: 'In the annals of crime, Andrei Chikatilo is undoubtedly one of the most sadistic killers ever to live. And he got away with murder for more than 12 years.'

It would be overly simplistic, however, for us to view Andrei Chikatilo as little more than a soulless monster – to neglect the conditions in which he was brought up and the environmental and medical factors that influenced his baser urges. Being born into poverty, raised in an environment of deprivation and forced to struggle with medical conditions – hydrocephalus, urinary incontinence and sexual impotence – that caused him embarrassing bodily dysfunctions culminated in psychological traumas that would remain with him for the rest of his life. Ultimately, of course, it was Chikatilo himself who made the decision to give in to his murderous desires and to take the lives of so many innocent people. With a mind that was perfectly capable of determining right from wrong, he sought no help and continued to prey upon the defenceless and vulnerable to satisfy his own needs. His actions were unforgivable and their impact profound. He is, nevertheless, a fascinating case study for anyone with an interest in crime, as he forces us to ask a very important question: to what extent is every criminal – or, indeed, every person, criminal or not – susceptible to the damaging impact of his or her environment? The answer to this question is all the more disturbing when we consider that any of us, placed in the wrong circumstances, could be capable of murder.

CHAPTER 15

Marcelo Costa De Andrade – The Vampire of Niterói

'He is like a wolf dressed in sheep's clothing. Look at him and you would never for a single second imagine what he is capable of doing with children.' Illana Casoy

Introduction

Brazilian murderer Marcelo Costa de Andrade is another example of a 20th-century serial killer who earned himself a monstrous moniker. Like many of the other killers discussed in this book, he had a tendency to target children and would ultimately be convicted of raping and killing 14 young boys. He earned himself the nickname of *'O Vampiro de Niterói'*, or 'The Vampire of Niterói' as a result of his sinister habit of drinking his victims' blood. Fortunately, for our purposes, a surplus of information exists regarding De Andrade's early years and crimes, as his notoriety as one of the most malevolent villains to come from Brazil meant that he was in high demand for interviews. The opportunity to enjoy the spotlight was something that De Andrade enjoyed.

The son of impoverished migrants, De Andrade was born in Rio de Janeiro on 2 January 1967 and grew up in the slum of Rocinha favela. Life for many people in the area was a struggle and this was certainly the case for De Andrade, whose family had very little money. There was rarely food on the table or running water. To add to this sad situation, many sources attest to the fact that, by the age of ten, De Andrade was beaten regularly by different members of his family, and was apparently also sexually molested by an older man. School attendance was a rare occurrence for him; when he did attend, he did not perform well and was bullied by his schoolmates. Instead of spending his time in classrooms, De Andrade roamed the streets, hustling and trying his best to bring in some money. Life was so bad for the young boy that aged ten he ran away from home for the first time, but came back to his family when he was unable to survive on his own.

By the age of 14, desperate to make a living, De Andrade entered into the world of prostitution and sold his body for money. Following a suicide attempt, he was reportedly sent to a reform school run by Funabem, a foundation for the welfare of minors. This chapter of his life was not to last long, however: he escaped after a few months and returned to making a living out of prostitution. By this time, it was becoming clear that De Andrade preferred male company and, at the age of 16, he began a serious, long-term relationship with an older man by the name of Antonio Batista Freire with whom he eventually moved in. This did nothing, however, to prevent him from attempting to commit his first sexual assault: at 17, he tried to force himself on his ten-year-old brother. Ten was to be the average age of the victims that De Andrade later targeted to kill.

A turning point in De Andrade's life came at the age of 23, when his relationship with Freire crumbled and he was thrown out of their home. With nowhere to go, he went to live with his mother and brother in the slums of Itaborai. He found a low-paying, menial job and developed a keen interest in religion. His mother reported incidences of his peculiar behaviour during this time, such as continually listening to tapes of his brother crying.

De Andrade became heavily involved with the Universal Church of the Kingdom of God (UCKG), to which he had been introduced by Freire at the age of 16. His devotion to this church continued throughout his criminal career and he would attend regularly for five-hour sessions, four days a week. The Church was a Pentecostal Christian denomination, founded in Rio de Janeiro in 1977, with a controversial reputation. In its short history it has received allegations of illicit activities, such as money laundering, corruption, witchcraft and promoting religious intolerance. The UCKG promoted a number of unusual doctrines, including that of the existence of evil spirits capable of possessing and controlling a human body – a belief that would later dominate the case of De Andrade. Interestingly, the Church also considered homosexuality to be a disease, although this did nothing to drive De Andrade away from his new-found faith. His beliefs, in fact, played a significant role in his psyche and he would later use religious sentiments as justification for his killings: to this day, he insists that he was possessed by the spirits of evil beings, who controlled him and forced him to kill, as they had a taste for children's blood.

Up to this time, De Andrade's behaviour invited little suspicion or concern. Despite his background and the fact that he had grown up in a troubled area, he was generally regarded as a good, harmless man, who had a gentle and childlike appearance and soft way of speaking.

His life was to continue in a relatively normal manner until De Andrade encountered a young transvestite, which triggered new and dangerous desires and behaviour. In an interview he gave to *Epoca* magazine in 2003, De Andrade said:

> 'One day when I was walking I met a 14-year-old boy. A transvestite. He propositioned me to go to a hotel with him. I had sex with him and kissed him on the mouth. I paid him 50 reals. I never got to see him again. But it sparked the desire for new boys. As I didn't find another one like him I ended up forcing myself on others.'

In April 1991, at the age of 24 and with this desire propelling him, De Andrade began his series of murders that would stun the country and leave 14 families reeling from loss.

Crimes

Between the years 1980 and 2010, there were an incredible one million homicides in Brazil, which may be attributed to the increased percentage of young men in the population, together with increases in drug use and the availability of firearms. As De Andrade had a preference for disadvantaged young boys, the streets of Brazil at the time were the perfect place for him to strike undetected. He had the advantage of having spent most of his life on the streets and knew them intimately. He knew how to blend in, and also knew the locations of secluded, abandoned sites to which he would lure his victims with the promise of sweets or money. His appearance and manner – that of a trustworthy, gentle and innocent man – was of great benefit to him during this time. He was someone that even the cautious children of Rio would have felt relatively safe to be with.

De Andrade's 14 victims were between the ages of six and 13, all murdered in the space of nine short months. He targeted boys that he found particularly attractive and was constantly on the search for those who had 'smooth legs, and a pretty face and body'. In an interview, De Andrade once explained his twisted rationale for selecting young boys as his victims:

'They are better looking and have soft skin. And the priest [of the UCKG church he frequented] said that children automatically go to Heaven if they die before they're 13. So I know I did them a favour by sending them to Heaven.'

He also explained, in a 2001 interview with forensic psychiatrist Dr Helen Morrison, that 'the children have bad lives here . . . if they are children when they die, they go to . . . a better place'. In De Andrade's mind, he was performing a humanitarian act by killing them, whereupon they would be saved from the misery of their poverty-stricken lives and able to spend eternity in paradise. This was also, in part, the reason why he never targeted girls, whom he believed did not go to heaven.

However, De Andrade's perverse sense of benevolence was inconsistent: during the same interview with Morrison, he discussed the murder of 11-year-old Odair Jose Muniz, whom he had met near a football pitch and subsequently raped and killed. He returned to Muniz's body hours after the murder with a machete he had borrowed from his mother ('to cut some bananas' he had told her) and chopped off the boy's head. Morrison asked why he had done this, to which De Andrade replied that he had done it so that the other children would make fun of Muniz, because he would not have a head.

De Andrade recalled his first murder without much clarity:

'The sadism went to my head. I ended up killing some of them . . . I do not remember their faces very well. The first one I caught was in Niterói. I only know that his name was Anderson. I offered him money. I said he could help me light candles in the church. I took him to a deserted place. When we got there I raped him. I then strangled him with his own shirt. I returned to the spot where the body was three times, to see if anyone had discovered anything. Nobody ever suspected me.'

This boy was eventually identified as Anderson Gomes Goulart, aged 11. In addition to raping and killing the boy, De Andrade cut open his skull to drink his blood.

De Andrade satisfied his sexual urges by raping his victims before killing them, usually by strangling them to death. On occasion, he also indulged in necrophilia with their bodies. Sometimes he took to decapitating his victims or crushing their skulls. He claimed to have drunk the blood of two of his victims, cracking their heads wide open and pouring the blood into a bowl to drink. He did this, he stated, as he thought that doing so would make him as young and beautiful as they were. He buried the bodies of the boys in shallow graves, after he had removed their trousers to keep as trophies.

De Andrade was evidently mentally unstable and regularly did things that would lead to his being detected and arrested. His spate of violence came to an end with one final and terrible murder, which took place on 11 December 1991. It was on this day that De Andrade came across brothers Ivan, aged six, and Altair Medeiros de Abreu, aged ten, young beggars looking for food or money to help support their mother, Zeli, a widowed mother of five.

De Andrade encountered the brothers at the Niterói bus terminal. He offered them money in exchange for them to accompany him to St George's, a local church, where he needed help lighting candles for a saint. The boys agreed, but once the three were away from public and prying eyes, De Andrade dragged them to a deserted beach on the outskirts of the Barreto Viaduct, where he tried to kiss Altair. When Altair attempted to escape, De Andrade grabbed him and threw him to the ground. The killer then focused his attentions on the younger brother. Once De Andrade began to strangle Ivan, Altair became so terrified that he was, by his own account, incapable of escaping.

'I was so paralysed by fear I could not run away,' Altair later said. 'I watched in horror, tears streaming down my cheeks, as he killed and then raped my brother.' Afterwards, De Andrade approached Altair with wide-open arms, saying, 'I have sent Ivan to Heaven. I love you.' Altair was forced to spend the night in terror with the man who had just murdered his brother, sleeping among bushes behind a petrol station.

The next morning, De Andrade took Altair to the tourist district of Copacabana, where the killer was employed handing out flyers for a jewellery shop. When they arrived, however, they found the office closed. Altair was able to make his escape here, hitchhiking home to the safety of his family. Initially, Altair's terror of De Andrade prevented him from being honest with his family about the incidents of the night before. He told his parents that he had simply 'lost' his brother.

Around the same time, a local fisherman discovered Ivan's body on the beach and immediately called the police. Homicide investigator Carlos Augusto Ponce de Leon arrived at the scene and his initial assumption was death by drowning. It was thought that the child had fallen asleep on the beach, been overcome by the rising tide and eventually drowned. This theory, however, was promptly discarded as soon as the investigators saw that the boy had his hands tucked neatly into his trouser pockets, which is not typical of a drowning victim. De Andrade, as we know, had a habit of revisiting his crime scenes, where he left offerings such as food for his victims. In this instance, he had returned to place Ivan's hands in his pockets, so that rats would not chew on his fingers.

An autopsy was performed on the little boy's body, which concluded that he had suffered death due to strangulation and that he had also been raped. Dr Antonio

Pedro Bocayuva, a forensic psychiatrist, spoke to the authorities about the case and offered his opinion that the modus operandi of this murder appeared to mirror that of several other minors who had been killed in recent months.

It was not until two days after Altair's safe return home that, following some careful coaxing by his sister, he revealed the truth about what had happened. His family went to the police with the information and a warrant was issued for De Andrade's arrest. The killer was apprehended at work on 18 December 1991. The 25-year-old reacted calmly to his arrest, reportedly saying to the police officers, 'I thought you would come yesterday.'

At the police station, De Andrade initially admitted only to the murder of Ivan. It was not until two months later, when De Andrade's mother was brought in for questioning, that the real truth came out. She reluctantly admitted that De Andrade had, in the past, asked to borrow a machete from her and had returned it covered with blood. It was only then that De Andrade confessed to his 13 other murders, bringing his victim count to 14. As proof of his crimes, he was able to lead the police to various burial sites in which the bodies of his victims were found.

Trial and Sentence

De Andrade's arrest prompted a great deal of media attention and he was not one to shy away from inquisitive reporters. He boldly told one that 'the soul and spirit of these children [will] go to live with God in Heaven'. Following a psychological evaluation, De Andrade was declared insane on 26 April 1993 and incapable of truly understanding the nature of his acts. For this reason, he was judged not guilty by reason of insanity. In June, a judge placed De Andrade in the Heitor Carrilho Psychiatric Hospital in Rio.

After nearly four years at this first institution, a breach in security led to De Andrade escaping on 24 January 1997. A guard accidentally left a door unlocked and the killer was able to simply slip out the front door. The media went into a frenzy, and for 12 agonizing days the public waited to see if any children would go missing. Thankfully, there were no reports of dead or missing children during this time and, on 5 February, the police were eventually able to track De Andrade down in Guaraciaba do Norte, a town in the north-eastern state of Ceara. He was clutching a bible and claimed to be on his way to the Holy Land. He told the police that, through killing his previous victims, he was now purified and completely lacked the urge to murder.

De Andrade is currently permanently detained in the high-security wing of Henrique Roxo Hospital, where he continues to insist that he is an evangelist. He states that he hopes one day to return to society where, with the love of a 'good woman' and God's light, he will be able to live an honest and lawful life.

Although De Andrade was once in great demand for interviews, his fame has dwindled over the decades and he now lives a lonely existence. The only relative to visit him is his mother, who dutifully comes once a year. De Andrade continues to show a complete lack of remorse for his crimes, which he maintains were committed for the right reasons.

Discussion

This religious side of De Andrade's character is something that Illana Casoy, a respected expert on the subject of Brazilian serial killers, does not believe in. She was able to meet and study De Andrade many times and believes his faith to be a farce. In his book *The World's Most Bizarre Murders*, James Marrison quotes her as saying:

'De Andrade is not a religious guy and he never was. He just heard a priest who said that a child under 13 years old goes straight to paradise if he dies without sins. He believed it literally.'

Following her talks with De Andrade, Casoy also asserted that his mind was remarkably naïve and childlike, stating that:

'His mind is more or less the same as that of a 12-year-old . . . He dreams of going to Disneyland or Moscow, winning a million dollars and having plastic surgery on his face so he would never be recognized by anyone. He never feels bad about what he did, just worried that it screwed up his life. He wasn't happy telling me what he did, but he wasn't exactly all that sad about it either. It's something that doesn't make any difference to him either way. He believes he was utterly tender to the children he killed and saved them from hell. He doesn't know it was really wrong or awful. He told me all of it as if he was talking about simple everyday things, but with specific and cruel details, and the tone in his voice never changed – it never changed for a single moment.'

Although this lack of remorse is often a calling card for a psychopath, there are subtleties in De Andrade's case that preclude him being classified as one. If we believe his assertions that he killed to save his victims from the depravity of their lives and to ensure their place in heaven, then he was, in fact, acting out of a kind of empathy and kindness – even a type of, in his own words, 'love'. If this is the case, his actions and their motivation could not be seen as those of a psychopath.

De Andrade talks tenderly of the boys he killed, but his claim that he acted out of goodwill does not entirely match his actions. If he wanted merely to send his victims to heaven, there would have been no need to sexually gratify himself with their corpses. This was an act of pure carnal desire on his part and one that is difficult to reconcile with his supposed religious morals and standards.

Casoy did, however, believe in De Andrade's insanity. She went on to state that, 'by meeting him I could really understand what it is to be an insane person. De Andrade has this mental illness and you get the feeling he doesn't know the true scale of what he did, the difference between right and wrong. There is no cure. Nobody knows what treatment he should receive, so they give him drugs to keep him under control, and that's about all they can do.'

The fact that De Andrade continued his work routine and daily life following the escape of Altair – who could not only identify him but also lead the police to his place of work – is further testament to his irrationality. The medical and legal professionals involved in De Andrade's case agreed: following his incarceration, De Andrade was subjected to annual psychological evaluations – and each year he was declared to be legally insane.

Casoy added that her experience in meeting with the killer was singular, terrifying and one she is never likely to forget: 'Meeting someone like Marcelo Costa de Andrade is very hard for any human being . . . He is like a wolf dressed in sheep's clothing. Look at him and you would never for a single second imagine what he is capable of doing with children. As soon as he told me that he took the shorts off every child he killed and kept them as trophies he asked me to bring him a gift – a pair of new shorts. I'd never give them to him. I hope he stays in the lunatic asylum for his entire life.'

It is tricky to place De Andrade within the Holmes and DeBurger typology: there was a definite sexual aspect to De Andrade's crimes, which places him in the Hedonistic category, specifically as a Lust killer.

The element of mental instability, however, certainly raises the question of whether he also belongs in the Visionary category. While he did not report psychotic symptoms of hearing voices or seeing visions directing him to kill, his religious beliefs might be considered to be delusions arising from psychosis. It is also possible, however, that his dominant belief that he was sending innocent boys under the age of 13 to heaven by killing them was an 'overvalued idea'. P.J. McKenna, in an article published in the *British Journal of Psychiatry* in 1984, described this overvalued idea in psychiatry as 'a solitary, abnormal belief that is neither delusional nor obsessional in nature, but which is preoccupying to the extent of dominating the sufferer's life'. *The Diagnostic and Statistical*

Manual of Mental Disorders (5th edition) (DSM-5) adds that the belief in an overvalued idea is held with less intensity than in a delusion. Insight is maintained in an overvalued idea, albeit poorly or erratically, which is inconsistent with psychosis, making it even harder to label De Andrade as a Visionary killer.

The Vampire of Niterói is a complicated killer and one whose story throws up many conflicting emotions. The lives lost in this case are an unequivocal tragedy. A rational, moral person might justifiably judge De Andrade and his actions as pure evil. To do this, however, would be to disregard his distorted beliefs and psychological issues – his entire inner world – and troubled childhood. Evil is not born in a vacuum; in fact, it is probably fair to say that evil is not born at all, but made. Multiple traumas compounded to turn a normal, innocent child into a remorseless killer whose name provokes fear to this day.

Earlier intervention and help given to many of the killers examined in this book may have prevented or put an earlier end to a series of terrible and senseless murders: in most cases, as in this one, it is society that ultimately pays the price.

CHAPTER 16

Jack Owen Spillman III – The Werewolf Butcher

'Mr. Spillman will never be on the streets again. We've guaranteed that.'

Rick Weber,
Okanogan County Prosecutor

Introduction

Jack Owen Spillman III is a fairly recent serial killer about whom relatively little information exists in criminological literature. This frustrating lack of information is strange, considering the media's insatiable interest in the darkest of criminals, but years after his incarceration, almost nothing has surfaced regarding Spillman, his psychology or his upbringing. His crimes, however, were so remarkably violent and terrifying that they are likely to never be forgotten. Compared to the majority of serial killers portrayed within this book, Spillman killed very few, but the manner in which he murdered, his blatant premeditation and the terrible way he handled his victims' bodies truly earns him his place among these real-life monsters.

Spillman differs from most other supernatural serial killers in that his moniker is derived not from public opinion of his crimes or the media, but rather from his own perception of his inner nature and instincts. Spillman identified with the vicious nature of the mythical werewolf and strived to emulate it as authentically as possible, stalking his helpless prey until he was able to attack and kill them. This, together with his lust for blood and debauched sexual desires, resulted in the brutal murders of three innocent female victims on two separate occasions: a ten-year-old girl on the first and a 48-year-old woman and her 15-year-old teenage daughter on the second.

Spillman was born on 30 August 1969 in Spokane, Washington. There is not much information available about his youth and adolescence, but what we do know suggests that his formative years were far from stable and had an inconsistent foundation. His mother, Judy, was married four times and had four children. There was some confusion regarding their paternity and Spillman and his siblings themselves were never entirely sure who their fathers were.

Spillman was not known to have been a very intelligent child, nor did he try to achieve academic excellence in any way. In fact, he dropped out of high school in the ninth grade. At the age of 16 years Spillman took a test using the Wechsler Adult Intelligence Scale – which measures intelligence for older adolescents and adults – he scored an 87 for performance IQ (low average) and a 74 for verbal IQ (borderline mental functioning). He also took the Peabody Individual Achievement Test, a test of academic progress, used with kindergarten to high school students to see how they compare individually to their peers in five areas: general knowledge, maths, reading recognition, reading comprehension and spelling. The results revealed that his highest performance level was fifth grade, with the average fifth grader being ten years of age.

Spillman remained in Spokane after high school, living in a trailer and working as a butcher. He was able to use the knowledge and techniques learned from this trade while committing his murders. His time as a butcher taught him exactly where and how to cut into a body with precision to achieve the effect he desired.

Even before he began his short series of violent murders, Spillman had built up a significant repertoire of crimes. His first criminal charge was of theft in November 1982. He later went on to be arrested for and convicted of indecent exposure, indecent liberties, illegal consumption of alcohol, malicious mischief, burglary and assault. In 1993, Spillman and a friend were arrested on rape allegations, after the victim escaped and named them as the men who had attacked her. The crime allegedly occurred after the three had met at a downtown bar in King County. The woman accepted a lift home with the two men and later described to the police how Spillman had held her down while his 26-year-old roommate had raped her. Before Spillman could do the same, however, she had been able to escape and report the attack. Charges were dropped against both men at a later date.

It was during a stay at Washington State Penitentiary at Walla Walla from July 1993 to February 1994 that Spillman would regularly discuss his innermost fantasies with his cellmate, Mark Miller. Miller told how Spillman had talked of wanting to be the world's greatest serial killer and described some debauched sexual fantasies that he would ultimately, unbeknownst to Miller, carry out. He read extensively about serial killers and police forensics, explaining that when he killed, he would take specific precautions against leaving behind incriminating evidence. He would do this by studying other killers and their crimes and analysing how they were caught and the mistakes they made that led to their discovery. He also mentioned what he believed to be an affinity with werewolves, claiming that he often thought of himself as one, carefully selecting and hunting down his victims over time. He often imagined torturing young girls in a cave and cutting out their hearts before consuming them.

Crimes

The gruesome murders that would see Spillman arrested and imprisoned took place on 13 April 1995 in East Wenatchee, Douglas County. The victims were Amanda 'Mandy' Huffman and her mother, Rita Huffman. The crime was not discovered until the following day when Rita's eldest daughter, finding that neither her mother nor her sister were answering the telephone, went to their house to check on them.

She tried the front door and found it locked, with nobody coming to the door to let her in. Knowing that the back door was usually left unlocked, she went around the house and let herself inside. She was immediately confronted with the ghastly murder scene of her mother and younger sister. She first discovered her sister, Amanda Huffman (only 15 years old at the time of her death) lying on her mother's bed, naked, posed in a sexually suggestive position and viciously mutilated. As she ran from the scene, she saw her mother, Rita Huffman, 48 years old, also naked, posed suggestively on the sofa and equally badly mutilated. In a state of shock and terror, she immediately went to the neighbours for help, who promptly contacted the police.

It was instantly clear to the police that the women in the house had been sexually violated and murdered. What was also evident was that the murderer had taken great delight in the act: the murders had been so violent and savage that they seemed more reflective of the actions of a wild animal than a human being. Furthermore, the attention paid to the bodies post-mortem and the deliberate and degrading display of them clearly indicated that the murderer had taken some time and pleasure in the act of killing them and then toying with their corpses. The time frame of the murders revealed that the killer had remained in the house for several hours after his victims' deaths, presumably to linger over and pose the bodies, indicating behaviour that can be very accurately described as psychopathic sexual sadism.

The resulting investigation revealed that Rita had been killed first, indicating that the teenaged Amanda had quite likely been held hostage for a short time. Rita had been stabbed a total of 31 times, with wounds to her upper chest, lower neck, left leg and back. These injuries had severed major blood vessels, resulting in a quick loss of consciousness and massive internal and external bleeding. She had also sustained wounds to her arms and hands consistent with typical signs of defensive behaviour: Rita had, most likely, attempted to fight off her attacker and had been well aware of what was happening to her. She had been stripped and terribly sexually mutilated: the killer had removed her breasts and eviscerated her genitalia, which had been removed and placed in her mouth. She had been sliced heavily from her vaginal area to the middle of her chest, exposing her internal organs. She was posed with her arms by her sides and legs spread wide.

Following the murder of Rita Huffman, the murderer had set his sights on her daughter. Evidence suggests that Amanda had been killed with a blow to the head. Her official cause of death, which had been in all likelihood swift, was that she had suffered 'massive cranial and cerebral trauma secondary to blunt impact on the left side of the head'. In addition, she had received sixteen stab wounds to her neck and had been viciously raped. Skin from her genital area had been sliced off and placed on her face. Also, an aluminium baseball bat had been inserted 12 to 16 inches into her vaginal canal. Amanda's bed sheets had been removed, most likely in an attempt by the killer to rid the crime scene of incriminating DNA.

The last time Rita's elder daughter had been in contact with her mother was at approximately 10pm the previous night. The post-mortem revealed that the time of death for the two victims was likely to have been between 11pm and 3am. This timeline was further narrowed down by a smashed watch on Amanda's wrist, which had stopped at 11.35pm, suggesting that a struggle had very likely occurred at that time.

There were no signs of forced entry into the house. This usually leads police to believe that the killer was acquainted with the victim and had been invited in; in this case, however, it was thought, quite rightly, to have been an indication that the killer had been watching the two women and knew that it was a habit for them to leave their rear door unlocked. Rita's boyfriend – who had been in a relationship with her for quite some time, though the couple did not live together – was questioned in order to determine his whereabouts at the time of the murders; he had an airtight alibi that testified to his innocence.

Incident reports from the night of the double murder indicated that, at about 2am, a man by the name of Jack Owen Spillman, a butcher who had lived in Wenatchee for approximately a month prior to the killings, had been arrested by a patrol officer in the car park of a Veterans of Foreign Wars (VFW) hall not far from the scene of the crime. He had been driving a black Chevy pickup truck with large tyres and a roll bar. Spillman had initially been arrested under suspicion of burglary. When the officer had approached him, he had raised his hands in surrender even before being told what he was being arrested for. Though his behaviour had been suspicious, there had not been sufficient evidence to detain him and he had been simply identified and released. It was only afterwards that the police looked into his criminal history and learned about his numerous past offences. They discovered that, prior to the Huffman murders, he had been the prime suspect in the disappearance and murder of a ten-year-old girl, Penny Davis, the daughter of a woman he had lived with, and that the case had never been solved. Further evidence also surfaced of his violent tendencies in the form of the torture and mutilation of animals: six months after Penny Davis's murder, Spillman had reportedly broken into another apartment home, mutilating a family's pet hamster and covering a child's room in its blood.

When the car park of the VFW hall was searched following Spillman's arrest, detectives discovered a 30 cm (12 in) knife covered in blood, concealed at the bottom of a dustbin. This particular knife appeared to match a three-piece knife set that had been found in the victims' home, from which one was missing. With this suspicious piece of evidence, in addition to his extensive criminal history, Spillman was placed under police surveillance for a week while the knife was sent for forensic tests.

The surveillance team stationed themselves outside Spillman's residence. On one occasion they saw him throwing an item into the dumpster outside his home. Chief Deputy Robin Wagg instructed waste management to pick up and search the dumpster and found that the discarded item was a blood-stained ski mask, which was particularly stained around the mouth area. Later, investigators were to learn that the stain around the mouth had resulted from Spillman having pressed his mouth to Amanda's wounds to drink her blood.

Following the murders, witnesses came forward to report a suspicious Chevy pickup that had been seen around the Huffman's neighbourhood and, according to Amanda's softball coach, outside Amanda's softball team's practice field. It had also been seen near the victims' home on the night of the murder. According to one woman who lived near the victims, she had seen the truck in the area the week prior to the murders and the man inside the truck had stopped her to ask if she was married and had a daughter.

It would come to light that 15-year-old Amanda had been Spillman's intended victim and Spillman had been stalking her for months, getting to know her routine, people with whom she spent time and the places she frequented. He had not intended for Rita to be a victim, but had been quite willing to make her one when the opportunity had arisen.

After obtaining a search warrant, the authorities investigated Spillman's truck and his residence. They found sufficient evidence to implicate him as a suspect. On the front seat of his truck, the detectives found the bloody gloves that he had worn when he had attacked the women. A surgical gown found in Spillman's possession matched fibres discovered at the crime scene: in an unsuccessful attempt to cover his tracks and minimize the presence of his DNA in the house, Spillman had worn the gown during the attack, and shaved off his bodily hair. As the crowning piece of evidence, the test results from the knife and the ski mask indicated that the blood found on them was a match with that of the victims.

Spillman was arrested on 20 April 1995. Immediately, the suspect invoked the Miranda warning and remained silent as the police questioned him, refusing to make a statement or co-operate. As such, he was held without bail in the Chelan-Douglas County Regional Jail. Spillman's girlfriend, who had been unaware of his crimes and criminal impulses, was questioned about his whereabouts on the night of the murders, but was unable to provide an alibi. Instead, her account was only more incriminating: she claimed that he had gone out for a drive at about 11pm and did not return until about 2am.

In the face of such overwhelming evidence and without an adequate alibi, Spillman ultimately agreed to talk.

Trial and Sentence

Spillman's trial for the Huffman murders had been arranged for August 1996. He understood the gravity of his crimes, the strong circumstantial evidence against him and that the prosecutors intended to seek the death penalty for him. He also knew that premeditation would not be difficult to prove in this case, as witnesses would testify to having seen him follow Amanda, and his former cellmate would attest to the fact that even years ago, Spillman had discussed his fantasies of torturing young girls, holding them hostage and cutting out their hearts. He was aware, furthermore, that if he were to plead guilty without trial, he would be likely to receive a more lenient sentence and avoid capital punishment.

As such, on 29 April 1996, Spillman pleaded guilty to three counts of aggravated murder. The third murder that Spillman confessed and pleaded guilty to was that of Penny Davis. She had been found dead in March 1995. Spillman had been a prime suspect for her murder, but there had been insufficient evidence to press charges against him at the time and the case had never been closed.

The murder of the ten-year old girl had occurred in Tonasket, Okanogan County in September 1994. At the time, she had been reported missing by her mother, who had been in a relationship with Spillman and lived with him. Following Penny's disappearance, Spillman had joined the search party organized for the little girl and pretended to take part in it. As soon as her body was discovered in March 1995, however, he had left the area. Her body, which had been found in a shallow grave 19 km

(12 miles) from her home, had also been mutilated and positioned in a sexually suggestive manner, in a strikingly similar way to Amanda's.

During questioning, Spillman expressed dissatisfaction about his experience with Penny, lamenting the fact that she had died too soon during his torture of her, when he had accidentally cut too deeply into her neck. He also claimed that, after burying her in the woods, he would occasionally return to her burial site where he would dig up her body and commit necrophilia with it.

Spillman waived his right to a jury trial in favour of a special sentencing proceeding. No evidence was introduced in the case and there was no defence. His defence counsel at the time claimed that if the case had gone to court, their best legal course of action would have been to attempt to present evidence of an alibi – which would, in all likelihood, have been flimsy at best. On the same day he entered his guilty plea, Superior Court Judge Carol Wardell sentenced him to life in prison without possibility of parole for the murder of Rita Huffman, 70 years for the murder of Mandy Huffman and 45 years and 6 months for the murder of Penny Davis. Of the sentence, Douglas County Prosecutor Steve Clem stated that, 'For the law-en-forcement officers, for the families, for the prosecutors, we all feel good about it.'

Spillman was sent to Washington State Penitentiary, where he is still a resident at the time of writing.

Discussion

The case of Spillman brings up many interesting aspects of the literature on serial killers. A history of animal abuse, for example, is something that has been prolifically researched in relation to serial killers since the 1970s, and is commonly regarded as one of the first warning signs of delinquency or violent, criminal behaviour. It is a history that is shared by many serial killers, a number of whom are examined in this book.

Another curious incident in Spillman's story occurred when he joined the search for Penny Davis after her murder. His actions may have seemed strange but it is, in fact, not uncommon for a killer to involve themselves in a manhunt for a perpetrator or search for their victim. Some assert that it results in a 'psychological high': the culprit is directly intervening in a police investigation, becoming intimately acquainted with its progress and aware of all the details that the police are lacking, which can give the perpetrator a sense of power and superiority. It also gives the perpetrator a practical way of monitoring and keeping up to date with the investigation. Discussing serial killers who hide their murderous impulses and maintain a façade of normalcy to their friends, family and society at large, Dr Michael Stone, professor of clinical psychiatry at the Columbia College of Physicians and Surgeons and host of *Most Evil*, an American forensics television series on murderers and homicides, has said that, 'in a way, we also become their victims, ensnared in their schemes, because it forces each of us to question the people we trust in our own community'.

Spillman's case, though horrifying, is also fascinating in terms of the sheer number of criminological categories he fits into so well. He has been described as a psychopathic sexual sadist, an organized offender and a Lust killer. More detail and information regarding his formative years would be greatly beneficial in understanding the evolution of his violent thoughts and his criminal behaviour, but simply by judging his actions and crimes, we are able to deduce and learn a great deal about the 'Werewolf Butcher'.

Spillman is classified as an 'organized offender', which is unusual as most organized offenders typically have an IQ that is classed as average or above average. Murderers who are in this category are, as the name suggests, highly organized and usually like to have the details of their crimes thought out and carefully planned to the best of their ability before the act takes place. They are extremely methodical and controlled, leaving very little to chance. Spillman took his time in committing his murders, patiently observing his victims, planning their murders and determining the probability and risk of getting caught. As his former cell mate attested, Spillman even conducted research into forensic science and other serial killers, voraciously reading about their lives and crimes. His knowledge of police forensics was such that he took pains to cover his tracks – by wearing a surgical gown which covered most of his body, shaving his bodily hair and attempting to hide the knife he used to carve up his victims – although, ultimately, his attempts were insufficient and there still remained more than enough evidence at the scene and at his own home to indicate his involvement. Further evidence of his premeditation can be found in the fact that he thought ahead and brought his own weapon – an aluminium baseball bat – with him to the crime scene.

With the information gained from studying Spillman and his crimes, it is relatively easy, using the Holmes and

DeBurger typology, to sort him into the Hedonistic type, specifically as a Hedonistic Lust killer. The Lust type of murderer kills with the expectation of achieving sexual satisfaction, which can occur either through sexual activity with the victim or by mutilating the victim's sexual organs. In Spillman's case, unfortunately, the victims were subjected to both. When mutilation is involved, it usually occurs post-mortem and may involve actual removal of the genitalia, as occurred in this case. Spillman very much epitomizes the Lust killer, who typically removes clothing from the body of the victim, poses the bodies in sexual positions and occasionally inserts objects into the victim's body. Lust killers also occasionally eat their victim's flesh or drink their blood, as Spillman did, all with the aim of sexual gratification. He had nothing else to gain from these murders; committing them appealed to some primal impulses that he compared to the savage predatory instincts of the violent, mythical werewolf.

Lust killers, furthermore, are typically male, have an ideal victim type (in Spillman's case, young girls) and stalk their victims before taking action. They characteristically have one or more fantasies in their minds that they are seeking to enact in reality. These fantasies usually grow and mutate over time – meaning the killer is never, and will never be, satisfied – and usually become increasingly violent and dramatic. Had he not been caught when he was, evidence suggests that, as a Lust killer, Spillman would likely have gone on to commit more crimes of a similar or increasingly sexual and disturbing nature; we have no way of knowing the extent to which his desires would have pushed him.

Jack Owen Spillman III was a killer whose crimes were clearly motivated by lust and sexual sadism. His victims were innocent girls and women who had done nothing to provoke his savage treatment of them, but whom he nonetheless stalked, mercilessly preyed upon and ultimately killed, leaving their bodies in a state of extreme indignity. That he was apprehended and imprisoned for life, preventing what would almost certainly have been further sexual assaults and murders, while protecting society at large from his murderous impulses, can be but little comfort to the friends and family of those who lost their lives in such a terrible way at his hands.

Conclusion

'In a way, we also become their victims ensnared in their schemes, because it forces each of us to question the people we trust in our own community.'   Dr Michael Stone,
Professor of Clinical Psychiatry,
Columbia College of Physicians and Surgeons

Throughout this book, the stories of a number of terrifying serial killers have been explored. Examining their crimes, the motivations behind them and the psychological factors at play is a process that is both disturbing and fascinating. These murderous men and women and the victims whose lives they so cruelly stole are not likely to ever be forgotten. There are many people throughout history who have left an unfavourable mark on the world and, although it is tempting to forget these individuals ever existed, in the long run it does society at large a disservice. After all, as Edmund Burke once said, 'Those who don't know history are doomed to repeat it.' If, by delving into the mind of a serial killer we can prevent similar recurrences in the future and develop our collective understanding of violent criminal behaviour and psychology, it is worth the study.

Superstition has played a significant role in many of the cases discussed, particularly the older ones. The stories of the Werewolves of Poligny, Gilles Garnier and Peter Stumpp, for example, would have played out very differently had there not been an institutionalized belief in the existence of werewolves at the time in which they lived. The infamy of Elizabeth Báthory, 'The Blood Countess', might not have been as pronounced as it was had she too not lived in a period when rumours of her supernatural associations were more likely to be believed.

Society has evolved since then. Superstition and an attraction to and fear of supernatural lore, however, continues to preoccupy our individual and collective psyches – Báthory continues to plague popular culture, appearing in numerous recent works of horror fiction as a vampiric villain. The jurors in the case of Richard Ramirez, 'The Night Stalker', were frightened beyond logic that he had somehow orchestrated the death of one among them from within prison, via his demonic minions. The victims of the confidence scams of Adrian Lim, 'The Toa Payoh Ritual Murderer', sought his professional advice as a medium due to their belief in his occult powers. There is a time-honoured and deeply entrenched emotional connection to the supernatural that is pervasive in our psychology, which we have historically turned to in order to explain phenomena beyond our comprehension. The actions of such twisted and depraved serial killers as the ones discussed here are certainly to be counted among such inexplicable phenomena and our habit of applying monstrous labels to these killers is, perhaps, a tribute to this connection.

There are some serial killers that have not been discussed in this book that we would have liked to include. One such example is Béla Kiss, also known as 'The Vampire of Cinkota'. Kiss was a Hungarian, born in approximately 1877, who eventually claimed the lives of 26 victims, including his wife and her lover. Each of his victim's bodies was found naked, pickled in a barrel filled with wood alcohol. A few were found with wounds in their neck, and it was assumed that Kiss had drunk the blood of his victims, earning him his vampire pseudonym. He was never caught or brought to justice. His case is a fascinating one, but there is little information available about his childhood, and a great deal of inconsistency between the different accounts of his crimes. As was the case with Báthory, people have had a tendency to fill the gaps in the information about his life and crimes with conjecture, which makes an honest, accurate retelling challenging. Two different men, for example, have been credited with fronting the investigation against Kiss. Different sources place him in different places of residence and three varying accounts exist of how his victims were discovered. Despite the fact that he is a relatively recent killer, his murders are already so shrouded in mystery that he and his victims may, one day, come to be thought of as an urban legend too strange to be true.

Another criminal we might have examined was John Brennan Crutchley, an American man suspected of murdering more than 30 women in the 1970s and 1980s. He earned the name of 'The Vampire Rapist' due to the fact that, as he sexually assaulted his victims, he would drain their blood before drinking it. John Crutchley is not included in this book as he was never formally convicted of his killings, but like Peter Kürten, 'The Vampire of Dusseldorf', and Richard Trenton Chase, 'The Vampire of Sacramento', he is nonetheless a striking example of the insatiable desire some people have for blood. In their case, bloodlust is a term that is more literal than figurative.

Some obvious patterns or themes emerge which link the serial killers discussed in this book, even ones from disparate time periods and geographical locations. Some of them, for example, suffered head injuries as children, which have been shown in neurological studies to correlate with the subsequent development of aggressive behaviour. Many of them suffered problems with sexual dysfunction or impotence during their formative years and their murders subsequently demonstrated a great deal of sexual frustration and sexual violence. A good number of them were struggling with mental illness of various forms, whether or not they went on to be judged as legally insane. They very often had unfortunate, even traumatizing, childhoods.

It is easy to suggest that, regardless of circumstance or upbringing, these killers still had a choice in determining their actions and behaviour, as we all do our own. Once one gains a deeper understanding of their stories, however, a very human instinct surfaces to also feel a degree of sympathy for them – not, perhaps, for the ruthless killers they became, but for the innocents they once were who were so deeply scarred by their environmental and psychological stressors that their lives were thrown wildly off course, beyond all definitions of normalcy and moral decency. The question arises, of course, of whether these men and women, given their terrible crimes and blatant disregard for their innocent victims and fellow human beings, deserve our sympathy at all. In society's centuries-long quest to distinguish these criminal monsters from ourselves, this may be the important difference that separates us from them: we are capable of tapping into a profound well of empathy, even for these murderers who committed such unthinkable crimes – a quality which most, if not all, of these 16 serial killers had forgotten, or never experienced in the first place. It benefits us to acknowledge this empathy and, perhaps, it makes us stronger – and more human – to exercise it.

The aim of this book was to investigate serial killers with a link to the supernatural, whether it be that the killers themselves felt an affinity with a creature of myth or whether they were assigned this link by society and the media. While there are many thematic similarities between these 16 cases and the killers may have had traits in common, their individual stories are extremely diverse. They differed in important ways, whether it was their background, the context of their crimes, the method of killing, the means of disposing of their victims' bodies or the motive behind the murders.

As discussed in the Introduction, a multitude of cultural, psychological, medical and developmental factors combine in the pathway to becoming a serial killer. Each of these 16 killers had his or her own complex pathway and the chapters of this book offer a glimpse into how different they can be. What unites all of them, however, is the fact that they committed such outrageous crimes that they were, symbolically, cast out of the human race and relegated to the ranks of vampires and werewolves and creatures of myth and horror. These men and women, who might have turned out so differently under different circumstances, earned themselves the legacy of being immortalized as real-life monsters.

References

Introduction

Dieperink, J. (2012)'*Wicked Artes': Human-to-Animal Transformations in Early Modern Europe.* Retrieved from: http://aladinrc.wrlc.org/handle/1961/10522

Giannangelo, S.J. (1996) *The Psychopathology of Serial Murder: A Theory of Violence* Greenwood Publishing Group, Westport

Kutzbach, K. & Mueller, M. (2007) *The Abject of Desire: The Aestheticization of the Unaesthetic in Contemporary Literature and Culture* Editions Rodopi, Amsterdam

Malinosky-Rummell, R. & Hansen, D.J. (1993) Long-term consequences of childhood physical abuse *Psychological Bulletin,* 114(1): 68–79

Moser, R.S. (2014) *Shocking violence II* Charles C Thomas Publisher, Springfield

Ramsland, K.M. (2006) *Inside the Minds of Serial Killers: Why They Kill* Greenwood Publishing Group, Westport

Reidy, T.J. (1977) 'The aggressive characteristics of abused and neglected children' *J. Clin. Psychol.,* 33: 1140–1145

Schlesinger, L.B. (2000) 'Serial homicide: sadism, fantasy, and a compulsion to kill' In *Serial Offenders: Current Thought, Recent Findings* (pp. 3–22) CRC Press, London

Stefoff, R. (2007) *Vampires, Zombies, and Shape-shifters* Marshall Cavendish, London

Chapter 1

Holmes, R.M. & Holmes, S.T. (1988) *Contemporary Perspectives on Serial Murder* SAGE Publications, New York

Poole, R. (2002) *The Lancashire Witches: Histories and Stories* Manchester University Press

Steiger, B. (2011) *The Werewolf Book: The Encyclopedia Of Shape-Shifting Beings* Visible Ink Press, Detroit

Summers, M. (2012) *The Werewolf in Lore and Legend* Courier Corporation, New York

Chapter 2

Baring-Gould, S. (1865) *The Book of Were-Wolves.* Smith, Elder & Co., London

Gibson, D.C. (2012) *Legends, Monsters, or Serial Murderers? The Real Story Behind an Ancient Crime* Praeger Publishers, Westport

Ruff, J.R. (2001) *Violence in Early Modern Europe 1500-1800.* Cambridge University Press

Steiger, B. (2011) *The Werewolf Book: The Encyclopedia of Shape-Shifting Beings* Visible Ink Press, Detroit

Chapter 3

Burton R. (1923) *The Anatomy of Melancholy* G. Bell and Sons, London

Fahy TA. (1989) 'Lycanthropy, a Review' *Journal of the Royal Society of Medicine* 82: 37–39

Garlipp, P., Godecke-Koch T., Dietrich D.E., Haltenhof H. (2004) 'Lycanthropy – Psychopathological and Psychodynamical Aspects' *Acta Psychiatrica Scandinavica* 109 (1): 19–22

Otten C.F. (1986) *A Lycanthropy Reader: Werewolves in Western Culture* Syracuse: Syracuse University Press

Gibson, D.C. (2012) *Legends, Monsters, or Serial Murderers? The Real Story Behind an Ancient Crime* Praeger Publishers, Westport

Stypczynski, B.A. (2013) *The Modern Literary Werewolf: A Critical Study of the Mutable Motif*: McFarland & Company, Jefferson

Chapter 4

Gibson, D.C. (2012) *Legends, Monsters, or Serial Murderers? The Real Story Behind an Ancient Crime* Praeger Publishers, Westport

Kord, S. (2009) *Murderesses in German Writing, 1720–1860: Heroines of Horror* Cambridge University Press

McNally, R.T. & Florescu, N. (1994) *In Search of Dracula: The History of Dracula and Vampires* Houghton Mifflin Harcourt, Boston

Chapter 5

Bufkin J.L. & Luttrell V.R. (2005) 'Neuroimaging Studies of Aggressive and Violent Behavior: Current Findings and Implications for Criminology and Criminal Justice' *Trauma Violence Abuse* 6(2):176–91

Flynn F.G., Cummings J.L. & Tomiyasu U. (1988) 'Altered Behavior Associated with Damage to the Ventromedial Hypothalamus: A Distinctive Syndrome' *Behavioural Neurology* 1(1): 49–58. doi: 10.3233/BEN-1988-1107

Gibson, D.C. (2009) *Serial Killing for Profit: Multiple Murder for Money* ABC-CLIO, Westport

Kerr, G. (2011) *World Serial Killers* Canary Press eBooks Ltd Retrieved from: https://books.google.com.sg/books?isbn=1908698160

Miller B.L., Darby A., Benson D.F. et al. (1997) 'Aggressive, Socially Disruptive and Antisocial Behaviour Associated with Frontotemporal Dementia' *British Journal of Psychiatry* 170:150–4

Tateno A., Jorge R.E., Robinson R.G. (2003) 'Clinical Correlates of Aggressive Behavior after Traumatic Brain Injury' *Journal of Neuropsychiatry & Clinical Neuroscience* 15(2):155–60

van Elst L.T., Woermann F.G., Lemieux L., et al. (2000) 'Affective Aggression in Patients with Temporal Lobe Epilepsy: A Quantitative MRI Study of the Amygdala' *Brain* 123(2):234–243

Wilson, C. (1995) *A Plague of Murder* Robinson Publishing, London

Chapter 6

Allely C.S., Minnis H., Thompson L., et al. (2014) 'Neurodevelopmental and Psychosocial Risk Factors in Serial Killers and Mass Murderers' *Aggression and Violent Behavior* 19(3): 288–301

Feinberg, J. (1998) 'Sickness and Wickedness: New Conceptions and New Paradoxes *Journal of the American Academy of Psychiatry and the Law* 26:475–85

Jenkins, P. (1989) 'Serial Murder in the United States 1900–1940: A Historical Perspective' *Journal of Criminal Justice* 17(5): 377–392

Joshi, S.T. (2006) *Icons of Horror and the Supernatural: An Encyclopedia of Our Worst Nightmares, Volume 1* Greenwood Publishing, Westport

Wilson, C. (1995) *A Plague of Murder* Robinson Publishing, London

Chapter 7

Enoch, M.D., and Trethowan, W.H. (1979) *Uncommon Psychiatric Syndromes* 2nd ed. John Wright & Sons, Ltd Bristol

Friedmann, C.T.H., and Faguet, R.A. (1982) *Extraordinary Disorders of Human Behavior* Plenum Press, New York

Godwin, George (1938) *Peter Kurten, A Study in Sadism* The Acorn Press, London

Noll, Richard (1990) *Bizarre Diseases of the Mind* Berkley, New York

Chapter 8

Australian Associated Press (1949, July 21) *Weeping girl visits Haigh* The Advertiser, p.1 Retrieved from http://trove.nla.gov.au

Clark, N. (2013, May 7) *The man who made dead people talk* Express Retrieved from http://www.express.co.uk

Greig, C. (2012) *Serial Killers: Horrifying True-Life Cases of Pure Evil* Arcturus Publishing, London

Root, N. (2012) *Frenzy! Heath, Haigh & Christie: How the Tabloid Press Turned Three Evil Serial Killers Into Celebrities* Random House, London

Chapter 9

American Psychiatric Association (2013) *Diagnostic and Statistical Manual of Mental Disorders* (5th ed.) American Psychiatric Association Publishing, Arlington

Biondi, R., & Hecox, W. (2005) *The Dracula Killer: The True Story of California's Vampire Killer* Diane Publishing Company, Darby

Bovsun, M. (2010, January 2) *Just Crazy for Blood: Richard Trenton Chase, a.k.a. the Vampire of Sacramento* New York Daily News Retrieved from: www.nydailynews.com

Jenkins, M.C. (2012) *Vampires: Unearthing the Bloodthirsty Legend* National Geographic Books, Washington DC

Lane, B., & Gregg, W. (1995) *The Encyclopedia of Serial Killers* New York: Berkeley

Lester, D. (2010) 'Suicide in Mass Murderers and Serial Killers' *Suicidology Online* 1: 19–27

Ressler, R. (1992) *Whoever Fights Monsters* St. Martins Press, New York

Schecter, H., & Everitt, D. (1996) *The A to Z Encyclopedia of Serial Killers* Pocket Books, New York

Schlesinger, L.B. (2000) *Serial Offenders: Current Thought, Recent Findings* CRC Press, London

Schlesinger, L.B. (2003) *Sexual Murder: Catathymic and Compulsive Homicides* CRC Press, London

Chapter 10

American Psychiatric Association (2013) *Diagnostic and Statistical Manual of Mental Disorders* (5th ed.) American Psychiatric Association Publishing, Arlington

Dahmer Urban Dictionary Retrieved from: www.urbandictionary.com

Dahmer Believed He Was Satan, Defense Says (1992, January 31) Los Angeles Times Retrieved from: www.articles.latimes.com

Masters, B. (2007) *The Shrine of Jeffrey Dahmer* Hodder & Stoughton, London

Ressler, R., & Shachtman, T. (1997) *I Have Lived in The Monster* St. Martin Press, New York

Schram, J. (2015, April 18) *Why I Killed Jeffrey Dahmer* New York Post Retrieved from: www.nypost.com

Shemtob, Z. *Consuming Loneliness: A Psychosocial Comparison of Two Criminal Cannibals* Retrieved from: www.zacharyshemtob.com

Stevens, D. (2005, June 27) *Dinner Conversation* Retrieved from: www.slate.com

Strubel, A. (2007) 'Jeffrey Dahmer: His Complicated Comorbid

Psychopathologies and Treatment Implications' *The New School Psychology Bulletin*, 5(1): 1–18

Chapter 11

Davidson, B. (2 January 1990) 'Trials that Rocked Singapore in the 80s' *The Straits Times* Singapore: Singapore Press Holdings, p.17

John, A. (1989) *Unholy Trinity: The Adrian Lim 'Ritual' Child Killings* Times Books International, Singapore

Sit, Y.F. (1983, June 25) 'Adrian Lim's Final Wish' *Singapore Monitor*, p.3 Retrieved from http://eresources.nlb.gov.sg/newspapers

Sit, Y.F. (1989) *Was Adrian Lim Mad?* Heinemann Asia, Singapore

Chapter 12

Makin, S. (2014) 'Does Marijuana Harm The Brain?' *Scientific American*, 25(05) Retrieved from http://www.scientificamerican.com

Sagar, K.A. et al. (2015) The Impact of Initiation: Early Onset Marijuana Smokers Demonstrate Altered Stroop Performance and Brain Activation *Developmental Cognitive Neuroscience* Retrieved from http://www.sciencedirect.com

Richard Ramirez (2015) Retrieved from http://www.biography.com

Carlo, P. (2006) *The Night Stalker: The Life and Crimes Of Richard Ramirez* Kensington Publishing Corporation, New York

Carlo, P. (2010) *The Night Stalker: The Life and Crimes of One of America's Deadliest Killers* Mainstream Publishing, London

Chapter 13

American Psychiatric Association (2013) *Diagnostic and Statistical Manual of Mental Disorders* (5th ed.) American Psychiatric Association Publishing, Arlington

Bell, R. (1999) 'All about Cannibalism: The Ancient Taboo in Modern Times Cannibalism Psychology' Retrieved from: www.crimelibrary.com

Marriott, T. (2013) *The Evil Within* John Blake Publishing, London

'Miyazaki unrepentant to the last/Serial child killer goes to execution without apologizing or explaining his thinking' (2008, June 18) *Yomiuri Shimbun* (Tokyo) www.yomiuri.co.jp

Oliviera, J. (2015) 'The Otaku Killer: Miyazaki Tsutomu' Retrieved from: www.scaredyet.net

Chapter 14

Berry-Dee, C. (2011) *Cannibal Serial Killers: Profiles of Depraved Flesh-*

Eating Murderers Ulysses Press, Berkeley

Cullen, R. (1993) *The Killer Department: Detective Viktor Burakov's Eight-Year Hunt for the Most Savage Serial Killer of Our Times* Pantheon Books, New York

Krivich, M., & Olgin, O. (2015) *Comrade Chikatilo: Russia's Most Notorious Serial Killer* Graymalkin Media, New York

Chapter 15

American Psychiatric Association (2013) *Diagnostic and Statistical Manual of Mental Disorders* (5th ed.) American Psychiatric Association Publishing, Arlington

Azevedo, S., & Dantas, E. (2003) 'Marcelo de Andrade – O sadism tinha subido à minha cabeçahar' *Epoca Magazine*

McKenna, P.J. (1984) 'Disorders with Overvalued Ideas' *British Journal of Psychiatry*, 145, 579–585

Marrison, J. (2010) *The World's Most Bizarre Murders* John Blake Publishing, London

Morrison, H., & Goldberg, H. (2004) *My Life Among the Serial Killers, Inside the Minds of the World's Most Notorious Murderers* Harper Collins, London

Murray, J., Cerqueira, D.R.d.C., & Kahn, T. (2013) 'Crime and Violence in Brazil: Systematic Review of Time Trends, Prevalence Rates and Risk Factors' *Aggression and Violent Behavior*, 18, 471–483

Chapter 16

Geberth, V.J. (2003) *Sex-Related Homicide and Death Investigation: Practical and Clinical Perspectives* Taylor & Francis, London

'Spillman Pleads Guilty To Killing Mother, Daughter Former Spokane Man Also Confesses To Murder Of Okanogan County Girl' (1996, May 1) *The Spokesman Review* Retrieved from: www.spokesman.com

Ramsland, K.M. (2006) *Inside the Minds of Serial Killers: Why They Kill* Greenwood Publishing Group, Westport

Ramsland, K., & McGrain, P.N. (2009) *Inside the Minds of Sexual Predators* ABC-CLIO, Westport

Index